APPLIED ETHICS AND SOCIAL PROBLEMS

Moral questions of birth, society and death

Tony Fitzpatrick

This edition published in Great Britain in 2008 by

The Policy Press
University of Bristol
Fourth Floor
Beacon House
Queen's Road
Bristol BS8 1QU
UK

Tel +44 (0)117 331 4054
Fax +44 (0)117 331 4093
e-mail tpp-info@bristol.ac.uk
www.policypress.org.uk

© Tony Fitzpatrick 2008

British Library Cataloguing in Publication Data
A catalogue record for this book is available from the British Library.

Library of Congress Cataloging-in-Publication Data
A catalog record for this book has been requested.

ISBN 978 1 86134 859 3 paperback
ISBN 978 1 86134 860 9 hardcover

Cover design by In-Text Design, Bristol.
Front cover: image kindly supplied by Magnum Photos.
Printed and bound in Great Britain by Hobbs the Printers, Southampton.

Contents

List of tables and figures

Tables

Figures

Acknowledgements

My gratitude to the many people whose ears I have bent and patience I have stretched over the years in debating many of the issues contained here. Also thanks to the anonymous reviewers of the proposal and of the draft manuscript. And staff at The Policy Press deserve recognition, not only for being efficient but also for remaining human beings in the process. You really don't know how academia is meant to work, do you?

Acronyms

DDE   Doctrine of double effect
DNR   Do not resuscitate
GNI   Gross national income
PVS   Persistent vegetative state
RCM   Relatively closed migration
ROM   Relatively open migration
VAE   Voluntary active euthanasia
VPE   Voluntary passive euthanasia

Introduction

The dog I had as a kid, Snoopy, had a talent for football and for chewing my stuff. This included assaulting my refractor telescope at regular intervals, though poor Snoopy was typically the loser in those battles. In truth, suburban Liverpool was not the greatest place for amateur astronomy and I was driven to observe other objects of heavenly beauty (God bless you, Mrs Mills, at no. 23) and develop interests that didn't depend on cloudless night skies. In reading about the history of science, my heroes became Kepler, Galileo and Einstein, figures whose bodies ate, slept and stumbled but whose intellects wheeled through farthest space and penetrated into the deepest heart of nature.

This fascination with reconciling the routines of the everyday with the immensities of the universe has never faded. Nor has the idea that the two converge through quite simple, almost childlike, questions. What would it be like to travel on a wave of light? Such elementary queries inspired the teenage Einstein, hiking through the Apennine mountains, and never left him alone thereafter. It is surely similar puzzles that bring us all to our passions, to enthusiasms we cannot stop exploring without becoming what Weber labelled a 'specialist without spirit'.

It is this fascination that drives me to write about philosophies and theories of social policy. I define the subject broadly, to encompass social relations, political governance, cultural identities and popular discourses that others might locate in alternative disciplines. But such matters do not affect the journey that lies before us, or the childlike questions I am still impelled to raise. On what grounds can our liberty be legitimately restricted? To what extent should individuals be protected from themselves?

We are therefore going to ask normative questions – 'what should we do and why?' – and to this end we will be playing with some of the most fundamental building blocks of inquiry. In British railway stations, it is common to hear announcements such as the following: 'We apologise for the late departure of the 10.23 to Kettering; this was because of delays to the incoming service'. Why was the outgoing train late? Because the incoming train was late! We cannot be satisfied with such circular explanations, especially given their frequent occurrence in public and political life. The aim in this book is therefore to interrogate some simple questions at their most foundational levels, the levels we often find it convenient to skip over or too intricate to engage with.

What are we going to be asking normative questions about (see Fitzpatrick, 2001, Ch.1)? For all of the interdisciplinary debates with which we increasingly have to grapple (Fitzpatrick, 2005a), much of this book deals with a centuries-old dilemma: what constitutes the legitimate boundaries of individual action? We will navigate some of the main tributaries into which this question flows, but it essentially reflects the beginning and end of our expedition. If social policy studies the production and distribution of public goods, and if the state has a considerable role to play in maximising welfare and social justice, why and to what extent can the state justifiably regulate and interfere with individual freedom to this end? Every generation thinks it has reached some kind of conclusive response to this query, and every succeeding generation delights in shattering that complacency before relaxing into its own. So while this book does not shy away from reaching some firm conclusions about the issues addressed, it should also help us to look beyond the fashions of the hour.

Yet in social policy circles it is not uncommon for people to be impatient with – or at best tolerably indulgent towards – what they see as philosophical diversions. 'We know what the problem is, why can't we just act?' This exasperation is voiced by many students, practitioners, policy makers and, yes, some academics. In fact, I share some of this impatience but it is important to stress why we should not succumb to it too quickly.

The difficulty for many is not only that the building blocks are arranged differently by different philosophical schools, but also that they disagree over what those blocks look like in the first place. It is one thing to be interested in fundamentals, another for those fundamentals to remain unresolved. If scientists were still arguing over whether Aristotle's arrangement of the four elements (earth, water, air, fire) was correct, we would still be trying to work out how quickly the celestial spheres orbit around the Earth. Yet philosophers still debate his moral and political ideas as if they cannot bear to move off the first square in a perilous game of snakes and ladders. It's not only hard-headed positivists who utter the Henry Higgins cry: 'Why can't a social scientist be more like a natural one?'. And often the answer is: philosophy. Hence the frequent appearance in social policy of middle-range theories, those that never wander too far from the practicalities of empirical verification.

But what these grumbles potentially miss is the importance of *process*. Our culture is one much more comfortable with outcome than process, with the end product rather than with its gestation. We expect statisticians to tell us what the rate of inflation is, not bore us with their methods of calculation; we want hospital managers to provide effective care, not share the details of committee structures. For a subject like social policy, highly empirical and concerned with providing definitive answers to service and research users, it is doubly so. More than this, we often feel uncomfortable with loose threads, with irresolvable stories, with content that bursts out of its packaging, with landscapes that elude their cartographers.

Philosophy is primarily about process, though. It is a caricature to imagine it as a series of questions that can never be answered, but philosophy certainly does not offer a simple means–end relationship. ('Tell me how to do the philosophy so I can concentrate on research design and fieldwork' is frequently the doctoral student's lament.) We do not 'do' philosophy in order to leave it behind and reach a determinate result. Philosophy is the critical method of all methodologies, the analysis of analyses, but is also its own end. It is inherently dialogical and deliberative. It can be methodical but is never linear. It loops back on itself, enjoying *both* the ladders *and* the snakes, convinced that the game contains no final, attainable square. We can identify losers (poor questions, unpromising lines of inquiry), but there is never just one winner. Philosophers can be incredibly opinionated, but rarely take their opinions for granted.

In previous books, I have tried to capture something of this 'process' through an array of perspectives designed to address a single puzzle. How can we be systematic without over-simplifying, for the sake of convenience, the complexities of the social world? How can we be comprehensive while avoiding the shapeless chaos of those complexities? The social world does not lend itself to just one methodology, empirical method, ideology, disciplinary path, thematic focus, conceptual framework or analytical procedure. Never confuse the roadmap with the places themselves. We shouldn't respect the latter so much that we get lost in their dense intricacies, but nor should we fear intricacy to the point of clinging to a crude map. Besides, most of us are general readers about most things most of the time, having to explore a landscape by circling around it at sometimes higher and sometimes lower altitudes. The use of multiple perspectives is an attempt to capture what we are looking at in the contemporary social world *and* the ways in which we typically look and learn. This can be unsettling to those who insist they already know where the gates are to this social maze and those impatient to get to the exit as quickly as possible.

The present book, too, wrestles with the above puzzle and I will describe how in a moment. First, let me admit to the impatience I have just signalled. Given the dangers and problems we face today (you can compile your own list of risks, horrors *and* opportunities), it is instinctive to want to intervene directly. When bodies are floating by, you should surely try to revive them instead of standing immobile, pondering the meaning of life and death. Isn't anything else an indulgence? Well, not quite. The point of 'pure' inquiry is that you can never predict how, if at all, its findings might be applied; as such, the criterion of 'applicability' should not restrict our inquiries. When he discovered X-rays, accidentally, Wilhelm Röntgen was conducting experiments most of the world would have regarded as pointless. 'What use is it?' A world in which we could always give a firm answer to this would be backward and dull beyond belief. Nevertheless, I too feel uncomfortable with philosophy that strays far away from the practical, the immediate, the tangible. This does not mean the philosopher is here to serve the policy maker (when this occurs the results are often excruciating), the layperson or the professional, but it can provide appropriate archives, tools and guidance designed to influence a social climate. For if we cut ourselves adrift from those labouring at the coalface, we have only inverted the snobbishness of Henry Higgins types.

Hence my interest in social policy. Having explored an array of social and political theories previously (Fitzpatrick, 2001, 2005a), this book deals with that branch of moral philosophy known as applied ethics.

Moral philosophy addresses the principles and concepts that do or should regulate human conduct. How ought we to behave? What do we mean by 'good'? Along with metaphysics it is the oldest form of philosophy. (When Democritus developed his theory of atomism, he was eschewing supernatural explanations of motion *and* human behaviour.) Today, it is common to distinguish between metaethics, normative ethics and applied ethics. The first deals with the *form* of moral propositions; is an insistence that 'murder is immoral' the articulation of an objective truth or a subjective emotion? Normative ethics deals with the rightness or wrongness of moral judgements and propositions, with the extent to which moral beliefs, values, schools of thought and value systems are coherently defensible. Applied ethics is concerned with practical problems (and is sometimes known as 'practical ethics'). To some extent, it therefore cuts across a fourth possible category of moral philosophy where ethics is attached to professional activities, such as social work, medical, legal and business ethics. Applied ethics can encompass these spheres but also transverses them and more easily permits lessons to be transferred from one to another. It draws on metaethics and normative ethics as appropriate.

Applied ethics really dates from the 1970s, a time when philosophers were becoming a bit exhausted with metaethics and when a host of social movements and developments needed the kind of urgent attention they were not receiving from political ideologies. Its full scope extends way beyond what is covered in this volume: including animals and the environment, corporate obligations, crime and punishment, discrimination and affirmative action, genetics, gun control, love and sexual behaviour, pornography and censorship, privacy, religious observance and war, among many other subjects.

A focus on applied ethics allows us to avoid the extremes mentioned above. It captures the abstract, dialogical process of philosophical investigation, while dealing with questions that, although practical, do not lend themselves to quick and easy resolution. It marries philosophy's concern with first principles to social policy's comfort zone with 'second' and 'third principles'. Our guiding, analogous test is always, 'Can I drink it?'. Water can take many different forms, but, from a practical, thirst-quenching point of view, we need to know what form can be safely ingested. In short, this book is concerned *with applying debates, theories and methods from moral philosophy to contemporary ethical issues relating to the disciplinary field (social policy) investigating the interactions of social problems, justice and wellbeing.* Its aim is partly prescriptive (to explore whether changes to existing policies, perceptions and practices are justified) and partly elucidatory (an excavation of why we do what we do). It is concerned with social problems defined as 'problematic questions requiring social debate' and not with social conditions (unemployment, homelessness, crime and so on) or the construction of social problems and certainly not with so-called 'problem groups' (the usual suspects with whom many politicians and journalists often seem obsessed).

As such, I have selected the topics to be examined using the following criteria. First, they are relevant not only to social policy, as defined above, but to what I consider are some of its most pressing contemporary issues. No doubt several more books could have been filled, but there should be enough here to enable you to lasso the many omissions. Second, I have targeted those debates within the field of applied ethics where the literature is fairly well developed. Finally, I have not intruded too much on subjects I have dealt with at length elsewhere. The book is not intended as an introduction to applied ethics, but, because I have attempted to be fair to those with whom I disagree, readers unfamiliar with the literature should find it to be something of an introduction nonetheless.

The book is effectively split into two parts. Chapters One to Five explore the three most prominent normative philosophies within contemporary ethical theory. Chapter One interrogates the possible foundations on which those philosophies can rest, arguing that the most appropriate is a 'social humanism' that supplies various analytical concepts that we return to throughout the book. Chapters Two to Four examine consequentialism, Kantianism and virtue ethics, respectively. Each provides an introduction to these normative philosophies, outlining its potential strengths and weaknesses and specifying its relevance for, and approach to, applied ethics. Chapter Five offers a summary of the story thus far and defends an eclectic, pragmatic way forward.

Chapters Six to Eleven then deal with various tributaries branching off from the key question noted earlier: what constitutes the legitimate boundaries of individual actions and why and to what extent can the state justifiably regulate and interfere with them? Chapter Six establishes the main parameters for subsequent chapters through an analysis of the harm principle, applying this to issues of smoking and drug taking. Chapter Seven extends this discussion to questions of choice and market provision, outlining a version of paternalism I call 'environmental paternalism'. Chapter Eight then brings family relationships and obligations into the picture. Having defended an autonomy-led approach, this is then applied to the two most controversial debates within applied ethics. Chapter Nine deals with abortion and Chapter Ten with euthanasia. Chapter Eleven then wonders whether we should pull the rug out from under those previous discussions by exploring several themes relating to global justice. Each chapter is organised around two to four focal questions that allow us to range widely without losing sight of our thematic purpose.

Those focal questions are:

- *Should smoking be banned in public places?*
- *Should bad habits be taxed?*
- *Should some drugs be legalised?*
- *To what extent should parents be able to choose their child's school?*
- *To what extent should we allocate public goods through regulated markets?*
- *Should the state actively promote marriage?*
- *Who should fund the care needs of older people?*
- *Should there be abortion on demand?*
- *What should the upper time limit for abortion be?*
- *Is stem cell research permissible?*
- *How can the right to choose be reconciled with the right to be chosen?*
- *Is euthanasia justified and, if so, when?*
- *How can we safeguard against euthanasia abuses?*

- *Should we restrict the welfare rights of recent migrants?*
- *To what extent is global justice in tension with (domestic) welfare states?*

Finally, terms like 'ethics', 'morals' and so on are used interchangeably. It will be obvious from the narrative when and why we are discussing abstract principles, rules of conduct, personal judgement, and so forth. We should not have to restrict our vocabulary to make this clear.

ONE

Foundations

Given some of the points made in the Introduction, it may seem indulgent to spend time on the foundations of moral philosophy. Yet at critical junctures throughout the book, we will sometimes have to bear such foundations in mind, particularly the set of ideas I will define and defend as 'social humanism'. To what extent are we obliged to protect people from themselves? Are we primarily sovereign agents or immersed in social relations? Does life begin at conception or later? Should we respect life per se or the person whose life that is? All ethical foundations help provide answers to such questions, ones that are vital to the debates ahead. We will therefore refer back to this chapter periodically as we progress.[1]

This chapter explores the three possible foundations that pretty much seem to exhaust the field of inquiry: the religious, the natural and the social. Our understanding of, and stance towards, modern moral philosophy will alter depending on the place we start from and the principal ideas we use when advancing further.

Religion

Religion has been one victor of a post-ideological world where political idealism has subsided and global societies face barely understood storms of insecurity from which many seek traditional shelters. Both faith and fanaticism have enjoyed a revival and while the latter can discredit theism it may also serve to emphasise the sanity and reasonableness of less strident forms of religious belief. Should we therefore place ethics primarily on a religious footing?

Reason

The argument that only religion can provide secure foundations for morality is well known. It is almost obligatory to quote Ivan in *The Brothers Karamazov*, to the effect that if there is no God everything is permitted. But the idea that without a love or fear of God humans have no convincing reason to act ethically is much older. St Augustine insisted, 16 centuries ago:

> When man tries to live justly by his own strength without
> the help of the liberating grace of God, he is then conquered
> by sins. (Quoted in Copleston, 1985, pp 83–4)

There is here no such figure as the virtuous atheist.

Secularists reply that there simply are no moral guarantees because *with* God why have so many atrocities *been* possible.[2] In one of Plato's earliest dialogues, Euthyphro and Socrates are discussing the nature of piety when the latter asks: '… is what is pious loved by the gods because it is pious, or is it pious because it is loved?' (Plato, 1954, p 31). If the former, piety has a distinct nature that we can understand without reference to the gods; if the latter, how can we be sure that we are acting piously since the gods often disagree with one another (as do humans when interpreting their wishes)? In a more modern idiom, either morality is independent of God, making Him redundant, or we cannot be sure that what God commands is moral. There are possible counter-arguments (Mann, 1998). Perhaps moral principles are indeed independent of God but He reveals the existence and necessity of those principles in a way that would not be possible in a Godless universe. Unsurprisingly, though, the persuasiveness of this assumption depends on whether you accept the initial premise from which it derives, that God is crucial to morality.

This question of God's essentialness feeds into a familiar dilemma in the philosophy of religion (Glauser, 2003): the difficulty of reconciling the existence of evil with God's omnipotence and God's omnibenevolence.[3] If evil exists, either God is powerless to prevent it – contradicting His omnipotence – or He wishes it to exist – contradicting His omnibenevolence. Theists and secularists respond to this problem differently.

Theists adopt several strategies. Perhaps what we call evil is no such thing. In his *Essay on Man*, Pope attests that:

> All discord, harmony not understood,
> All partial evil, universal good

This sleight-of-hand is inadequate, since the strength of religion presumably lies in offering us reasons not to be evil instead of wishing it away. A more cogent strategy is to regard evil as a necessary concomitant of free will. Either it is better for humans to have free will, albeit at what seems to be a terrible price, or it is in the nature of humans to possess free will. However, if it is *better*, theists are indeed allowing God's omnibenevolence to collapse since He can no longer be denoted as *all* benevolent in permitting a universe where innocents suffer (Jordan, 2004); whereas if free will is unavoidable, God appears constrained by certain necessary truths and therefore His omnipotence collapses. So if God's omnipotence or omnibenevolence are in doubt, what is to distinguish Him from an advanced alien species that is simply farther up the evolutionary path than humans?

Theists reply to this last point by arguing that being constrained by logical necessities does not mean that God is not omnipotent, merely that circles can never be square and two plus two can never equal five (Swinburne, 1998; Wielenberg, 2004). Yet even supposing this reasoning applies to *logical* necessities, why assume they apply to *moral* necessities also? Mackie (1971, p 101) once wondered why God did not simply create beings that always freely choose to be good. Plantinga's (2000) reply (see also Mawson, 2004) is that such a constraint would contradict the very notion of free will. But as we will see later, such an absolutist conception is not required and freedom may well be compatible with a 'soft determinism' (cf. Cain, 2004). If so, why could God not simply close off certain possibilities from our moral psychologies, certain destructive desires, for instance? (And why permit the suffering caused by natural events like earthquakes and tsunami?) If I have no desire to kill people does that mean I am less free than a serial killer? Even if we accept Plantinga's counter-argument, it provides an explanation of why we act *freely* but not reasons why we should act *morally* (Schellenberg, 2004). If freedom, and the risk that it will be used for cruelty, is a necessary part of the best possible world that God was able to create, perhaps evil is justified because it enables good to exist elsewhere.

Faith

Perhaps we are going about this the wrong way. Perhaps rationalistic debate is inevitably inconclusive and we must put our trust in faith. This might simply amount to faith that God loves us and so does not deceive us. The problem is in deciding what distinguishes faith in God from faith in astrology, pixies or tarot cards. If we eschew reason and evidence, don't we open the floodgates to each and every superstition?

Instead, perhaps avoiding such creeds lies not in treating faith as a direct line to truth but in embracing the paradoxes to which faith itself gives rise. Simone Weil (2002) posits a tug of war between grace and gravity, the former pulling us towards, and the latter away from, God. But for Weil it is not the case that evil consists in distance *from* God, since violence, torture and cruelty *are themselves signs that God loves us*, that He is pushing us away in order to reclaim, through our love for

Him, the space He has given us to occupy. She therefore throws herself into the paradoxes that many theists smooth over. For instance (Weil, 2002, pp 75, 90):

> ... to love God as the author of the evil we are actually hating.

> An innocent being who suffers sheds the light of salvation upon evil. Such a one is the visible image of the innocent God. That is why a God who loves man and a man who loves God have to suffer.

To be good is to focus on the nothingness of God by inviting the afflictions of evil upon oneself rather than upon others. Weil's politics is therefore a peculiar 'communistic conservatism' (see, for example, Weil, 1987, p 18); communist because both wealth and poverty distract from the spiritual, she thought, but also conservative because it is through temporal continuity (an orientation to the past) that the social becomes subordinate to the spiritual.

What might we say about this? What can we say that would not appear heartless about a woman who was gifted and tortured enough to starve herself to death? In truth, not a lot. It is possible for many theists and atheists to find value within her work, a poetic expression of intuitions so deep that God becomes synonymous with existence itself. Yet if your admiration for such insights does not result in a feeling of *God* filling your soul, this approach need be no more compelling than rationalistic accounts of religion. Sceptics are inevitably compelled to dissect the subjective peculiarities and historical contexts of the mystic and of the faithful. In Weil's case, this consisted in an inclination towards emotional and physical masochism, in addition to an eclectic leftism that reflected the political pessimism of the inter-war years (McLellan, 1989, pp 32-7). Weil's philosophy was a mysticism but one that cannot, by itself, impel us towards religion, faith and God given the fact that some have adopted elements of mysticism without abandoning a secular tone, for example, Huxley (1936) or Murdoch (2001).

Usefulness

So perhaps, finally, we have to appreciate religion in terms neither of rationalism nor faith but in terms of pragmatism (Hardwick and Crosby, 1997). What matters is less the truthfulness of religious beliefs and more the impact they have on the believer: the social stickiness of doctrine rather than its word-for-word veracity. Since religion as a social institution is often a force for good, and since belief in God is embedded deep within the human psyche, better to work with the grain of religious endeavour as a moral and cultural glue that holds societies together by protecting people from their worst impulses. It is true that religious extremism can be a source of violence and intolerance, but atheists like Hitler, Stalin and Mao hardly suggest that extremism is a trait of theism alone. Better to associate an ethos of divine love with the modern principles of tolerance and pluralism.

This upbeat pragmatism might generate both conservative and leftist positions (Bane and Mead, 2003). The conservative typically prefers some notion of obligation towards others (family, neighbourhood, country) that the modern secular state is accused of undermining; not only the welfare state but also often the excesses of the minimal, free market state (Mead, 2005a). By stressing what people are owed rather than what they owe, by encouraging the qualities of selfish hedonism rather than those of thrift, hard work and respect, the modern state has unravelled the bonds of dutifulness and attachment. The solution is to remoralise society, though to what extent this demands the reintegration of state and Church is something that divides religious conservatives. The leftist, meanwhile, is less hostile to the doctrines of social justice that have propelled many social reforms over the last century (Weithman, 2002). Yet here too there is a worry that the moral codes that underpinned the work of most 19th-century reformers have eroded, with secularists unable to find substitutes for religious principles, preferring instead a hollow mechanical materialism. Social justice therefore requires that a new social ethic be woven through familiar theological resources.

This defence involves a kind of sociological consequentialism. It sets religion up as a social narrative whose value resides in its beneficial effects. The problem with this, as we see in Chapter Two, is that they who live by the consequence can die by it too. First, if we are primarily concerned with social cohesion, why not prefer more effective alternatives? The Hitler/Stalin/Mao argument often thrown at atheists partly misfires because it ignores the extent to which those dictators' purpose was to create political quasi-religions that would supersede rather than replace the Church. Such systems may have rejected belief in God but they did not reject the *need* for an infallible authority, and it is the 'need for' rather than belief per se that is capable of perverse interpretation. What is not thereby ruled out is an atheism that acknowledges the benefits of religion but nevertheless supports a long-term, progressive secularisation of its social narratives.

A second problem is that this defence is some senses *downgrades* religion, such that the precise content of religious beliefs matter less than whether they 'work' or not. If a nation's cultural/historical tradition is Muslim, Islam should be supported; if it is Jewish, Judaism should be supported. At best, this is a healthy embrace of value pluralism. At worst, it is a relativistic detour around some important substantive questions that many Muslims, Jews and others think of as crucial to their identities. Even then we are not off the hook, for being immersed within a Christian tradition offers, by itself, no guidance as to whether we should be conservatives or liberals, for or against school prayer, pro- or anti-abortion.

In short, a 'what-works' justification may supplement but not dispel essential normative questions. Is there a God? Is God the source of morality? Why does God permit evil? Is faith sufficient? None of this is meant to dismiss religion's contribution to moral debate, as the following pages will demonstrate. But my aim is to suggest why religion alone provides an insufficient foundation for an adequate account of moral theory and so of applied ethics.

Nature

Should we therefore look to the natural rather than the supernatural? This distinction is loaded, for, as we will see shortly, the former can be taken as a manifestation of the latter. Yet the modern era is also that which began to understand the natural as *distinct* from the supernatural. My intention here is not to convey the entire tradition of naturalism but to explore some of the principal ways in which it has been considered the ground of morality (Trigg, 2005, Chs 1 and 2).

One important strand of that tradition concerns natural law and tracks back to Aquinas in the 13th century. Aquinas conceives of natural law as the bridge between divine and human law. One end of that bridge is fixed and unalterable, determined by God and knowable through the action of right reason and the exercise of virtue, reason being the apprehension of God and virtue the willingness to live with and in God. The other end of the bridge is varied, diversity being the imperfect and always incomplete movement of that which is not-God towards the goodness of God's perfection (Aquinas, 1993, p 271). Natural law therefore encompasses the divine essence *and* the pluralism of diverse forms:

> ... it is this distinctive sharing in the eternal law by reasoning
> creatures that we call the law we have in us by nature.
> (Aquinas, 1993, p 418)

For others, though, natural law leads away from God and not only
to the 'autonomy' of nature (Aquinas too had viewed nature as
autonomous) but to its 'solitude' in a Godless reality, the emptiness
feared by Pascal in which all voices, prayers and heresies go unanswered
and unacknowledged. In the early 17th century, Grotius (2005, p 89)
insisted that natural law and moral orientation do not depend on God
(though Grotius was by no means an atheist); the individual comes to
the foreground and so does a specific conception of human nature.
Rights are the means by which moral beings exercise their capacity and
obligations derive from relationships into which we enter voluntarily.
Grotius therefore anticipates the traditions of classic liberalism and of
the social contract.

We have two versions of natural law, then: one that relates nature
to the supernatural (Aquinas) and one that detaches it from the
supernatural (Grotius). These versions persist into the present day with
naturalism lately coming back into fashion. The *non*-naturalist turn was
first taken by Moore (1993) in his opposition to the 'naturalistic fallacy';
according to Moore what *ought* to be the case cannot be inferred from
natural facts because he believed morality does not mirror natural
properties. Naturalism's resurrection is partly because, whatever its
deficiencies, this non-naturalistic turn has increasingly seemed even less
persuasive; partly because the metaethical concern with language does
not fulfil desires for applied ethical debate and partly because while
the naturalistic fallacy states a problem, it does not necessarily rule out
the possibility of solution (MacIntyre, 1971, pp 109-72; Hudson, 1983,
pp 249-94). The rest of this section will therefore be concerned with
two contemporary versions of naturalism (*Social Philosophy and Policy*,
2001): one derived from the tradition of Aquinas (cf. Finnis, 1980) and
one that is Darwinian.

Natural law

MacIntyre (1999) has recently attempted to fuse his previous work
(inspired by Aquinas and Aristotle) with an environmental ethic where
we are enjoined to recognise our similarities to other animals even as we
transcend these by our moral capacity to recognise the vulnerabilities,
injuries and dependencies of others and, through practical reason,
act accordingly. It is into this sensibility that MacIntyre inserts his

virtue ethics. If by nature we mean the possession of certain capacities and the desire to flourish by fulfilling those capacities, then humans differ from non-human animals in degree rather than kind. The good therefore involves the realisation of one's natural characteristics, the precise nature of which will obviously differ from species to species and for humans will imply a capacity to reason and weigh alternatives. Within any socio-historical tradition, children receive instruction from authorities (mainly parents and teachers) who articulate and manage that tradition. The acquisition of moral competence comes ultimately through habituation in the intellectual and ethical virtues specific to one's tradition so that they literally become 'second nature'. MacIntyre (1999, p 111) therefore follows Aquinas in identifying a natural law that implies orientation to a particular community through obedience to certain rules but also, because rule following does not exhaust morality, the exercise of practical reason made possible by education in the virtues.

We will take a closer look at MacIntyre's philosophy in Chapter Four. What is clear, though, is that while a more convincing account of the 'natural' occupies his ideas than was previously the case, he has to take several non-natural steps to reach the ethical position he defends. For example, he maintains that an environmental ethic reinforces the suspicion that humans are *interdependent* (MacIntyre, 1999, Ch 9). Breaking with others (socially, culturally) may sometimes be permitted but should be the exception; disagreement about social means requires a deeper, more fundamental agreement about those ends that are indispensable to social order and without which divergence of opinion is likely either to be sterile or potentially anarchic. Perhaps some of this can be accepted but it largely ignores the extent to which other philosophies, ones relying much less on virtue ethics per se, already incorporate such understanding. The liberalism with which MacIntyre has such a fraught relationship also accepts the need for shared ends. But the ends proposed by liberals are 'looser' and more pluralistic than those to which MacIntyre and others attach themselves. When 'nature' is so imbued with social understandings, influences and practices, there can be no 'bible' of natural law to read from. Therefore, either an authority-based morality gives way to dogmatism (religious or otherwise) or it makes room for deliberativeness and contestability, leading us away from the notion of ethical unitariness, and towards a more generous, pluralistic liberalism that MacIntyre has frequently rejected. Therefore, virtue ethics cannot simply be read off from nature. Human interpretation and influence always gets in the way.

Darwinism

Are there better links between nature and morality? The most obvious contender traces the development of our moral sensibilities from human evolution. Simply put, morality is an evolutionary adaptation: we are moral beings because morality is to our evolutionary advantage. If our origins are natural rather than divine, so are our social and moral relationships, meaning we have to look to nature's 'internal dynamics':

> Ultimately our moral sense or conscience becomes a highly complex sentiment – originating in the social instincts, largely guided by the approbation of our fellow-men, ruled by reason, self-interest, and in later times by deep religious feelings, and confirmed by instruction and habit. (Darwin, 2004, p 157)

This basic idea remains the same in contemporary Darwinism (Ridley, 1996; Thompson, 1999). What simple organisms do by instinct drives the evolutionary process towards more complex forms and leads eventually to beings, ourselves, who are capable of reflecting on and refining those instincts by developing systems of moral belief and behaviour. Morality emerges as instinct evolves into conscience and kinship relations into social structures. Evolutionary ethicists contend that those instincts settle into a middle way somewhere between egoistic and short-term selfishness, on the one hand, and pure self-sacrificing altruism, on the other; a community of the former collapses because it fails to develop networks of reciprocal trust, the latter collapses because it is vulnerable to defectors and free riders (Sober and Wilson, 1998). A middle way therefore consists of an enlightened self-interest in which the urge to compete and defect is tempered by widespread recognition of the necessity of cooperation.[4] This recognition involves an emotional attachment to kin but does not halt at the family's edge. As the community expands, so relations of trust and reciprocity spill across the boundaries of kinship to those with whom other forms of relationship are shared (Singer, 1999). A more systematic form of ethical attitude and behaviour develops as the others with whom we share some kind of communal bond become more familially and geographically distant. Religion and morality are the advanced means by which that dispersal is given a collective unity, schemas of reward and punishment by which 'the tribe' is redefined.

Critics complain that this account reduces our moral sense to biology and so to meaninglessness. For theists, unless we have the freedom to act (or not) in accordance with God's will we are nothing more than biologically programmed, soulless robots. For secularists, not only those on the left, a strident, asocial evolutionism exhibits socially biased conceptions of nature, such as Ridley's (1996, p 20) expectation that if our basic instincts are selfish, the scope for cooperation and justice is always highly limited. But evolutionary ethicists respond that while morality may have its roots in biology, this does not make it fictional or merely functional. Instead, because it is the means by which we take control of our natures and drag ourselves farther up the evolutionary ladder morality is both desirable *and* in possession of a distinct rationale and set of criteria (Pinker, 2002, Chs 14 and 15). Morality is as cultural as it is biological, the means by which we evolve beyond our basic programming.

Nevertheless, if morals have a naturalistic origin, they presumably continue to carry naturalistic properties. There are two possible interpretations of this. One is multidimensional in its argument that scientific and ethical paradigms are loosely connected. Stephen Jay Gould (2002, pp 66-7), for instance, assigns science and religion to distinct domains, each of which may have something important to contribute *to* the other but neither of which should be collapsed *into* the other. Midgley (2002), too, argues that moral and religious thinkers have important insights to contribute that only a purblind evolutionism could dismiss as deriving from an immature phase of social development.

This interpretation is certainly valuable in dismissing the more facile claims of sociobiology, evolutionary psychology and so on. Wilson (1998, p 296), for example, views science and religion/ethics as combatants in a contest that science will undoubtedly win. This kind of crude scientism remains popular:

> Modern humanism is the faith that through science humankind can know the truth – and so be free. But if Darwin's theory of natural selection is true this is impossible. The human mind serves evolutionary success, not truth. To think otherwise is to resurrect the pre-Darwinian error that humans are different from all other animals. (Gray, 2002, p 26)

Virtually every page of Gray's *Straw Dogs* sounds like this, being barely more than an anti-liberal updating of sociobiology.

Yet Gould and Midgley might be accused of wishful thinking, nevertheless, of asserting what they find desirable rather than what is scientifically credible. A second possible interpretation, therefore, sees nature as dynamic, as integral to the cultural development by which humans become more self-aware and self-directing. For Pinker (2002, pp 192-3), although our brains may have been wired to receive ethics' 'intrinsic logic', so explaining the universal sharing of certain moral rules, that is not the end of the story since visible within that universalism is a diverse spectrum of moral perspectives, from Leviticus to the *Critique of Practical Reason*. This model therefore offers a closer connection between evolution and ethics without collapsing the latter all way into the former. It assigns a degree of relative autonomy to freedom and culture. How cogent is this?

This is not a question that many Darwinists have been traditionally well prepared to answer (Fitzpatrick, 2005a, pp 116-9). For instance, many have asserted that (1) genes are the key determinants of their organic 'carriers' and that (2) genes seek to replicate themselves, but that (3) humans are nevertheless free to rebel against their genes. A difficulty lies in reconciling these hypotheses. The latter is consistent with the notion that genes seek to replicate themselves if such rebellion is necessary for replication. But if this is the case, the first hypothesis, on which the second depends, is undermined. Conversely, if we insist that genes are the key determinants of their organic 'carriers', our ability to transcend our genes may well be limited. Either way, genetics and freedom do not appear to make peaceful bedfellows.

However, more convincing attempts to reconcile genetics and freedom are now being made. In *Freedom Evolves*, Dennett (2003) elaborates on what has been largely implicit within modern Darwinism. During their earlier stages of evolution, humans were indeed genetically programmed, he claims, like non-human animals. But humans are capable of adapting to their environment better if they possess some degree of autonomy; because enlightened self-interest is superior to egoistic self-interest humans developed the ability to shape how, where and when such cooperative schemes of enlightened self-interest can form. To put it simply, they were genetically programmed to transcend their genetic programming and become self-determining. *Human nature has changed over time* This process of historical self-transcendence is what Dennett refers to as culture: the sharing of knowledge so that we can develop the foresight our genes lack. He is not asserting that such self-determination is absolute, since our cultures of freedom were shaped by those basic, animalistic, genetic codes, but he does maintain that free will is consistent with a 'soft' form of determinism. Dennett has therefore provided an interesting account: (1) used to be important but is less so now, (3) is more important now than it used to be.

We therefore have a naturalistic explanation for ethics that involves two phases. During the first phase, certain rules of behaviour were instilled in us for the sake of survival. The Golden Rule (treat others as you wish to be treated) seems to be necessary for social cooperation and appears to be fundamental to all moral philosophies, for instance. But as we exert more control over ourselves and our environments, we have to think through our moral assumptions and their social implications. In this second phase, morality is less about survival (which is not to claim that the first phase has faded entirely) and more about us making ourselves into the kind of beings we think it desirable to become (Dennett, 2003, pp 260-1). We are nature made self-conscious.

Is this convincing? Well, not in its present form, for several reasons (cf. Gillett, 1999). For while he deploys history as an explanation, Dennett's account is curiously ahistorical. It is perhaps asking too much of him to offer even a brief history of freedom, culture and ethics (that is, how the first phase shaded into the second), but such a history is required if this model is to be anything other than an abstraction. Dennett's reluctance may also be due to his preference for mimetic explanations of culture.

An idea to which Dennett (2006) and Dawkins (2006) constantly return, the meme is the alleged medium of cultural transmission. The meme is to culture what the gene is to biology: it is a cultural replicator, the means by which cultures remain stable over time and share their essential features with other cultural systems. Dennett (2003, p 266) shoehorns this concept into his historical account, arguing that memes have themselves evolved and become self-conscious forms of informational exchange. Yet, if so, why continue to refer to culture and morality as *mimetic*? Doing so risks reinvoking the crude determinism with which Dennett has been charged, with humans becoming 'hosts' and 'nesting places' for memes (Dennett, 2003, pp 178, 186); it also bypasses a wealth of social science literature on social structures and cultural reproduction. Dennett is entitled to observe that we are wired with certain cultural responses but to explain these as quasi-genetic rather than as a distinctly *social* wiring is to collapse the social back into the genetic and revive the contradiction between our genetic programming and our ability to transcend it.

Therefore, Dennett (2006, p 188) lacks any real sensitivity to sociological and sociocultural debates, perhaps, like Pinker (2002), imagining that these offer simplistic 'blank slate' approaches. For instance, he regards belief in God as deriving from the primitive instinct to see agency operating everywhere in nature (Dennett, 2006, Ch 5), yet he seems to accord little space to actual agents acting consciously on the world. It is one thing to attribute a poisoned river to the anger of a river god, entirely another to attribute it to the destructiveness of a materialistic society.

To summarise, Darwinian naturalism potentially offers a foundational account of freedom and culture, and so of ethics, but one that is unlikely to be convincing unless the social is not reduced to its genetic origins but seen as having distinct practices and relations of its own. In my view, evolutionary ethics suggests the basics of a moral philosophy without an entirely convincing theory yet being available. In other words, naturalism is not the whole story.[5]

Social humanism

To be convincing, naturalism must lead us towards humanism or the idea that value and meaning derive from humanity rather than nature per se. This is not to claim that humanism is necessarily anti-religious, simply that for those inclined towards spirituality questions of faith must be seen on a human scale. Think of Kierkegaard's (1985, p 143) insistence that since God's commandments are subject to human interpretation our decisions are inevitably subjective as *we* choose the foundations on which we are to live. Nor is humanism anti-naturalistic, for, as we saw above, humans are themselves part of nature's evolution but, through the medium of culture and civilisation, have become to some degree self-evolving.

Yet humanism has hardly been the intellectual fashion of late. Strange, considering how in the first half of the last century the humanistic tradition was flourishing (Davies, 1997), whether under the guise of humanist Marxism or existentialism (Sartre, 1948). This flourishing proved to be a sprint that preceded an exhausting collapse.

Humanists arguably left themselves weakened by detaching humanism from its religious and natural origins. Bertrand Russell's strident rejection of Christianity would have been more persuasive had he developed the convincing ethical theory for which he strove (Monk, 2001, pp 352-4). And Sartre's sense of revolt about nature, expressed most forcefully in *La Nausée*, expresses a nihilism that captured the zeitgeist but could not in the long term satisfy the human need for attachment and connection.

Whatever the reason, humanism came under attack on many fronts: from feminists who detected within 'the human' masculine properties (synonyms like 'mankind' and 'man') that subtly elided and oppressed women (Le Dœuff, 1991, pp 190–2); from ecologists who insisted that humanism was inevitably anthropocentric and so ignored the intrinsic value of nature (Eckersley, 1992, pp 56–7); and from structuralists who regarded humanism as hopelessly agent-centred (Lacan, 1989, Ch 1). Such ideas in turn inspired post-structuralists to treat the human as a transitory and already fading effect of a particular historical conjuncture, humanism being a doctrine of sameness and so of finitude and death (Foucault, 1989, pp 312–8).

A humanism that takes on board at least some of these critiques is potentially a strengthened and renewed form of humanism, therefore (Norman, 2004, Ch 4), one not necessarily reliant on a conception of the human as the *sole* source of all value and meaning, while conceiving of the self as relational and intersubjective (as dependent on the dependencies of others). The name I give to this revived, sociologically sensitive humanism is *social humanism*. The 'social' here performs several functions. First, it offers a frame of reference distinct from that of religion and nature without (like Russell and Sartre) necessarily having to disinherit the religious and the natural as sources of society's ongoing development. Second, the 'social' is shorthand for the relational, interdependent model of humanness to which we have alluded, the idea that humanity is more like a stream that can direct its own flow than an object that restricts and blocks the current.

Consequently, many feminists have embraced the humanist tradition, seeing feminism as opening a new chapter rather than closing an old book (Nussbaum, 1999a). Meanwhile many ecologists have advocated an ecocentrism that neither treats humanity as unique nor overlooks the special position we occupy as beings whose power over nature gives us particular responsibilities towards it (Bookchin, 1997). While the turn towards difference and discourse may repel the more egocentric forms of individualism, they do not provide reasons for treating agency per se as an illusion (Soper, 1986).

While this book's aim is not to outline and defend a comprehensive theory of social humanism, the intention is to demonstrate how and why its key ingredients are relevant to debates within moral philosophy and applied ethics. To this end, social humanism will be defined according to three principles, two of which are elaborated below with the third following in Chapters Three to Five.

Freedom as appropriation

Autonomy is a central principle for many of the chapters that follow. But what does it mean? Libertarian freedom? Absolute self-determination?

How is it consistent with the emphasis on human evolution outlined earlier?

It is possible that Dennett was correct to interpret freedom as the later stage of an evolutionary process that led from an earlier, animal-like wantonness to the medium of culture and civilisation by which humans become more (but not entirely) self-evolving. Dennett hints at a compatibilism, though the critiques offered earlier (regarding agency) suggest he does not embrace it as such. Compatibilism is the idea that freedom and determinism are reconcilable; incompatibilism says that they are not. Incompatibilists split into libertarians, for whom our actions and beliefs are undetermined (Balaguer, 2004), and determinists, who argue that freedom is illusory (Yadin, 2004). Disagreements between these schools are often of a semantic nature, for what, ultimately, does freedom mean (Kane, 2002; Honderich, 2002)?

If we interpret freedom as 'origination' – or what Kant called 'absolute spontaneity' (Rawls, 2000, pp 280-90) – we are likely to be incompatibilists, for this is the idea that actions and mental events originate solely from within the person holding and performing them, with no 'external' causes at work. Libertarians are persuaded by this notion of 'freedom as origination', while determinists are not. Alternatively, we might view origination as too stringent a requirement and instead see freedom as the 'internal' accommodation and appropriation of external causes, ie *compatibilism*. For example, I cannot avoid feeling hungry or tired occasionally but the means of relieving such appetites are to some extent within my grasp.

Which should we prefer, freedom as origination or as appropriation? We will proceed on the basis that compatibilism is closer to the truth, first because we have defended the view that naturalism offers the basics of an account of morality's origins. Humanists certainly contend that naturalism does not exhaust ethical debate but may also allow that the basic impulses, drives, instincts and desires that drove earlier phases of human evolution are still at work; that they are neither mere social constructions, nor have been socialised away over the course of several millennia. Second, if we accord importance to the social, we cannot ignore the extent to which social structures and institutions constrain and compel certain forms of behaviour. We are all to some extent the products of our social environments without necessarily being its prisoners (see below). Finally, as we will see in Chapter Three, the most impressive attempt to base ethics on incompatibilism fails.

Yet including compatibilism within social humanism leaves it open to a common objection. If we are constrained by nature and social environments, surely we are led towards a philosophical and political determinism where the personal responsibility of individuals is neglected. In short, 'freedom as appropriation' translates into a politics and ethics of freedom as submission to a given order, or to our biological/ psychological programming. But many authors have observed how a recognition of natural and social determinism is a recurrent theme in political radicalism, for it can inspire not fatalism and pessimism but a collectivist ethos of struggle and solidarity whereby people work together to overcome conditions that might otherwise defeat them as isolated individuals (Dubos, 1998, pp 127-35). Indeed, radicals have erred badly when they have ignored the deterministic features of the human condition and proposed that social environments can be remade at will. A more nuanced account of responsibility balances the personal with the environmental (Scanlon, 1998, pp 277-94).

So, autonomy is here defined as freedom as appropriation. Rather than absolute self-determination, it implies, first, accommodation to natural and social determinisms (in a 'soft' sense) and, second, the struggle to transcend those determinisms. The more we act consciously with others, the more self-determining we are likely to be.

Dialogue

The second principle of a social humanist ethics therefore concerns its intersubjective nature. Ethical theory has long been trapped in a series of binary questions – such as 'Are ethical propositions universal *or* relative, objective *or* subjective?' – where even ambitious attempts to transcend these dichotomies have merely preserved them. Since the 1980s, a number of theorists have attempted to relocate ethics conceptually. Habermas (1990; see also Rehg, 1994), for example, outlined what he called 'discourse ethics', complaining that earlier ethical universalists like Kant had only offered a thin form of universalism, and that ethics has to recognise the mutuality of actors in their social and discursive contexts. Ethical debate is therefore more of a public conversation, a dialogue of back-and-forth interaction where participants speak, listen and deliberate. For Habermas, this conversation can reach at least provisional, practical conclusions if we imagine ourselves in an 'ideal speech situation' where the force of the better argument wins. Neutrality and impartiality are not chimerical.

Critics complained that this dialogical universalism was barely an improvement as it still assumed models of rationality, communication and agency that empty the self of its context-dependent identities (see Brandom, 2000, Ch 3). There can be no such thing as an ideal speech situation, for instance, even as an heuristic device, since this presumes a consensual space of open interaction where everyone is included in the dialogue, when what we actually face is an incommensurable series of exclusions, power struggles, pluralistic spaces and ubiquitous differences. Discourse implies meaning and there just is no universally accepted framework of meaning; to converse is to disagree over the nature of the conversation and not only its conclusion. If social interaction is therefore less like an Athenian debate and more like a chaotic set of skirmishes, ethical theory has to reflect this too. Such critics allege that the 'intersubjective universalism' of Habermas really just falls back into the objectivist errors of Kantian idealism. Instead, we ought to acknowledge the more modest but realistic aims of a 'transcultural' politics where different cultures agree to live side by side without the delusions of a foundational once-and-for-all agreement (Gray, 2000).

Such criticisms have themselves been subject to challenge. Most notably, Benhabib (1992; see also Scanlon, 1998, pp 338–49; Rehg, 1999; Bracci, 2002) has sought to accommodate some, although not all, of the charges made against Habermas while retaining discourse ethics as a conception of interactive universalism. She takes seriously his claim to be reconfiguring the traditional binaries of dichotomous thinking, without the poststructuralist conceit of shattering everything into infinite, irreparable fragments. The self is indeed 'situated', and so not the disembodied abstraction of classic liberal philosophies, yet that situatedness is itself a resource *enabling* autonomy and rationality to operate rather than disabling the entire corpus of liberal humanist values. Rules of justice cannot be detached from communal standards; our identities may indeed be saturated within the contexts of their sociation and meaning may well always be contestable, but none of that absolves us of the ability or the responsibility to come to ethical agreements that are rationally defensible. We may always and everywhere be faced by 'otherness', but this in itself depends on universal norms of recognition, where those 'others' share some common ground even though the details of the resulting interaction are not spelt out in advance. For Benhabib, discourse ethics acknowledges the chaotic multitude of discursive interaction without preventing us from calming the noise to manageable levels in crucial areas of human life (constitutions, laws, democratic processes, public debate and association, international relations).

I have argued elsewhere that we ought to adopt a stance of 'creative agnosticism' towards these various perspectives (Fitzpatrick, 2002a), the idea being that what matters is the innovative interaction between them rather than a resolution in favour of just one side – they are dance partners rather than prize fighters. My point is less to resolve the intricacies of discourse theory and more to emphasise the point that if, as indicated above, humanism is based on a recognition of human interdependency, one implication of this is that truth never resides in a single location but is dispersed and distributed across a social field. Therefore consensus and moral agreement do not require homogeneity and rigid unity but a looser affiliation scattered across a number of diverse domains of understanding and social interaction.

Intersubjectivism is therefore a critical method by which moral and social problems are approached through open, ongoing forms of dialogue that interpret truth neither as *merely* subjective but nor as deriving from Olympian, objective facts. It refers us to the interactive contexts of speakers and listeners without allowing us to become lost in those contexts. Meaning is consensual and communal without being relativistic. Intersubjectivism dovetails with 'freedom as appropriation' in that both concepts envisage philosophical inquiry and social progress as explorative and never-ending quests. The self is not an asocial or non-natural atom and individualism is not necessarily synonymous with possessive individualism; the self is instead relational, always engaged in a discovery of that to which it does or can relate, of the connections between agents and of the social and natural tendrils along which our subjectivities extend. Ethical debate therefore resembles a social conversation.

The *social* of 'social humanism' therefore encompasses at least two principles: a *compatibilism* that aids understanding of the extent to which we are constructed by the environments that precede us, where freedom involves the collective struggle to shape the environments that will outlive us; and an *intersubjectivism* that regards ethical debate as open, discursive, pragmatic, participative and eclectic.

A third principle of social humanism will be outlined in Chapters Three and Four before we return to it more systematically in Chapter Five.

Conclusion

The first two sections of this chapter gave various reasons why religion and naturalism do not, alone, provide sufficient support for a convincing ethical theory. Hopefully, this has not caused those who disagree to launch this book across the room in disgust. The social humanism approach outlined above, at least in part, has a distinct rationale that some are entitled to explore without reference to religion and nature, but that others will want to shore up with reference to one or both. What this chapter has not sought to do is put forward a theory of moral foundations that is unnecessarily exclusive. This approach will therefore frame the pragmatic stance taken with regard to ethics in Chapter Five.

Notes

[1] We could also spend time examining issues of universalism, relativism and so on. But while elements of these are touched on below, and in chapters to come, such discussions would require too much of a diversion into metaethics.

[2] Secularism and humanism are here defined as philosophical terms. Secularists are those who reject or are largely sceptical of theistic explanations of reality. This is not to claim that most theists are not down to earth in their political, social and personal commitments. Secularists are therefore humanists in that they seek explanations on a human scale. Such explanations include human evolution and are distinct from the Sartrean emphasis on personal subjectivity. Again, this is not to claim that theists are not also humanitarians.

[3] I use the term evil for convenience, but there is obviously a discussion to be had on whether it serves as shorthand for cruelty, malevolence and so on or whether it is bound up with notions (like hell and Satan) that secularists cannot use.

[4] De Waal (2006) offers a slightly different account: that because primates demonstrate considerable empathy towards one another (not only family and tribal members), our moral sense can be said to derive from these emotional recognitions of natural sentiment. However, his basic model is similar to that which sees behaviour in more self-serving terms, with relatively little space given to reason and agency. Incidentally, one of his inspirations, Adam Smith, illustrates a danger here. While Smith (1976, pp 50-3, 61-3) refuses to condone the worship of wealth and the wealthy, he regards social inequality as inflexible due to sentiment and disposition. This kind of conclusion is all too easily reached when nature is reified.

[5] Why am I therefore claiming its superiority to religious-based ethics? Because if God cannot provide his followers with clearer, firmer foundations for morality, especially after several thousand years' worth of attempts, it seems reasonable to hold religion to a higher standard!

TWO

Consequence

We will draw on the discussions of 'ethical foundations' in chapters to come as we now turn more to normative issues. In this and the following two chapters, we will review the three most influential theories of moral philosophy. These will inevitably be succinct as our aim is simply to equip ourselves with the basic tools necessary for the debates in applied ethics that follow. These chapters will therefore introduce the key dimensions and ideas of each theory, outline their main strengths and weaknesses and indicate what each contributes to applied ethics. Nothing systematic will be said about addressing social problems and social policy per se until Chapter Five.[1]

The basics of consequentialism

Consequentialism states that what makes an action good or bad depends on the effects that action engenders (Sen and Williams, 1982; Pettit, 1993; Darwall, 2003a). There is something intuitively satisfying about this, for who can deny that consequences are important? Yet in its 'pure' form, consequentialism insists that the intention of the person who acts is irrelevant; if I make a hoax phone call that sends a fire engine to a building where, entirely coincidentally, a fire has just broken out, my action was good because it minimised the damage that would have resulted. The intentional nature of the act is also irrelevant to purists; if my lying to you makes you happy, because you believe the deception, that lie cannot be intrinsically immoral. It cannot be *intrinsically* anything, since actions are moral or immoral only to the extent that they serve non-moral values – happiness in this example.

An immediate objection, therefore, is that consequentialism empties morality of the *moral* actor. If good or bad motives are beside the point, I act morally or otherwise depending on how effective I am at weighing consequences. Bentham (2000, Ch 4), most obviously, thought of morality at least partly as a calculus. And because effects depend on a vast confluence of factors, sheer luck intervenes at every stage of human activity. On trial for assaulting a blind woman, I am acquitted by the Court of Consequentialism when the blow she received suddenly restores her sight. Can the im/morality of an action be similarly dependent on unanticipated contingencies? Might I in the long term be justified in smashing a vial of smallpox in Times Square because the reduced population may promote environmental sustainability a century from now?

Consequentialists have a reply to this (Hooker, 2002). It involves acknowledging that making individual acts the unit of assessment leaves the theory vulnerable to such criticisms. If, however, we judge consequences according to a set of rules, perhaps they can be avoided. This is not rule following for its own sake, but the idea that beneficial consequences are most likely to result when certain socio-moral regulations are adhered to (which would include the possession of good intentions). It is possible to imagine circumstances when stealing a loaf of bread would be legitimate, yet we should not sanction stealing because of the anarchy that would probably result. Therefore, the rule 'do not steal' should be followed and exceptions made only in those rare circumstances when stealing appears reasonable.

But this rule-consequentialism is far from being irrefutable (Benn, 1998, pp 73-4). For 'act-consequentialists' are entitled to observe that because exceptions to the rule are sometimes justified, the 'rule-consequentialist' is continuing to assess effects according to actions. If the only way to assist a dying child is by breaking into a chemist in the middle of the night, the rule-consequentialist accepts that the rule against stealing may be violated. But if so, all that separates the act-from the rule-consequentialist is the emphasis they give to actions: the former assesses them all or most the time, the latter some of the time. In other words, we can only decide which rules to follow by deciding which *actions* have beneficial effects and so which *actions* those rules should serve. Rules, therefore, are simply injunctions to perform those classes of actions most likely to have beneficial consequences. (And if a rule-consequentialist denies this, if he maintains the chemist should *never* be broken into, then presumably he *is* justifying rule following for its own sake and has abandoned consequentialism.)

An even trickier issue concerns the assessment of consequences. What value do consequences have to promote in order to be considered good? How is that value to be measured? It is in response to these questions that the most famous school of consequentialism – utilitarianism – arose.

Utility

Utilitarianism was initially influenced by the 18th-century philosopher David Hume, although Bentham admitted that this amounted to something of a misunderstanding on his part (Mack, 1961, pp 102,

120-1). Both thinkers treat utility and happiness as important and therefore regard the generation of beneficial consequences as central to moral judgement. Both were naturalists and held some notion of 'the good' to be more foundational than the dictates of rights, reason and justice, although they also parted company in key respects. Where Hume thought moral actions to be in some sense oriented to 'dense' public and social conventions, Bentham is more individualistic, believing that public rules can and should be aggregated from personal experiences. So where Hume turns towards ancient philosophers, with their emphasis on virtue, narrative and complexity, Bentham is content to borrow from the 'calculative', machine-like moral systems of Mandeville, Tucker and (arguably) Smith. A discussion of Hume is therefore delayed until Chapter Four.

For utilitarians, the property actions should maximise and so be measured against is that of utility. Benthamite utilitarians define utility as happiness, or an excess of pleasure over pain, leading to the famous declaration that:

> Prejudice apart, the game of push-pin is of equal value with the arts and sciences of music and poetry. (Bentham, 1962, p 253)

Nevertheless, he does not deny that these pleasures can produce differing *intensities* of feeling.

Bentham's greatest student, however, J. S. Mill (1962, pp 258-61), was wary of such crude formulations and sought to defend utilitarianism as sensitive to the quality of various pleasures. Those, he observes, who have experienced higher *and* lower pleasures know that even small quantities of the former are superior to large quantities of the latter. True, there are those who forego the higher for the lower but they can only do so as their capacities diminish and are never truly voluntary. Mill's hedonic utilitarianism therefore depends on an elitism (of experience, not birth) where no one can voluntarily choose the lower pleasures even in combination with the higher. In his famous account of personal depression, Mill (1989, pp 97-8, 117-8) makes it clear that it was only a greater sensitivity to feeling, imagination and the 'internal culture' of character that saved him from the harsher elements of utilitarianism as practised by his father. He also proposes that happiness cannot be effected by aiming for it directly but only by realising some mediating property through which, it can be anticipated, happiness will also result.

Despite these welcome additions to Benthamite doctrine, many came to believe that hedonic utilitarianism was simply too limiting and psychologically reductive, with most subsequent utilitarians abandoning happiness as a definition of utility, although the concept has made a recent comeback (Tännsjö, 1998; Layard, 2005).

Many alternatives have been proposed, two of the most important being 'welfare' and 'preferences'. Welfare utilitarians assess actions according to whether they produce better or worse states of affairs or social outcomes (Sen, 2003).[2] The question therefore turns on what counts as a better state of affairs (Card, 2004). What does welfare or wellbeing mean exactly (Fitzpatrick, 2001, Ch 1)? One popular candidate is that of need, that is, actions leading to outcome A are better than those leading to outcome B if more needs are satisfied in A than in B. The problem here concerns how we compare and rank needs. Is my need for a holiday the same as yours for an operation? Is the rich man's need for food the same as the poor man's? Presumably not. But if not, against which scale should we rank those needs? Sen, for instance, has argued that what matters is the capability to achieve certain functionings. A parcel of goods (say, a wage of £300 per week) will engender different capabilities depending on the attributes of the person who receives those goods. Welfare is therefore defined not according to wealth and income but according to the relevant set of capabilities and functionings. In this respect, Sen (1999) has recently accorded particular importance to freedom and political voice (also Nussbaum, 2006).

But whether we define wellbeing in terms of needs or capabilities, or something else, assessing one outcome against another is notoriously problematic (Goodin, 1995, pp 168-75; Foot, 2002, pp 63-9). Perhaps, then, we should be more concerned with the process that leads to a particular outcome than with the outcome itself. While needs are difficult to measure and compare, the same cannot be said for preferences. People have whatever wants they say they have and the strength of those desires can be discerned by how much effort they expend in realising them, as measured by their purchases in the market, for example. So according to 'preference utilitarians', consequences are good when they satisfy people's preferences.

One problem with the market individualist version of preference utilitarianism (Narveson, 1967) is that markets skew information towards those with the most economic power (Reeve, 1990). You may feel empowered by the credit card I have just sold you but unless you really know what is meant by '6.1% APR over 30 months' only I fully appreciate the level of debt you may incur. Consumers frequently have distorted and short-term information about how best to satisfy their preferences. A simple appeal to preferences may also crowd out arguments about social justice. Years ago, the political scientist Charles Murray appeared on a British television programme in which the distinction between the deserving and undeserving poor hinged on their levels of satisfaction; the former had adapted their preferences to their low income and so were content ('poor but happy'), while the latter possessed unrealistic preferences, leading to discontentment, and so contributed to the 'dependency culture' as they expected the state to take up the slack.[3] Market individualists are therefore only interested in 'given' preferences and are indifferent to how those preferences were formed and whether they were formed within a socially just environment (Elster, 1982; Goodin, 1995, pp 130-1). Preferences, they imagine, always precede considerations of justice.

So one problem with preferences is that they can be subjective, distorting and ideologically one-sided. Other forms of preference utilitarianism exist, though. Hare (1981) proposed that moral judgements are universalisable in the sense that they ought to be made impartially, regardless of our position in the scheme of things. Utilitarianism therefore requires the maximisation of the preferences of the greatest possible number of people rather than the dominance of one person's preferences over another's. This approach can seem promising, but the problem with detaching preferences from the market individualist model is that we are again left with the problem of measuring the potentially immeasurable.

Griffin (1986), for instance, defends a conception of utility as the 'fulfilment of informed desires', which, he says, contributes to a theory of distributive justice that limits the operation of property rights. Yet can desires ever be *fully* informed? Do I fulfil my desire to become fitter by walking to work when that walk takes me past a main road filled with cars spewing out carbon monoxide? And even if desires can be fully informed, so what? If I know that smoking this cigarette will reduce my life expectancy by 3.27 minutes, how do I weigh my desire to smoke it against my desire to live as long as possible? My being fully informed about the quantity and quality of life factors is of itself little help in deciding between different courses of potential action (Scanlon, 1998, pp 114-15) Griffin believes that such conflicts *can* be resolved by balancing personal with impersonal factors and developing a 'preference set' that ranks desires in order of importance. But this depends on abstracting from the messy specifics of human life and does not escape from what I will call the 'consequentialist dilemma': the more precise the calculus, the less it reflects the richness, complexity and sheer ambiguities of life (Griffin, 1986, pp 114-23).

With such problems in mind, perhaps consequentialism should adopt an agnostic response to questions of value or utility and analyse the possible worlds created by performing actions or applying rules in terms of their distributional patterns.[4] If total value matters less than social distribution, perhaps intricate issues of value definition can be bracketed. This means that society x, which contains 1,000 utility units owned mainly by the richest 10%, is less preferable to society y, which contains 500 units shared out roughly between all citizens, due to the diminishing marginal utility experienced by the 10% (cf. Sidgwick, 1981, pp 444-8). This is one answer consequentialism might give to the criticism that it does not respect individuals, that, for example, it permits torture if the pleasure of the torturers outweighs the pain of the tortured. For while *rights* may be 'nonsense on stilts' (Bentham, 1962, p 501; cf. Frey, 1984), individual *wellbeing* matters considerably. So it could be that whereas a philosophy of rights engenders a politics of atomistic individualism, one based on wellbeing recognises the importance of individuals (my wellbeing is mine) but also of their interdependency (the level of my wellbeing is dependent on yours).

Anti-utilitarian critics have two rejoinders, however. First, what if society x's affluent are genuinely deserving of their wealth while everyone else deserves their poverty? Surely any redistribution that transformed x into y would be unjust to the deserving (Nozick, 1974, pp 153-5). To this, the consequentialist might respond that rather than merely generating distributive patterns, actions are themselves dependent on the distributive patterns that preceded them. A just allocation of property rights, for instance, might ensure that all subsequent distributions are themselves reflective of (consequentialist) justice. The principle of desert (along with happiness, welfare and preferences) *can* therefore be subsumed within a distributional account (cf. Feldman, 1997, pp 154-74).

A second rejoinder alleges that any redistribution could only occur until the increasing disutility of those from whom wealth is being taken exceeds the increasing utility of those to whom it is being distributed. But if we ought to be concerned with people's needs and capabilities, such consequentialist redistribution may cease before we have reached a socially just level (determined on non-consequentialist grounds). Individual rights might demand a politics of distributive justice that goes beyond anything a principle of social utility can offer.

However, this objection might be countered by consequentialists if our aim were to maximise *average* utility. Here, we might discount the increasing disutilities of the wealthiest so that the maximum level of average utility can be achieved (Sidgwick, 1981, p 415). But Rawls (1972, pp 167-75) objected to this principle of 'maximum average utility' as too risky, as possibly leading to sacrifices of basic liberties where it could be demonstrated that such sacrifices would boost average utility. Yet consequentialists observe that it *may* be reasonable to consider maximum average utility as a rational response to the original position *if* such basic liberties are guaranteed and *if* the least advantaged are also protected by weighting utility in their favour (Wolff, 2002) – a solution that pushes towards some notion of equality of utility or perhaps equality of welfare. In other words, there may be scope for a rapprochement between consequentialism and Rawlsian justice.

In this brief introduction[5], I have mentioned various criticisms of consequentialism's basic position but indicated at each stage how and why its defenders can use them to develop more nuanced and sophisticated versions of consequentialism. Having appreciated what these are, we are now ready to step back and understand the main pros and cons of consequentialism.[6]

Pros and cons

As already noted, consequentialism has an intuitive appeal. Most of us regard an assessment of consequences as crucial to moral deliberation and so consequentialism provides guidance in this respect, without necessarily excluding additional moral theories. Consequentialists also demand that when something is condemned as wrong actual evidence of its negative consequences, such as harm to others, be produced. It is not enough to cite feelings or traditions or commandments; rigorous proof must be provided (Kymlicka, 2002, pp 11-12). Consequentialism allows us to catch out those whose moral disapproval barely rises above the 'ugh' factor. When a devout theist, for instance, condemns homosexuality as destructive of the 'normal' family consequentialism helps us to see through the self-serving bias of such opinions by demanding rational, verifiable, scientific evidence of actual effects.

There are, however, three criticisms of consequentialism that we must review. First, there is the 'consequentialist dilemma' with which utilitarians have spent much time wrestling. Note how the above argument depends on the verifiability of that which makes a consequence good or bad. But if it is to be empirically verifiable, utility also has to be elemental; the more complex our definition of utility, the less measurable it becomes. The appeal of happiness (in Bentham's formulation) or market preference is that they allow such quantification and so permit 'interpersonal comparisons of utility' (Fitzpatrick, 2001, pp 12-13). If you outbid me at an auction for an 18th-century clock, this might allow the satisfaction we would each derive from the clock to be quantified according to how high we were willing to bid. But if happiness and market preferences give rise to the kind of problems mentioned above, we have to develop more sophisticated conceptions of utility.

Yet the more we do so, the more problematic verification and measurement become. For example, Hare (1981, p 92) distinguishes between harming and suffering. If I know my wife is having an affair, I suffer; but if I never learn of the affair, while I do not suffer *I am still harmed.* Yet if there is no experienced harm, how on earth could such disutility be confirmable or measurable? My *reputation* may be harmed if everyone knows about the affair but me, yet the *I* that is being harmed is not reducible to my reputation or to the views of others towards me. What if the affair were only unearthed 1,000 years in the future? Would it also make sense to say that I could be harmed 10 centuries from now? The consequentialist dilemma is therefore this: to measure effects, we must offer potentially reductive conceptions of utility/value, hence simplifying a complex picture; but the more we resist such simplification, the less we can yield useful measurements of relevant values and effects.

Second, consequentialism arguably leans towards 'agent-neutrality', one implication being that consequentialism requires us to act like moral saints. If we are required to maximise utility, then obligations we may bear towards specific others become irrelevant. If £20 would either save the life of someone in Africa by providing them with hygienic water or pay for a birthday present for my sister she doesn't really need, strictly speaking consequentialism demands I choose the first course of action. In one sense, this gives rise to a humanitarian philosophy and politics. If we ought to be concerned with 'protecting the vulnerable', in Goodin's (1986) phrase, the vulnerability of distant strangers may matter more than that of acquaintances or fellow citizens. Yet where does this 'self-other asymmetry' end (Slote, 1992, Ch 1)? If I can live a frugal existence on, say, £200 per month, am I not obligated to donate the other £2,000 of my monthly income to international charities? Are you not similarly obligated? This level of consequence-creating responsibility hardly seems realistic and, indeed, even the most stringent internationalists rarely go that far (see Singer, 2002a, Ch 5; and Chapter Eleven of this volume).

But if agent neutrality demands moral sainthood, it might also demand we become moral defaulters. If you invoice me for a £20 DVD

I purchased, am I not obligated to break my promise to pay because, again, your need is less than that of the stranger in Africa? Are not the obligations of contracts and promises contingent on calculations of utility? We might, of course, invoke the rule-consequentialist requirement that 'all contracts and promises be honoured'. But as we saw above, rule-consequentialism allows for exceptions to the rule and does not permit us to avoid either utility calculations or the contingent, violable aspects of our obligations towards others. Consequentialism therefore enjoins us simply to maxmimise the good without paying attention to those significant others with whom 'agent-relative', social reciprocities have been formed.

Third, and most famously, comes the objection that conseqentialism does not respect the separateness of people. In a remote part of the jungle, the exploration party you lead is captured by natives and, as a test of your courage, you are told to execute one of your compatriots. If you do, everyone else will go free; if you do not, everyone will die. While regarding both options as undesirable, a consequentialist will interpret the death of one as less undesirable than the death of the whole group. In this extreme example, the non-consequentialist is likely to come to the same conclusion about the lesser of two evils, but the consequentialist may nevertheless be criticised for removing from the deliberative process what Bernard Williams called 'integrity' (Smart and Williams, 1973, pp 98-117). This refers to the integrity of the person you are about to sacrifice, the idea that their existence should not depend on a straightforward utilitarian calculus, and your own integrity, since, as a moral being, you cannot disconnect your actions from your core beliefs simply because you are under duress. Non-consequentialists observe that the aggregations typically performed by consequentialists easily allow a large number of trivial harms to be given greater moral weight than a small number of major ones. In short, consequences may be important yet consequentialism may not offer the best form of moral reasoning for taking them into account (Scanlon, 1998, pp 229-41).

Do these objections supply knockdown arguments against consequentialism? Not necessarily. Let us revisit each in turn. The 'consequentialist dilemma' has attracted more work in the field of welfare economics than this chapter can possibly summarise and evaluate. There appear to be many candidates for values that are both complex *and* susceptible to measurement. To take perhaps the most famous example, Sen's work on capabilities has been massively influential in the field of international development, influencing the United Nations Development Programme and providing a basis for cross-national comparisons (*Economics and Philosophy*, 2001). Since governments deal with statistical abstractions and simplifications in order to govern, perhaps we can and should permit comparisons of outcomes and distributive patterns, albeit at a generic level.

Some consequentialists have also challenged the earlier assumption about agent-neutrality by introducing agent-relative arguments into the picture (Pettit, 1997, pp 94–6; Portmore, 2001). This means that in judging the consequences of possible actions we not only aggregate potential utility gains against utility losses at an impersonal level, but also consider the particular impacts on the actors concerned. In the jungle scenario, what is relevant is not only the number of deaths but also the consequences for the person sacrificed (reduced to the status of a sacrificial lamb) and for the leader (who has been given a moral responsibility without full moral autonomy). We might therefore weigh the interests of these individuals in our deliberations, making it less obvious which of the two courses of action should be taken. According to Scheffler (1994, p 93; cf. Slote, 1985; Mulgan, 2001):

> Hybrid theories constitute a bona fide, stable alternative to consequentialist and fully agent-centred conceptions.

We should certainly question exactly how stable such hybridity can be, for it seems highly unlikely that we can simultaneously maximise the good *and* maximise individual rights. Nevertheless, as noted in Chapter Five, this search for hybridity has become a common feature of contemporary debates. So consequentialists are neither required to be moral saints nor moral defaulters. It is possible to combine a humanitarian concern for everyone while acknowledging that we have particular allegiances to family, friends and fellow citizens (Sidgwick, 1981, pp 431–2); similarly, those with whom we enter into contracts have legitimate claims on our sense of moral responsibility.

Therefore, consequentialists have a potential answer to the 'separateness of persons' argument, for agent-relativity allows a recognition of integrity to enter into our assessments of what we should do, without neglecting that in the event of having to make lose–lose decisions we need to be both compassionate and tough, personal and impersonal, in choosing the least worst alternative: Scheffler (1994, p 88) again:

> Either way, someone loses: *some* inviolable person is violated. Why isn't it at least permissible to prevent the violation of five people by violating one? An appeal to the value of an unviolated life or the disvalue of the violation of a life cannot

possibly provide a satisfactory answer to this question. For the question is not whether to choose an unviolated life over a violated one; the relative value of violated and unviolated lives is not at issue.

As in the previous section, there are some persuasive criticisms of consequentialism to be advanced but arguably none so strong that consequentialists cannot reasonably respond to it. We will be able to make a stronger assessment of consequentialism's worth once we have looked at the theories and debates covered in the next two chapters. But we are already able to outline the concepts and methods that consequentialism contributes to the subject of applied ethics.

Applied ethics

Let us assume that consequentialism should be used to *inform* the decision-making process with regard to applied ethics. There is an argument that consequentialist theories should only be used for the post facto evaluation of actions on the grounds that most people are not consequentialists, and never will be, so that the assumption and imposition of consequentialist criteria would distort the moral reasoning we bring to bear on ethical problems (Pettit and Brennan, 1993). Such post facto evaluation seems hardly worth the effort, however, unless it permits all of us, as policy shapers, to learn from experience and decide better next time.

If courses of action are to be judged according to their consequences, those pertinent to applied ethics should be similarly assessed (Häyry, 1994, Ch 4), which, at its heart, means treating consequentialism as a decision-making framework based simply on our favouring what is likely to further the interests of those affected by our actions (Singer, 1993, p 14). Key to the consequentialist approach is a rejection of the distinction between acts and omissions.

When you act, you intervene in some significant way in a set of relevant circumstances; when you do not act, you do not intervene. But although one involves performance and the other non-performance, consequentialists insist that they are both of moral significance whenever deliberateness is present. Actions and omissions do not always imply deliberateness, of course. When, for instance, I pull you out of the way of a speeding car, I may have *re*acted at such a pace that no conscious forethought was possible. Alternatively, I may fail to act through lack of deliberateness; for example, I hear cries for help that I honestly mistake for TV sounds and so ignore them. But, according to consequentialists, when deliberateness is present, moral significance attaches to it whether the deliberateness generates an act *or* an omission.[7]

The non-consequentialists among you may be getting uneasy by now. There is little that is problematic about assigning moral significance to freely chosen actions, since these are executed in conformity with some ethical standard and with reference to some notion of personal responsibility. But surely the same cannot be said of omissions. At every moment of my life there is an endless number of things I am omitting to do. While typing these words, I am not sending any money to charity, not helping grannies across the road, and not finding a cure for AIDS; in fact, not doing an endless series of laudable acts up to the *nth* degree of infinity. Does this mean I am partly to blame for underfunded charities, stranded grannies and the continuation of AIDS? This is either too stern an allocation of moral failure, or a trite observation that we are all partly responsible for everything.

In fact, consequentialism cedes ground here and does not require heroic self-sacrifice for the sake of the greater good (but see Unger, 1996). Indeed, many consequentialists agree that there *is* a distinction to be made between acts and omissions. My not sending a crate of food that would be enough to save five lives to a hurricane-ravaged area is not the same as sending a crate of poisoned food that *kills* five people. The former may be a regrettable omission but also reflects the impossibility of my doing everything for everyone; the latter, by contrast, is murder.

Yet consequentialists maintain that while there is a distinction to be made, the difference between acts and omissions is not that considerable (Singer, 1993, pp 206-13). If you have been pushed into a well and break your leg, I am morally obliged to help you even though I am in no way responsible for your being there in the first place. My ignoring your pleas for help might make me as culpable as the person who pushed you into the well. So if some omissions are morally significant, and some are not, where do we draw the line? Some omissions will be closer to the poisoned food scenario – if I spot that your house is on fire but neglect to act and so possibly contribute to a family member's death, for example. Other omissions will barely be of significance at all, as when I do not perform an action whose consequences would be beneficial but negligible. There is no 'line', in other words, but a series of gradations that can perhaps only be established on a case-by-case basis. In short, if what matters are consequences, the consequences that follow from omissions *can* sometimes be as important as those that flow from actions. As long as we apply a bit of common sense, we can judge the morality of many non-actions.

Therefore, consequentialists do not necessarily reject the 'doctrine of double effect' (DDE) per se, but they do launch a large dollop of scepticism in its direction (Woodward, 2001; also see Chapter Three of this volume).

The DDE is traceable back to Aquinas and allows a distinction to be made between those effects that were and those that were not intended. Killing in self-defence is permitted, for example, if my intention was self-preservation but I accidentally killed my attacker in the process. One effect was intended (the self-defence), while the other (the killing) was not, although it may well have been foreseen. However, if I shoot you in the back while you are clearly running away, there is no double effect and so no reasonable defence against a charge of murder. The doctrine is particularly familiar in two areas of applied ethics.

In the first example, your brother is terminally ill and in a great deal of pain. He has expressed a wish to die but euthanasia is against the law. However, the doctor administers ever-higher levels of morphine to ease your brother's pain, foreseeing that this will also have the effect of hastening your brother's death. As we will see in Chapter Ten, this is a common occurrence and on those occasions where doctors have been prosecuted the defence has argued, almost always successfully, that the intention was to relieve pain rather than end life. The morphine-induced death may have been *foreseen* but not *intended*, a distinction that is recognised in many systems of law and, indeed, by the Catholic Church (Vatican, 1994). One problem is that medics who really do set out to murder their patients might be able to hide behind the doctrine, as might those whose incompetence resulted in your brother's death. We will engage with this debate fully in Chapter Ten.

In the second example, terrorists bomb your capital city, causing thousands of deaths. In reprisal, you launch missiles against the terrorists' hideouts but because they reside in urban areas several hundred innocent civilians are killed along with them. Do those civilian deaths equate to murder, on a par with those committed by the terrorists? All things being equal, the doctrine says not: that while it was foreseen that your retaliation would kill civilians, it was not your intention to do so. Indeed, any credible theory of a just war says not that civilian deaths must always be avoided but that they must be minimised (see Walzer, 2000, pp 152-9). The DDE suggests there is no moral equivalence between yourself and the terrorists.

Consequentialists, however, question the distinction between intending and merely foreseeing along the lines suggested above. In the first example, your brother's death may have been a *later* effect but it became inevitable once the decision to increase his morphine had been made. The intention was to spare him pain, but since the pain had become inseparable from his life you also wanted to spare him the pain of living. Intention therefore applies to both effects (pain relief and death) and so there is no significant moral distinction between killing and 'letting die'. Where this takes us to isn't clear. Some consequentialists will oppose euthanasia (perhaps on rule-consequentialist grounds that we should never kill), while others will insist that since our aim should be to relieve pain, and since doctors are carrying a moral burden the rest of us are unwilling to shoulder, we ought to formalise the rules even if this means practising euthanasia overtly rather than (as at present) covertly.

Similar considerations apply to the retaliatory strike. The civilian deaths were intended in the sense that, even if you could not calculate exact numbers, you knew some would result. Those people would have been alive today had you not acted as you did. They are dead because at some level you thought their deaths to be acceptable. (Note, however, that this is an argument against DDE but not necessarily against the retaliation; a consequentialist might still decide to retaliate if he anticipates that more people will die in the long run if the terrorist attack is allowed to go unpunished.)

So while there are distinctions to be drawn between acts and omissions, and intending and foreseeing, consequentialists argue that we cannot derive sound conclusions from them when debating applied ethics and ought instead to recognise the significant overlaps between each term.

A further contribution that consequentialism makes to applied ethics relates to interests. It seems reasonable to observe that all beings capable of experience have an interest in avoiding harm, suffering and pain. There may certainly be exceptions to the rule but for the most part these are 'bads' that we all prefer to avoid. Applied ethics should therefore be concerned to diminish the incidence of such bads. Yet this apparently simple point has some contentious implications. Do the interests of all sentient beings matter equally? If we can propose that some non-humans (such as chimps and the great apes) rank on a level with humans due to their evolutionary similarities, perhaps certain humans rank *below* that level. For example, some coma victims might be incapable of feeling either pleasure or pain and so possess no interests that register within our calculation of moral consequences; severely disabled babies might experience so much pain that we are better off 'putting them down', just as we would show mercy to an injured dog or horse. Such conclusions have been reached by Singer (1993, Chs 4–7) and are the reasons why he is such a controversial figure. We will explore some of the relevant issues concerning harm in Chapters Six to Ten.

Conclusion

There are many points to be made in favour of consequentialism, and many to be made against it. It revolves around the commonsense notion that consequences are highly important when it comes to judging the goodness or badness of an action. Critics observe that while consequences are certainly important, they are far from being of such overwhelming concern that they crowd out other factors relevant to moral deliberation. Key among these are the integrity of the agents affected and the individual and social particularisms that make a consequentialist calculus problematic. Critics allege that the importance of consequences does not translate into making consequential*ism* the basis of morality. Then again, we have seen that consequentialists voice a range of counter-objections to their critics. If these objections possess even some plausibility, while we may not possess any knockdown arguments *for* consequentialism we do not possess any knockdown arguments against it either. It therefore seems reasonable to retain consequentialism as a vital point of reference when debating both moral philosophy and applied ethics. This is not the end of the debate, however, and we will continue to review the main themes and critiques of consequentialism in the next two chapters and beyond.

Notes
[1] For analyses of utilitarianism and public policy, see Goodin (1995) and Bailey (1997).

[2] Note that Sen himself would reject the label of 'welfare utilitarian'.

[3] I hope I didn't dream this TV programme (think of the therapist bills if I did).

[4] This takes us back to states-of-affairs arguments.

[5] And it is brief. I have not covered motives, satisficing versus optimising criteria, the direct/indirect distinction or future generations (on the latter, see Fitzpatrick, 2003, pp 131-3).

[6] Further critiques will be presented in the next two chapters and so are not replicated here.

[7] Judging each case is difficult, of course. For instance, to what extent can I cite ignorance of a situation as a factor when I am responsible for that ignorance? My not knowing what happens to political prisoners in the jails of a dictatorship is no excuse if I have ignored the information which is available.

THREE

Right

Consequentialism is typically contrasted with 'deontology' where the moral obligation to perform an act is thought to come from principles that make little or no reference to consequences. Deontology therefore departs from the 'teleological' character of consequentialism: the latter is concerned with the ends of action, the former with rules and principles that 'precede' actions. In this chapter, we will run through the classic expression of deontological thinking (Kant), look at recent Kantian 'contractualists' and then develop our understanding of applied ethics.

Kant's ethics

Grounds

Although complex, the basics of Kant's ethics are fairly well known (O'Neill, 1989; Baron, 1995).

Seventy-five years before Mill's *Utilitarianism*, Kant (1996, pp 156-8) anticipated and dismissed its central premise. Pleasure and desire are all of one degree, he claims. Some may possess greater *intensity* than others but to imagine that certain pleasures and desires are of a higher order is to allow them to intrude on to a level that can be reserved only for reason. Given a choice between Bentham's and Mill's utilitarianism, Kant might have preferred the former. But ultimately, of course, he would have supported neither, since consequences are too capricious a foundation for morality:

> ... the ground of obligation must be looked for, not in the nature of man nor in the circumstances of the world in which he is placed, but solely *a priori* in the concepts of pure reason. (Kant, 1991, p 55)

Moral actions are those performed not simply *in conformity* with the moral law, as revealed to reason, but *for the sake* of that law. Inclination and motivation are irrelevant since, as aspects of nature, they are subject to vicissitude; to do good is to act from duty in accordance with the 'good will'. Since duty is a question of principle, rather than of realising whatever consequences are held to be preferable, the job of ethical philosophy is to determine what those principles or maxims are. This leads to Kant's first formulation of the categorical imperative in the *Groundwork* (Kant, 1991).

Hypothetical imperatives demonstrate an 'if ... then' quality: if you wish to succeed, then you ought to work hard. In such propositions, the property of 'ought' and 'should' is dependent on the nature of the object the 'if' is referring to. By contrast, the categorical imperative is not dependent on contingent desires:

> ... I ought never to act except in such a way that I can also will that my maxim should become a universal law. (Kant, 1991, p 67)

Before proceeding, we must dispense with a common misunderstanding that treats the above as equivalent to the Golden Rule of 'treat others as you wish to be treated' (MacIntyre, 1981, p 46). One objection is as follows. Kant is proposing that for something to be moral it must be universalisable. So what if my preferred maxim states that it is acceptable to steal from others? I am fine with this maxim because while I thereby allow others to try to steal from me, I am so confident in my abilities as a thief that the gains will outweigh any losses. On this account, stealing is therefore a universal law.

This objection to the categorical imperative misses the point, however. Remember that Kant is omitting anything that by being empirically dependent – consequences, personal gain, inclination and so on – does not correspond to the objective necessity of the good will.[1] It is not a question of what *I will* as a subjective holder of preferences but of what *is willable* by rational beings. Kant (1991, p 84) therefore reformulates the categorical imperative in such a way that subjectivism is eased out of the picture:

> Act only on that maxim through which you can at the same time will that it should become a universal law.

By identifying me as a rational being, the categorical imperative thereby demands that I recognise and respect the rationality of others:

> Act in such a way that you always treat humanity, whether in your own person or in the person of any other, never simply as a means, but always at the same time as an end. (Kant, 1991, p 91)

To treat others as means only is to institute a heteronomy in which people are conceived as nothing more than indistinct projections of my own subjectivity. To conceive of others as ends in themselves is, by contrast, to institute a principle of autonomy that binds rational beings together under common objective laws in a 'kingdom of ends'. This is the core of what for many is the most persuasive model of liberalism: one based on the freedom of rational beings who observe the laws and duties of universal reason in a moral and social system of mutual respect, a liberalism that sits squarely between libertarianism, on the one hand, and a sentimental politics of tradition, community and the common good, on the other.

Many of the standard criticisms of Kant's ethics kick in at this point (MacIntyre, 1967, Ch 14): that the categorical imperative is too formal and rigid, abstracting from anything we recognise as deriving from particular social contexts, in all of their density and complexity, offering only desiccated guidance for moral decision making; that Kant's version of duty is emotionless, less the principle of moral saints and more that of moral robots, which by ignoring motives asks people to *do* good without necessarily *being* good; and that by excluding consequences from his moral philosophy (let justice be done though the heavens fall) Kant is ensuring that the heavens will indeed fall. The general thrust of these attacks is not necessarily incorrect but certainly incomplete until we have appreciated how and why Kant developed his basic ideas.

Freedom, for Kant, is a philosophical absolute. Given the 'unreliability' of the empirical dimension of nature, freedom must be independent of the causation that prevails in the sensible world. Freedom cannot be itself if it is in any way a subject of determination. This suggests that we exist across two dimensions (Kant, 1991, pp 111-21): the world of appearance, sensibility, causality (phenomena) and the necessary, transcendent world of supersensible things-in-themselves (noumena). The latter is the habitation of the good will and so the ground of the former, the means by which nature is subordinated to rational law. It was these hints that Kant elaborated on in the *Critique of Practical Reason* (see Kant, 1996, pp 174-9).

Critique addresses itself in part to the question of how these worlds are related (Kant, 1996, pp 215-21). If causation implies time and freedom implies timelessness, how does time intersect with that which is 'not time'? How, for instance, can we be free of the ripple effects of the interventions we ourselves have previously made into the temporal world of nature? As will be argued further below, Kant does not give a satisfactory answer to this problem of intersection. For example:

> ... I do not see how those who insist on regarding time
> and space as determinations belonging to the existence of
> things in themselves would avoid fatalism of actions ...(Kant,
> 1996, p 221)

Kant refers to fatalism here because, for him, any hint of determinism
renders us as marionettes that inhere within nature as *accidents*. Indeed,
we cannot even treat God as the causal origin of actions, although,
says Kant (1996, p 222), God *is* the reason we are free in the first
place, the 'cause of the existence of the acting beings (as noumena)'
and therefore the means by which the sensible and transcendental
worlds are reconciled and the problem of intersection set aside. So,
having rejected ontological and cosmological arguments for God's
existence, Kant (1996, p 241) settles on an instrumentalist defence
to reconcile phenomena and noumena:'... it is morally necessary to
assume the existence of God'; 'this being must be postulated' (Kant,
1934, p 368).

Virtues

It is this issue of reconciliation that constitutes a starting point for Kant's
final work of moral philosophy, *The Metaphysics of Morals* – specifically
how the transcendental translates into the world of appearances. In this
book, he is clear that the doctrine of right must neighbour a doctrine
of virtue.

Kant (1996, p 191) had earlier contrasted 'the good' with the moral
law. In *Metaphysics* this becomes:

> Right is therefore the sum of conditions under which the
> choice of one can be united with the choice of another in
> accordance with a universal law of freedom. (Kant, 1996,
> p 387)

The freedom to choose in accordance with the moral laws of universal
reason (the right) therefore predominates over the particular content
and values of the choices we make at any one time (the good). This
distinction between the right and the good has been highly influential,
yet recent scholars observe that we should not use it to neglect the
arguments about virtue, and indeed happiness, that Kant makes in
Metaphysics (Baron, 1997; Ramsay, 1997, Ch 2; Louden, 2000; Stratton-
Lake, 2000).

Virtue for Kant (1996, pp 517-27) seems to imply 'free self-constraint', that is, the freedom to choose ends but ends that are consistent with the principle of universal duty. Virtue is not the fulfilment of one's animal nature but the reluctant cultivation of natural predispositions – reluctant because it involves an educative process of struggle and commitment. Towards others, virtue implies the promotion of their happiness, the removal of whatever obstacles are preventing the growth of their virtuous dispositions. What makes a doctrine of virtue necessary in the first place are the limitations of the right, for while the latter can specify the *maxims* of actions, it cannot prescribe the actions themselves. There is an obligation to obey the moral law but no *a priori* rule that says that obligation involves *these* particular ends and objects rather than *those*. The right is a 'perfect' duty that cannot be rationally ignored, whereas the good consists of many possible (and therefore imperfect) duties that may approximate to the moral law but can never conjoin with it exactly. There is therefore a disparity or disjunction (what Kant calls a 'playroom') between our duty to obey rational, universal laws and the actions through which that obedience manifests itself at any one time – how wide a disparity is a matter of some dispute (see Hill, 2002, Ch 7). It is that gap that makes a doctrine of virtue necessary: we have a duty to seek perfection through imperfect acts.

Kantian virtue therefore consists of an inner strength, the disposition of free beings to constrain themselves. Does this mean that Baron (1997) is correct that Kant recognises the value of the good (for example, happiness) without falling into the errors of consequentialism; or that he has a more persuasive conception of virtue than self-proclaimed virtue ethicists (see Chapter Four)? Yes and no. Kant was obviously not the puritan of rationalist abstractions, whose moral philosophy involves impersonal computations of duty, that popular myth perceives him as being. In bringing together elements of the right, the good and virtue, he strikes a surprisingly eclectic and contemporary note. Yet for all this Kant does still give priority to the right (Rawls, 2000, p 231).

For example, he is quite clear that his account of virtue differs from Aristotle's. For the latter, virtue is a mean between two vices, while for Kant (1996, pp 532-3), virtue has to be referred always to the maxims of universal law. It is not enough to claim, for example, that prudence is an avoidance of both profligacy (excessive spending) and parsimony (excessive thrift); instead, we require a maxim that, based on the categorical imperative, is more reliable than such empirical comparisons and generalisations. The *phronesis* (or practical rationality) on which Aristotelian virtue is based is, for Kant, too thin and capricious a means of support. Virtue possesses us rather than the other way around.

So, while Kant does not ignore the good, he gives priority to the right. This amounts to a distinct moral perspective within which resides a theory of applied ethics. Kant's reference here is to a 'moral anthropology', the point at which the right is applied to the empirical world of natural causation.

Take the famous example of lying. That you should never tell a lie is a Kantian maxim. In the event of Harry coming to your door seeking Roger, you should tell Harry the truth about Roger's whereabouts (that he's hiding in the attic) even if you know that Harry means to kill Roger. Kant acknowledges the overwhelming temptation we would have to lie and misdirect Harry. But what if, he imagines, Roger has slipped out of the attic without your knowing and then runs into the path of Harry, who, had you been truthful, would now be rummaging through your house? There are, in short, so many potential ramifications and permutations that we are better off sticking to principles (treating Harry and Roger as ends-in-themselves) rather than trying to estimate consequences, even when it feels instinctive to do so.[2] Even rule-consequentialism would be impermissible because to contemplate exceptions to the rule is to invalidate the universalism that makes something a principle in the first place. If as a result of your honesty Harry murders Roger in the attic, so far as your intervention is concerned, this is an accidental harm for which you cannot be held responsible. Kant (1996, p 612) is in other words distinguishing between intending and foreseeing and arguing that we can be held accountable only for the former:

> ... if you have kept strictly to the truth, then public justice can hold nothing against you whatever the unforeseen consequences might be.

We will revisit this DDE again later but it is worth anticipating an obvious criticism. To maintain (presumably correctly) that not every relevant consequence of a lie can be anticipated surely does not mean that *no* relevant consequences can be anticipated with reasonable certainty. Refusing to incorporate those reasonable certainties into one's decision making is, for consequentialists and even many Kantians (Korsgaard, 1996, pp 348–58), a dereliction of duty. If Harry kills Roger in the attic as a result of your honesty, you are surely more responsible than if he kills Roger in the street as a result of your deception, since the former implies greater foresight than the latter. Kant would reject this objection, of course. The assessment of contingent circumstances must be subservient to the right, he says, not the other way around. The moral law always comes first.

Criticisms

Putting this debate aside for now, how convincing is Kant's ethics? We can see that the criticisms mentioned on p 47 are a bit too simplistic. Kant's attention to virtue and happiness means that his philosophy is not quite the purview of soulless moralisers, perpetually calculating their ethical duties, that it is often represented as being. Indeed, Herman (1993, Ch 2) even regards Kant's ethics as a reflective process such that considerations of the good may resonate back and alter our conception of the right; the categorical imperative is less a commandment and more a regulative and deliberative ideal. Yet while Kantians are obviously entitled to reformulate ethics in this way, it must be questioned how faithful this reading is to Kant's actual text. His own examples of universal laws (against lying, for example) do remain quite formal and formulaic, especially in the rejection of consequences as factors relevant to moral deliberation.

What are also crucial are the dualisms Kant repeatedly makes between reason and nature, necessity and contingency, freedom and causality, infinity and time. His books are strewn with a Cartesian insistence on the superiority of one dimension over another (Kant, 1996, pp 269–70) and although the term 'essentialist' has become hackneyed with recent overuse, Kant, for all of his work on history (Wood, 1999, Chs 7 and 9), does display a palpable fear of the ideal being diluted by the impurities of the empirical. This dread is reaffirmed during the period when his doctrine of virtue is being developed. He makes, for example, the reasonable point that:

> However evil a man has been up to the very moment of an impending free act so that evil has actually become custom or second nature it was not only his duty to have been better [in the past], it is *now* still his duty to better himself. (Kant, 2001, p 391) [emphasis in original]

And because 'ought implies can', Kant is obviously making the point that he is still free to choose. There is an absolutism at work here, a common intuition that final responsibility for their actions rests with anyone who can be said to possess moral consciousness.

Yet does such absolutism 'go all the way down', that is, does it apply equally to each and every aspect of the self? I suspect that most of us would wish to place greater emphasis on what Kant calls 'custom or second nature', so that (in epistemological and psychological as well as political terms) our freedom is always reconfigured by the weight of the social environments, habits and predispositions, genetic constitutions and cultural routines that flow through and around it.

Take what he says about social policy, broadly defined. Kant (1996, pp xviii-xx, 573) derides those who laud as virtuous wealthy people who give to the poor when the needs of the latter are in fact due, not to a lack of charity, but to the 'goods of fortune' and the 'injustice of government'. Yet his intent here is to correct the whiff of hypocrisy rather than challenge the injustice of social inequalities. As far as the latter is concerned, Kant (1996, pp 468-70) advocates a kind of *state-enabled* system of charity. Freedom for Kant therefore appears to be asocial, indifferent to hierarchies of economic power – a version of the freedom to sleep under a bridge or dine at the Ritz, for example.

A contractualist like Scanlon (1998, pp 277-94) arguably offers a more persuasive account than this by distinguishing between 'attributive' responsibility (the attribution of an action to an agent) and 'substantive' responsibility (deeper claims about what people owe to one another).[3] To hang moral blame entirely on the former is to ignore the substantive differences in opportunity possessed by different individuals. The attributive and the substantive therefore only begin to correspond under conditions of fair opportunity; yet by seeing freedom in absolutist terms only, idealist philosophers such as Kant risk becoming the rugged individualists of human ontology.[4]

In short, rather than being an 'in itself' or an 'all or nothing', we might see freedom as a hybrid, a question always of degree, where the attributive is mixed with 'impure' elements that hem, stifle and encumber possibilities without ever erasing them entirely. This perhaps means reinvoking the argument of Chapter One: of viewing freedom as an appropriation, as compatible with a 'soft' conception of determinism.

But maybe this is too critical. After all, even the most thoroughgoing materialists make room for a conception of the ideal, so perhaps Kant's transcendentalism is simply making a space for the ideal that, as a concurrent feature of rationality, materialist philosophies would otherwise lack. Perhaps hybridity is precisely what Kant himself is theorising (Allison, 1990, pp 3-6). The problem with this defence is that Kant wishes to make the difference between reason and non-reason a matter of kind and not of degree. MacIntyre (1999, pp 57-61) observes that non-human animals demonstrate certain powers of reasoning. If so, does Fido participate in the transcendental noumena when he decides to chase the red ball instead of the blue one? Or is only *human* rationality attached to the ideal? What, then, about the primitive reasoning powers of babies? Does the noumena snap into place when we reach a certain age?

In other words, while Kant should certainly not be interpreted as articulating two *separate* wills operating in two *separate* worlds (noumena and phenomena) (Hill, 1992, Ch 5; Rawls, 2000, p 277), his account of freedom *is* dualistic and firmly anchored in the transcendent. Kantians praise him for harmonising the transcendental realm of freedom with that of temporal matter (Korsgaard, 1996: 182-3) but are less vocal about why they have to be separated out in the first place, especially in this post-Darwinian age when plausible accounts of evolutionary ethics are available (see Chapter One).

This criticism of Kant's ontology echoes that of Paul Guyer. Guyer makes clear that Kant's intention was to resist the absolute idealism of Spinoza and Fichte, which he believed did not take enough account of contingency. Yet although Kant anticipated some elements of Darwinism, and even hints that purely mechanical accounts of natural development are conceivable, his is a theory whereby organisms nevertheless receive their ends and purpose by an intelligent designer. Guyer (2005, Chs 11-13) establishes that this assumption about nature's teleology does not survive post-Darwinian scrutiny. For instance, Kant naively supposed that matter is inert unless 'motivated' by a non-material 'outside' (God, in other words).

Kantian idealism therefore perpetuated the Cartesianism rampant throughout European philosophy, floating our moral and rational consciousness free of its material moorings, where the phenomenal world is illuminated from outside by the lights of the ideal. So while Kant (2001, p 393) recognises that understanding incorporates an 'anthropological' dimension, since our moral characters encompass a 'contingent existence', its origins, he maintains, lie outside of time. Kant is therefore an incompatibilist, a non-naturalist who invites nature into ethics only as something of a reluctant and belated guest (Rawls, 2000, pp 283-90).[5]

Contractualism

This does not necessarily mean we should reject Kant's ethics in its entirety, or the tradition to which it gave rise (Wood, 1999, pp 178-82). What happens if we retain Kant's ethics without the underlying ontology? One response to this question has appeared in the form of contractualism (Scanlon, 1998; Darwall, 2003b, 2006) and it is to this we now turn.[6] John Rawls sits squarely in this tradition and his moral philosophy will be our main point of reference.

Contractualism recommends that we base our moral principles on what *rational individuals would reasonably consent to under conditions of liberty and equality.*[7] Contractualists are less hostile to heteronomy and hypothetical imperatives than Kantians, proposing that *reasonableness* does not always reduce to *reason* (see Scanlon, 1998, p 6). Contractualism treats moral propositions partly as a matter of rational analysis and partly as the outcome of social interaction and deliberation (something akin to the intersubjectivism mentioned in Chapter One). Difficulties in assigning meaning to 'reasonableness' and 'reason' suggest that contractualists face an uphill task.

Why, first of all, make rationality important? Reason is only one of many characteristics of humanness and perhaps not even the most essential one. Reason is the slave of the passions, alleged Hume (1969, pp 460-1), and the 20th century was dominated by theories that maintained that reason is indeed subject to any number of non-rational forces: the unconscious (Freud), historical materialism (Marx), the will to power (Nietzsche), to name but a few. And why, then, make the individual your starting point when many have argued that the self is a humanist mirage that disappears when you look at it too directly? The stipulation of what people *would consent* to is surely contentious also. Perhaps morality requires more than a show of hands, given that people can be misled, wrong or just plain biased in their opinions. If we are concerned with what they *would* consent to, are we not opening the door to prejudicial and paternalistic assumptions? And what does reasonable mean? How can we test for it? Opinions – even collective, consensual ones – on when reasonableness is and is not present are likely to be shaped by what we agree with: subjective interests and personal beliefs. Can discussants really meet together under conditions of liberty and equality? Surely some are going to dominate others, ensuring that their view prevails. Surely some will be more articulate than others. How can this hypothetical condition really be translated into an open space of moral deliberation?

These are all legitimate observations and questions, but do they thereby defeat the contractualist project? Rawls (1972, pp 251-7) observes that his principles of justice are Kantian in inspiration and that the original position represents the deliberative space of autonomous beings determining laws for themselves according to rational precepts. The veil of ignorance ensures autonomy by stripping away those contingent features of our natures or social positions that could skew deliberation; it therefore ensures impartial deliberation among *equal* beings and so might be thought of as a kingdom of ends. The principles of justice are presented by Rawls as categorical imperatives. For instance, while the ends that people pursue can and should be left to them, reason suggests that certain *primary* resources (rights and liberties, opportunity and powers, income and wealth, self-respect) are those that everyone requires in order to pursue their particular conception of the good.

Both Kant and Rawls are therefore concerned to detail the conditions of our autonomy. Kant's aim, he says, was not to recommend a morality of duty-bound austerity but one of the self-respect and mutual esteem that comes from acting according to the highest principles, rather than transitory inclinations and desires. In *A Theory of Justice*, Rawls (1972) associates the original position with the noumenal self by claiming that it permits rational choice free of all social and natural contingencies. Once the veil of ignorance is removed, we still have some decisions to make over how to apply our principles to the phenomenal world. The main difference is that while Kant gives the impression of being able to work out universal maxims from scratch, Rawls maintains that the original position is a collective enterprise, an ethical commonwealth of reasonable consent into which is incorporated a basic understanding of social conditions, such that, for example, we cannot reasonably decide that everyone should be a billionaire and own a palace.

There is therefore something of a question mark over what Rawls (1972, pp 48–52) called 'reflective equilibrium'. This is a methodological process of assessing and revising our considered judgements against the many principles of justice offered by moral philosophy. If, for instance, we agree with Rawls' defence of the maximin principle, this might cause us to revise our views about particular policies, such as tax rates, property rights and so on. Surely it is also the case, however, that our existing judgements will influence which moral theory we are most persuaded by and so which principles of justice are supportable. Rawls leaves this possibility as an open question while acknowledging that:

> ... it is obviously impossible to develop a substantive theory of justice founded solely on truths of logic and definition.... Moral philosophy must be free to use contingent assumptions and general facts as it pleases. (Rawls, 1972, p 51)

But if reflective equilibrium is a reflexive dynamic in which principles and judgements are interdependent, how does this square with Rawls' Kantian warning about the need to strip away social and natural contingencies from the original position?

The puzzle disappears when we note that Rawls (1993, pp 8–15) later revised his theories of justice so that the original position becomes a political construct rather than a metaphysical conceit. By the early 1980s, he had distanced himself from Kant's 'comprehensive doctrine' and preferred, instead, to ground justice as fairness in the familiar ideals and standards of public culture. This means identifying a political conception of justice that all reasonable citizens can endorse because they recognise it as sustaining not only their own particular values and ideology, but also all those with which they disagree. Political justice therefore specifies what the 'basic structure' of society should be (its main political, social and economic institutions determining the distribution of liberties, powers and opportunities) in order that a 'reasonable pluralism' can subsist. Rawls is trying to specify the principles that allow disagreement and opposition without permitting such forces to fly off into disunity and anarchy. Reciprocity is the key here, since people will bind themselves to fair terms of cooperation if they can see that others are doing so as well (Rawls, 2001, pp 6–9). Reasonableness presupposes that rational beings possess a conception of what is to their advantage but it also limits the ends individuals can pursue to whatever does not threaten society's basic structure and public culture (Rawls, 1993, pp 58–62). Rawls therefore defines as well ordered a society that maintains *an overlapping consensus of reasonable doctrines*.

Contractualism must therefore be concerned more with consensus, with orientation to an encompassing social perspective, than with moral and metaphysical absolutes (Rawls, 1993, pp 125–9). Contractualism is political rather than metaphysical and reflective equilibrium becomes liberated from the need to avoid *all* social and natural contingencies (Rawls, 1993, pp 95–7; 2001, pp 29–32). In fact, the latter are now the clay out of which the tools of the original position mould the principles of political justice.

Some have regretted this concession to a quasi-communitarian approach (Barry, 1995, p 54) and this chapter will shortly question the extent to which liberalism can indeed relegate ontology to the sidelines. But has Rawls successfully addressed the general questions fired at contractualism earlier? By eventually rejecting Kantian ontology, Rawls neatly sidesteps many of the standard objections to contractualism. Rather than half-floating in a noumenal universe, reason is practical through and through, orientated to values and the good without thereby discarding the priority of the right (Scanlon, 1998, pp 114–26). Rawls' rational individuals are social beings, dependent on one another in a web of reciprocal relations, yet each still possesses a discrete integrity. The possibility of error and bias is therefore written into Rawlsian contractualism. This is less of a definitive map and more a sextant that requires repeated sightings and orientations, since

> ... not all the moral questions we are prompted to ask in ✳ everyday life have answers. (Rawls, 2003, p 208)

To ask what people would reasonably consent to implies abstracting from and reconfiguring our social embeddedness, in order to test our considered judgements against rigorous conceptions of fairness, *without* ignoring social context.

Does this mean, then, that Rawls' contractualism has succeeded? Not entirely.

Assessment

The value of Rawls' position lies in the fact that he has addressed a central problem with contractualism: why should we agree that *agreement* is morally significant (Blackburn, 2001, p 126)? A contract per se cannot be the basis for secure moral principles, since we need a reason to enter into that contractual relationship in the first place. Such a reason cannot be derived from the principles the contract itself yields, as that would be circular, deploying the outcome of our agreement as that agreement's rationale. It was to avoid this circularity that Kant invoked the moral law that subjects, *as sovereigns*, give to themselves. As already noted, however, Kant's ontology betrays certain weaknesses.

There are other solutions to the circularity of the social contract – I am going to sidestep the virtue ethics examined in Chapter 4. First, we might prefer to define individuals as essentially self-interested and so derive cooperation from a Hobbesian contract where self-interest is protected from itself through schemes of mutual advantage. In other words, *we cannot avoid* being bargainers and contractors. Alternatively, we might define individuals as driven towards certain ends, whether this be desire for the good (virtue) or for utility (happiness, wellbeing, preference-satisfaction). Here, a contract is that which enables our ends to be realised. Finally, we might follow Rawls in invoking the social traditions and public cultures into which we have already been socialised. Assuming that we ignore the Hobbesian approach as amoral, why not prefer the second option – the utilitarian alternative?

We might, for example, claim that consequentialism and contractualism are not that distinct after all (Pettit, 2000; cf. Scanlon, 2000). For example, Cummiskey (1996) argues that the categorical imperative assumes a theory of the good that has two tiers. The first says that we should promote our capacity for rational agency, that is, the conditions (liberty and life) necessary for a rational choice of ends. This 'rational nature' tier is lexically prior to the second, which states that we ought to promote the effective realisation of people's rationally chosen ends – their happiness, in other words. This is Kantian in that it disallows sacrificing life or liberty for the purpose of happiness; however, it is also consequentialist, both because happiness is nevertheless important, and because it *is* permissible to sacrifice life or liberty if that is the only way of protecting the life and liberty of others. The moral force of Kant and Kantianism therefore derives from seeing the right and the good in conjunction with one another:

> A conscientious moral agent acts from a sense of duty, not from self-interest or inclination, but for all that Kant says, she nonetheless may strive to maximally promote the good. More specifically, even if a formal principle determines the normative content (or end) of moral principles, it may nonetheless be the case that the right action maximally promotes that content (or end). (Cummiskey, 1996, p 10)

Yet, as noted earlier in this chapter, Kantianism does not exclude the good, it only omits the possibility of giving final priority *to* the good. For instance, it is good if I warn you about the banana peel you are about to slip on, but our primary responsibility is to ensure that the ground is not littered with banana peels in the first place (Watson, 2003, pp 252-3). The responsibility not to drop banana peels is prior to the generalised responsibility that bystanders have to effect the good by warning you of the danger. This means that whereas the good can sometimes restrict the right (recall Rawls' account of reasonableness), the right cannot be reduced to a generalised duty of beneficence; it restricts the good far more than the good restricts it. Kantianism therefore embodies a firmer principle of causation and responsibility than the consequentialist injunction to produce beneficial effects.

But if we are left with Rawls' emphasis on social traditions and public cultures – the third option – there is a twofold danger.[8] First, this option underestimates our freedom of movement. If we take our cue of what is morally and socially acceptable from existing mores, we risk excluding valuable political and cultural models that diverge from current assumptions. For instance, I have argued elsewhere that the contractualism of those such as Rawls and White (2003) does not adequately question the productivism of existing capitalism (Fitzpatrick, 2005b). We might therefore triangulate Rawls's emphasis on public culture and political justice by adding a third term (utopian realism or practical radicalism?) that enjoins us to think more imaginatively about social possibilities.

The second danger is that Rawls on one level abandons the ontology he needs on another. By (thankfully) rejecting Kant's transcendental idealism, Rawls perhaps swings too far in an anti-ontological direction and so undermines other aspects of his thought. After all, Rawls (1972, p 12) inspired the school of 'luck egalitarianism' by stating that the initial distribution of talents and endowments was arbitrary from a moral point of view, such that legitimate social inequalities could not derive from inequalities of chance and undeserved circumstance. And while Rawls (2001, pp 61-79) rethought the details of what this implied, the basic emphasis on luck remained. But this distinction between what we do not deserve (because based on chance) and what we do (being based on choice) surely requires an engagement with issues of free will and determinism. So while the arguments in Chapter One may or may not have been persuasive, to treat liberalism as a purely political doctrine that can bracket potentially empowering ontological debates is to risk colouring it with the hue of philosophical and political conservatism (for example, Gray, 2000).[9]

Applied ethics

What does all this mean for applied ethics (cf. Oderberg, 2000a, Ch 3)?

Kant proposes that the moral law consists of universal maxims that are categorical and so not dependent on inclinations. Thus, in contrast to consequentialism, which recommends courses of action that may vary according to contingent circumstances, Kantianism argues that we must look beyond such contingency to that which can be generalised across all circumstances. For the domain of applied ethics, this means that our decisions should not vary according to cultural and geographical differences, e.g. the age of consent in Washington and that in Turkmenistan should be identical.

This kind of stringent universalism has come under attack in recent decades, but with the extremer forms of postmodernist and poststructuralist critiques themselves becoming rather tired there are two points to make. First, the abandonment of universalism per se creates more problems than it solves,[10] and second, more sensitive versions of universalism are available (see Chapter One). Indeed, it is this that has perhaps motivated recent scholarship whereby Kant, as we saw earlier, makes room for conceptions of virtue and the good. So although the right continues to have priority, implying that we assess ethical questions according to generalisable rules and principles rather than consequences, it is not necessarily insensitive to substantive questions of value. Therefore, our applied ethics might seek to embody Kant's kingdom of ends without reducing our principles to formalist abstractions or imagining 'duty' to imply a robotic obedience to puritanical laws. Applied ethics therefore occupies the 'playroom' of judgement and imperfect duties. It implies the priority of the right and the kingdom of ends but leaves open the question as to precisely which actions correspond to universal principles. To this account contractualists add the notion of reasonableness, which implies, first, hypothetical agreements under social conditions of fairness and, second, some reference to actually existing conceptions of what is fair and reasonable. In considering applied ethics, then, we both abstract from and return to the standards of our social traditions and public cultures in a process of reflective equilibrium – albeit with the caveats outlined at the end of the previous section.

More specifically, and as noted on p 50, Kantianism enjoins us to distinguish between intention and foresight, and therefore between acts and omissions, and to emphasise the supremacy of the former over the latter. This returns us to the discussion at the end of Chapter Two. Kantian defenders of the DDE observe that only in this way can individuals' sovereignty be defended (Scanlon, 2003, pp 40-1).

Take the following example. You are about to undergo a potentially dangerous operation. If your surgeon is a Kantian, she will presume in favour of some principle that is based on your sovereignty as an individual; perhaps an expressed wish such as 'keep me alive at all costs', or 'do not resuscitate in the event of *x* happening'. If you lapse into a vegetative and painful condition, the surgeon is always obliged to obey that principle. However, there are possible circumstances where the surgeon has more discretion (perhaps you had not previously expressed a wish) and can only be guided by a recognition of your inherent moral worth. Here, the surgeon may decide to administer ever-higher doses of morphine to relieve your pain. But even if the (foreseen) cost is to foreshorten your life, your moral worth may nevertheless have been respected since she did not *intend* to kill you and so her decision did not violate your membership of the kingdom of ends. This membership was respected on the grounds that it requires attention to quality of life (how painful it is) as much as, if not more, to quantity of life (how long it lasts). The surgeon would therefore have acted reasonably out of respect for your humanity as an end in itself.

Now imagine that your surgeon is a consequentialist. The distinctions between intention and foresight, between acts and omissions, are no longer recognised and he weighs your sovereignty more equally against other considerations. What if you have lapsed into a deep coma as a result of surgery? If it is consequences that matter, your surgeon is better placed to judge these altered circumstances than either your current or previous self. Perhaps, rather than simply foreseeing your death by relieving pain, he takes active steps to end your life. For the Kantian, there is a line here between killing and letting someone die that either should not be crossed or at least should not be crossed without presuming in favour of someone's inherent moral worth. For the consequentialist, by contrast, there is less difference between killing you and letting you die, meaning that he may cross this line too quickly and too casually, arguably confirming that consequentialists have insufficient respect for human life. And if it is consequences that matter, the consequentialist surgeon may also allow decisions about your life to be determined by its expense to the hospital, the emotional state of your relatives or the lack of transplant organs for other patients whose prognosis is more favourable. While the Kantian will presume in favour of your status as an end, the consequentialist will include these other, more contingent factors in his deliberations.

The debate does not stop there, of course, and readers are referred back to Chapter Two for reasons why too severe a distinction between acts and omissions, intention and foresight, are themselves problematic. Given that consequentialists admit that these distinctions have some salience, it might be that in many instances disagreements between them and Kantians are more fine-grained than the illustrations used above suggest. We will revisit such issues in Chapter Ten.

Conclusion

Kant's ethics is more subtle than brief introductions to his moral philosophy often suggest. While occupying a deontological position, he nevertheless reaches out towards aspects of virtue ethics and, according to some Kantians, even offers a rapprochement with consequentialism. Indeed, if we abandon his ontology on the grounds offered earlier, the differences between Kant and those other philosophies may subside further. However, recent contractualists like Rawls argue that Kantianism retains a distinct identity that, by abstracting from the contingencies of natural and social circumstances, provides a more secure basis for moral deliberation than consequentialism, although Rawls's concession to communitarianism is not without its problems.

We are now ready to explore the third of our moral philosophies, virtue ethics.

Notes

[1] Note that Kant (1996, p 201) states that we must have respect for the moral law, although this is a rational respect rather than one of corporeal conditions, for example, hope of gain or fear of loss.

[2] How does this stringency square with Kant's conception of an anthropological 'playroom'? Perhaps it is that while Kant would not sanction lying, he might permit a certain looseness with truth telling. For example, while you should not lie to Harry if he asks a direct question, neither should you necessarily go out of your way to inform Harry of Roger's location if no such question is forthcoming.

[3] The extent to which Scanlon is a Kantian is a matter of some conjecture. Scanlon (1998, pp 5-6) himself denies it (cf. Onora O'Neill, 2003) but this view relies on a (brief) critique of Kant's *Groundwork* and does not take into account the other, virtue-based, aspects of Kant's subsequent development.

[4] Incidentally, this critique anticipates the third 'social' principle of the social humanism offered in Chapter One. More will be said about this in Chapters Four and Five.

[5] These criticisms imply that we cannot talk of autonomy per se. Instead, we have to make room for a conception of humans as socially interdependent, as neither fully autonomous nor heteronomous. Readers are again referred back to the social humanism outlined in Chapter One – compatibilism and intersubjectivism – made there partly in anticipation of Kantianism.

[6] Be aware of two associated terms. 'Constructivism' is an anti-realist metaethics that contractualists may take various positions towards. Contractualism is sometimes used interchangeably with 'contractarianism', although it could be said that they are distinct because the latter sees moral principles as being derived from self-interested bargaining and so supports a morality of mutual advantage. Contractualism is concerned more with inherent moral worth.

[7] For a more intricate analysis, see Scanlon (1998, pp 153-5), who prefers to talk not about consent but about what agents could not reasonably reject.

[8] There is perhaps a fourth option that is more community-lite than Rawls' and owes more to Scanlon. This is Darwall's (2006, Ch 12) 'second-person standpoint', which derives moral obligation from interpersonal claims of respect. However, my initial reading of this philosophy is that it, too, cannot avoid ontological deliberation about free will for very long, a point that Darwall (2006, p 70) seems to accept but does not deal with at length.

[9] For a contractualist engagement with ontology (though not questions of free will), see Scanlon (1998, pp 55-64; Matravers, 2003).

[10] By universalism is meant that which transcends particularism, rather than, as Butler et al (2000) have it, being a patchwork of the latter.

FOUR

Virtue

Although consequentialism and Kantianism recommend how to *act* morally, some allege that they do not necessarily encourage us to *become* moral beings. Virtue ethicists (hereafter known as 'virtuists') regard moral action as intimately woven with the notion of moral character. Unless we imagine that *doing* is somehow separate from *being*, the question 'What should I do?' links to the broader question 'Who am I?'. Your inquiry after my health means more to me if you are genuinely concerned than if you are simply trying to produce beneficial effects or are inquiring from a rationalistic sense of duty. If virtuism is often vague in making recommendations for acting (unhelpfully vague, according to its critics), this is because it focuses on the even more complex questions of how best to live. Every action derives from and is a sign of the moral health of our characters, our disposition to embody certain values.

Although contemporary virtuism dates back to the 1950s, it is only since the late 1980s that it has established itself in the canon (Crisp and Slote, 1997; Copp and Sobel, 2004; Williams, 2005; van Hooft, 2006; cf. Nussbaum, 1999b), despite the fact that it springs from one of the oldest traditions of thought.

Aristotle and Hume

The purpose of this section is not to provide an introduction to Aristotle (Rorty, 1980; Broadie, 1991; Kraut, 2006) or Hume (Penelhum, 1992; Norton, 1993) but to outline those components of their ethics that have been most influential on contemporary thinking.

Aristotle (1955, p 63) defines the good as 'that at which all things aim'. Like consequentialists, he is concerned with the ends of action (teleology) but unlike them he does not believe that those ends can be defined and measured in terms of utility, pleasure or preference. The good already resides within our motivations but is realised (or not) by our actions depending on whether we possess the correct dispositions or qualities of character (the virtues). What do people seek, he asks? What do their actions reveal the best life for man to be?

He observes that humans are characterised by certain 'functions' that flourish most completely when expressed through virtuous actions. Just as a tennis player's function is to achieve excellence by playing well, or a carpenter's by making good furniture, so a human's function is to live excellently. This property of living well is *eudaimonia* (literally 'good spirit'), commonly translated as 'happiness' but which has to be understood as a contented, balanced state of being rather than as a transitory experience of pleasure (Aristotle, 1955, pp 326-8). Human good is the fulfilment of that function through the application of virtue. Since it is reason that allows us to understand what it is to live well or excellently, and because reason is what distinguishes the human from the non-human, virtue means living in accordance with reason. It is therefore virtuous reason that engenders eudaimonia and so represents the flourishing of human function.

The moral virtues apply to the action-oriented lives of humans and manifest themselves as forms of practical wisdom (*phronesis*), or reason guided by appreciation of the good to produce virtuous actions in any given circumstance. You cannot simply recognise the moral virtues 'at a distance', since to appreciate what they are implies that you must already be able to practise them (Aristotle, 1955, pp 336-7). In one respect, this makes the moral virtues an educative and deliberative process. In another, after the specific injunctions of consequentialism and Kantianism, it lends Aristotelian ethics a certain vagueness. The student being tutored in the moral virtues must accept the authority of those already 'in the know', yet moral character does not involve following a rulebook of maxims. So it is possible to list moral virtues such as courage, honesty, temperance and so on, but what they *mean* in any given context will always depend.

How attractive are these ideas (Louden, 1997)? It is clear from Aristotle that living well is not simply a question of adhering to moral codes and injunctions. Practising the virtues is more of an art than a science; we must act according to experienced inclination but without any guarantee that things will come right. If this sounds too open-ended to modern ears, we have perhaps been clinging too tightly to rigid moral commandments and need to relearn the fluidity and dynamism of what it means to live virtuously (Nussbaum, 1986, pp 300-6).

For the same reason, Aristotle is arguably of little use when it comes to formulating the universal rules that mass societies seem to need.[1] We are more reluctant than he to leap from facts to values, descriptions to norms. And even if we do make that jump, we should not necessarily identify a human essence or function to be realised through the development of particular virtues (Lawrence, 2006, pp 54-61). Such a stress on moral character may apply to a community of like-minded people (such as Aristotle's Lyceum) but perhaps offends against the pluralism of mass liberal democracies (cf. Swanton, 2003). In the latter, there is no such elite and/or cultural homogeneity, since public morals more often resemble a looser affiliation of values in rough equilibrium vis-à-vis one another. The individualism and pluralism of mass democracies may not aggregate into a clear, singular set of publicly recognised values, characters and dispositions (Williams, 1985, pp 50–3). There are perhaps so many ways of living well and being good that a doctrine of the right needs to be stressed, such as an impartial universalism to prevent diversity from decaying into anarchy, rather than an overarching, perfectionist theory of the good into which all human activities are compressed (see the criticisms of MacIntyre in Chapter One).

As someone closer to our era than Aristotle, Hume (1998) arguably offers a more helpful resource in this respect. Rooted in a concept of utility, Hume defines as virtuous those qualities that are most likely to be useful, by promoting the good of ourselves and others. The human sentiment of benevolence and compassion expresses such qualities, since they lead us towards sympathy with others, and therefore towards social harmony, so overcoming the attraction of the darker characteristics of human nature, selfishness and negativity. Hume is more aware than Aristotle of the fact and importance of sociocultural pluralism and, as such, aims to detach moral universalism from moral objectivism. Whereas the latter involves the search for principles independent of and prior to society, the former is derived from the social conventions within which the 'internal' ethical sense of humans matures over time as societies form traditions, laws and institutions (the conduits of our ethical education). Morality is therefore a matter of those habits learned within a social framework of rules and customs in accordance with natural sentiment, and moral universalism consists of those qualities (gratitude, cheerfulness, politeness) to which all conventions assent as a matter of empirical fact, a common denominator underpinning all differential sociocultural contexts and about which an impartial observer would approve.

Has Hume therefore provided an 'impartial universalism' without recourse to a (Kantian) doctrine of the right? Not quite. Part of Hume's aim is to elevate sentiment above reason (1998, pp 158–63). Sentiments provide us with our ends, he claims, while reason selects the appropriate actions by which those ends can be realised; reason can sometimes redirect sentiment but can never supply the motivations that are essential to virtuous behaviour and ethical assessment. For instance, I help my friend because I am inclined to and not because I dutifully obey a system of rules. Hume (1998, pp 170–2) does acknowledge that inclinations can be harmful and so require reference to a 'whole system' of actions, but believes that convention offers the requisite framework. But what if our convention is defective? Perhaps we can cross-reference conventions against one another but, without an external frame of reference through which we can properly distinguish defects from non-defects, this hardly solves the problem, perhaps leaving our 'impartial universalism' vulnerable to infection from flawed moral assumptions. And in loading so much on convention, Hume is arguably as guilty as Aristotle of over-homogenising the moral community – after all, he promoted atheism in an age when it was far from 'conventional' to do so. In short, Hume runs up against the same problem that all communitarian philosophies encounter (see below). While we might reject the excessive rationalism of Kant, Hume's sentimentalism arguably swings too much in the opposite direction.

If these criticisms hold, perhaps we ought to be concerned primarily with acts and/or duties after all. If you save me from drowning, why should I be concerned whether you are a virtuous person or not? As we saw in previous chapters, consequentialism and Kantianism can make some room for character and virtue without losing their primary emphasis on effects and rules, respectively.

We can gain a better idea of whether these critiques apply to virtuism per se by examining one of the key theorists of recent times.

MacIntyre

Two of MacIntyre's greatest inspirations are Aristotle and Hume and, like them, we need only explore selected aspects of his work (Horton and Mendus, 1994; Murphy, 2003).

MacIntyre's (1981) socio-moral philosophy is established in opposition to modernity and enlightenment, since these, he proposes, have left us without the shared vocabulary needed to communicate across the privatised boundaries of the self. Modern thought resembles the incoherence and blind collision of ethical/cultural fragments. By separating reason from function, modernity has individualised rationality and detached it from its social moorings. What we *do* no longer translates into who we *are*, as the self floats free of the teleological background that used to orientate it. We no longer identify with our social roles, nor with the background traditions that once conferred meaning. By jettisoning tradition, the modern self celebrates its mobility and freedom at the cost of shared moral spaces; its alienation is due to this simultaneous empowerment and disempowerment. Left to direct itself, it has no direction. The standards and understandings that constitute a communal tradition erode, until modernity is left with only the semblance of traditions patched together through attenuated rules, laws and principles that, by trying to speak to and for all, speak ultimately about nothing.

MacIntyre condemns liberalism for abandoning an overarching conception of the good and so leaving us with oases of neutrality, abstract rationality and individual choice that inadequately mimic their communal ancestors and so signify our wanderings through a cultural desert. Liberalism is merely another tradition, rather than that which is external to, and so adjudicates between, traditions; one that does not recognise its philosophical self in the mirror of history (MacIntyre, 1987, pp 335-48). MacIntyre therefore calls for the reintegration of the self with its ends (*telos*) and the telos with the social roles belonging to communal traditions whose meanings derive from themselves and not from some extra-communal universalism. His ambition is nothing less than a communitarian reinvention of social virtues.

MacIntyre weaves his account of the virtues in and around two concepts: the narrative self and 'practices'.

The liberal self is associated with choice: choice of possessions, objects and lifestyles, and ultimately of country, belief, values and even identity itself. By seeing choice as unlimited, the liberal self is left without reasons to choose *this* rather than *that*. Choice becomes meaningless. The narrative self, by contrast, strives for continuity and stability by being oriented to the givenness of communal context. The story within which we become characters preceded our entry on to the stage, and will survive our exit, but is in small part articulated by us the more we allow it to occupy our beings. This occupancy is never final, but consists instead of a search for the good life. The narrative self is therefore a virtuous self, able to entwine apparently disparate elements into a coherent whole.

The conduits of communal and personal coherence are those 'practices' – 'any coherent and complex form of socially established co-operative human activity' (MacIntyre, 1981, p 187) – whose meaning depends on the social context within which they inhere. If you and I play chess, we must adhere to the meaning of the pieces and the rules of the game. By suddenly deciding that pawns can move two spaces, we abandon the very point of playing. The meaning and standards of the game are internal to it; similarly, excellence in the practices means realising internal qualities rather than pursuing objectives extraneous to it. If we play chess solely to earn money, we are treating it no differently from a vast range of other activities. Virtue is that which recognises a practice's internal properties and motivates us to achieve excellence in them in order to weave the narrative self into its communal tradition.

A tradition is therefore a source of shared understandings, of practices, selves and virtues whose interaction feeds back into and develops the tradition from which they emerged.

To what extent does MacIntyre evade the criticisms directed at Aristotle and Hume? MacIntyre (1981, pp 162-4) acknowledges that ancient readings of human nature are at best incomplete; for where Aristotle appeals to nature as the source of human function, MacIntyre's version of natural law is aware of how reductivist this can be and so promises a teleology that incorporates a diverse, sociological understanding (see Chapter One). Similarly, MacIntyre is alive to the necessity of formulating virtues in the context of a modern world of plurality, complexity and sheer scale. The parochialism of Aristotle's ethics is abandoned, as is any pretence that ethics can be shorn of deep, philosophical conflict. That said, this was the MacIntyre of *After Virtue* (1981) and his subsequent turn to Thomist Catholicism left some supporters feeling alienated and many critics delighted to have it confirmed that *this* is what he meant all the time (Nagel, 1995, pp 203-9).

There are several key criticisms of MacIntyre's philosophy. He has been accused of offering a falsified history of western thought in order to justify what is largely a gloomy story of moral decline (Wokler, 1994; Schneewind, 1997). Furthermore, despite MacIntyre's nods towards pluralism, he is arguably too willing to treat traditions as discrete, homogenous categories (cf. Porter, 1993). In *Three Rival Versions of Moral Inquiry*, for instance, MacIntyre (1990) contrasts three traditions: one represented by the ninth edition of the *Encyclopaedia Britannica*, one by Nietzchean genealogy and one by Thomist Catholicism (embodied in Leo XIII's *Aeterni Patris*). This might make for some knockabout fun, but is hardly representative of socio-historical complexity; although this criticism perhaps matters less than the suspicion that each of us belongs to a *multiplicity* of traditions. Those who can keep a straight face while claiming to derive from just one culture or value system are rare creatures indeed. But if this is the case, if our social identities are flooded with multi-traditional pluralities, MacIntyre's virtuism becomes problematic (Cohen, 2000); the narrative self is being forever broken apart, practices are not characterised by a simple internal/external distinction and there is no singular correspondence between our social roles and personal identities.

In addition, and despite his earlier socialism, social justice is barely evident in MacIntyre's work. The pursuit of excellence, the flourishing of human function and the cultivation of virtues are all no doubt worthy objectives but what relevance have they to environmental degradation, global poverty and social exclusion? Where, in short, is the political economy of virtue ethics? Where is the just distribution of material and public goods? Where is the guarantee of participative equity? Without answers to these questions, virtuism risks resembling the worst kind of cultural elitism in which the privileged preach morals to their socioeconomic 'inferiors' (more about this on pages 77-80). MacIntyre (1999, pp 114-18, for example) occasionally drops hints but little more.

Finally, there is one particular challenge that MacIntyre himself has addressed at length (Herdt, 1998). If there are no extra-contextual or extra-communal standards, if the universalism of modernity is a delusional façade masking a philosophical imperialism, if liberalism is itself a tradition rather than the means of adjudicating *between* traditions, are we not left with relativism? Is there any appeal the exponents of varying traditions can make other than 'this is what I am and believe'? In resolving conflicts between traditions, is there anything other than rhetoric to which we can appeal (or anything other than force, once rhetoric breaks down)? And what should we do about immoral traditions or about immoral practices within otherwise respectable traditions? If we are communal beings through and through, how can I identify, let alone condemn, such customs? Is not the torturer entitled to say: 'This is my practice, performed for the glory of God's truth. Don't interfere'?

MacIntyre's response in *Whose Justice? Which Rationality?* (1987, Ch 20) is to claim that traditions can be compared rationally according to their own 'internal' standards. History seems to suggest that those traditions prevail that can incorporate and adapt the distinct strengths of their 'competitors' while retaining their own conventions and identities. He therefore proposes that such an appeal to reason can form the basis for dialogue between otherwise incommensurable traditions without the liberal pretence that a universal language is needed to effect such intercultural translations.

Here lies the core of MacIntyre's fraught relationship with liberalism. He appears to be saying that while a universal vocabulary is not possible, certain rational standards are. Yet MacIntyre's conception of dialogical reason is either exceptional or it is not. If it belongs solely to the tradition MacIntyre prefers, what chance is there that it will appeal to those deeply committed to others? If the word of God is paramount, faith (not reason) and obedience (not dialogue) will be your bible. But if inter-tradition communication is possible, why could this not be a hook on which liberal universalism can also be hung (Levy, 1999)? Not a one-size-fits-all liberalism, but perhaps the kind of interactive, context-sensitive universalism defended in Chapter One in the discussion about 'intersubjectivism'. Can we not just repeat Habermas' (1977) point that a hermeneutic fusion of interpretative horizons points us beyond the hermeneutic methodology per se towards a critical theory of human liberation? If MacIntyre denies this, he might be guilty of 'selective historicism', denying to liberals and universalists the kind of cross-cultural understandings he himself makes.

So while it is facile to condemn MacIntyre's virtuism as relativist, his strong communitarianism does embody considerable problems. But do these criticisms, particularly the last one, condemn virtuism per se to irrelevancy?

Foot and Slote

To address this further, let us look at two other influential virtuists.

Like MacIntyre, Foot (1978, Ch 8) has long been concerned with denying that facts are separable from values (Hudson, 1983, pp 315-33). Borrowing the term from Geach, she regards goodness as 'attributive', that is, the meaning of good derives from the noun to which it is attached. For instance, a good phone box is that which has a soundproof door, clear instructions and works efficiently; those properties stem from the function a phone box is meant to perform. But there is nothing that requires a phone box to be red or blue or brown. Goodness is *attribute* in a way that colour is not. Can we apply the same reasoning to humans? Foot (2002, pp 162-8) insists that we can. The presence or absence of goodness, she says, depends on the specific characteristics and operations of the species under consideration. This 'autonomous species-dependent goodness' means that a good beaver builds an effective dam and a good horse runs swiftly. The human species may be more diverse but Foot believes that we have enough in common for similar inferences to be drawn, since without basic mental and physical health we are deprived of the capacity to flourish (cf. Doyal and Gough, 1991). Virtues do not correlate simplistically to activities and there is considerable room for indeterminacy; nevertheless, a virtuous person possesses the practical rationality to see that certain considerations give reasons for action.

So where MacIntyre focuses on communal traditions, the virtuism defended by Foot makes the species its primary reference point. Yet in doing so, Foot (2001, p 44) works at a level that comes across as asocial:

Men and women need to be industrious and tenacious of purpose not only so as to be able to house, clothe and feed themselves, but also to pursue human ends having to do with love and friendship. They need the ability to form family ties, friendships, and special relations with neighbours.

This is difficult to disagree with, and is equally something with which the average fascist could agree, since all but the most saintly of us demarcate those deserving of our love, friendship and neighbourliness. Yet while operating at this species level, Foot (2001, pp 72-7) sneaks in her own beliefs, such as that suicide and illiteracy denote a lack of virtue. So while MacIntyre perhaps concedes too much to communal particularism, Foot may concede too little (Copp and Sobel, 2004, pp 534-43).

Michael Slote has arguably done more than Foot to wrestle with the often-conflicting imperatives of the local and the universal, without (like MacIntyre) yielding too much to the former. Slote (1992) abandons teleological evaluations as being too dependent on luck; yet since luck is an inevitable aspect of human affairs, it is much better, he thinks, to abandon notions of blameworthiness and instead restrict ourselves to judging actions, motives and characters in terms of their admirability or otherwise.

The problem here lies in the 'we' to which appeal must be made when considering what it is that *we* find admirable or detestable (Kultgen, 1997). Slote (2001, pp 95-100) has addressed this issue more recently. He observes that where deontological reasoning *may* apply at a personal/local level – for example, the refusal to kill even if it would save lives – such reasoning fails when the stakes are higher, for instance when we face large-scale human catastrophe. If the fate of nations is involved, a 'moral shift' must occur. This public/political level involves a form of caring (a patriotic attachment to one's country) analogous to the care people demonstrate towards friends and family. The moral shift is therefore negotiated through an ethic of care. Being virtuous means being motivated to care for others and a just society is one in which institutions and laws reflect this motivation. Slote (2001, pp 136-7) contrasts the care ethic with one of impartial, universal benevolence, for while the latter (exemplified by consequentialism and Kantianism) demotes the moral import of particular attachments, a care ethic treats them as inherently significant. Of course, it is naive to imagine that I can have with strangers half a world away the same emotional bond I have with my wife and children, but this does not mean that the moral community halts at the nation's edge, simply that universal feeling is built outwards from the particular (Slote, 2001, pp 187-8).

How persuasive is this and, compared with MacIntyre and Foot, does it represent a more effective balance of the universal and particular?

From care to justice

One problem is that Slote is rather too uncritical of the extent to which a care ethic can perform all of the work of liberal, universal justice (Gelfand, 2004, pp 598-600; cf. Darwall, 2002). It is easy to denounce the Gordon Gekko version of capitalism [so called after a power-hungry stock broker in the 1987 film *Wall Street*], since Gekko's motto (greed is good) obviously does not derive from a motivation of care (Slote, 2001, pp 119-20). But as the more subtle defenders of capitalism often argue, most employers, shareholders and managers do not leave their ethical sense at home; in making profits, the directors of oil companies do not actually wish to destroy the planet (for where else will their grandchildren live?) but to keep the economic wheels moving and prevent sociopolitical collapse. These wishes seem consistent with the motivation to care. Yet it may also be perfectly consistent with a market system that *is* wrecking the planet, *is* exploiting workers, *is* oppressing developing countries and *is* allowing 4,000 children a day to die because of unsafe water.[2] Few people *intend* to create these results, but the in/justice of our actions, our interactions and their effects are not necessarily reducible to our intentions (Brady, 2004). If motivations are therefore of minor importance when it comes to identifying unjust conditions, perhaps we need to fall back on either consequentialism or Kantianism.

Therefore, even if our motivations matter, how can we interpret them accurately and assess their actual significance? As far as their interpretation is concerned, presumably it is not simply a question of X-raying our internal psychological states, since surely what matters are those states over which I have control; yet you do not have to delve very far into the philosophy of mind to appreciate that distinguishing between voluntary motivations (reasons) and involuntary ones (causes) is far from easy. With regard to the significance of our motivations, Driver (2001, p 59) points out that different motives have different meanings and effects depending on their context. She accordingly maintains that virtuism is only useful if it is abridged to a consequentialism that takes those contexts seriously.[3] So as well as the difficulty of assessing someone's motives, there is the considerable problem of judging entire social systems on that basis. Slote (2001, pp 101-2) is remarkably unspecific about the *politics* of care, noting that it might be egalitarian and might as easily justify inegalitarian distributions.

Readers should understand that this is not to dismiss a care ethic, but to query whether it should be so closely associated with virtue ethics – see Nussbaum (2006) for an attempt to reconcile a care ethic with at least some aspects of contractualist thinking (cf. Fitzpatrick, 2008). In attempting to reconcile care and justice, by rooting them in the particularity of attachments, Slote's approach dovetails with others within the care literature (Tronto, 1993; Noddings, 2002). Yet in earlier critiques I have suggested that there are significant problems in relegating universal principles of justice to a subordinate role as this group appears to do (Fitzpatrick, 2003, pp 114–18; cf. 2005a, pp 44–7; also Halwani, 2003). Others like Nancy Fraser (2001) have similarly argued that an incorporation of care and justice has to give greater prominence to the latter. This means taking Kant seriously.

A Kantian theory of care can presumably be inferred from what he says about justice. Kant (1996, pp 335-6, 351) does not exclude reference to moral education or what he calls the 'sweet feeling of beneficence'. Instead, he argues that the former first requires a 'good state constitution' and that the latter can only be embraced once the unconditional duty to respect human rights has been assured. Virtue is obviously desirable, but because we have to allow for the possibility that most social members will not achieve such lofty heights, attention to what Rawls calls the 'basic structure of society' is paramount. While hoping for angels, we have to organise society, in the first instance, to protect ourselves against devils.

To sum up, Slote wrestles with the kind of particularist/universalist issues that are central to contemporary philosophy and for which neither MacIntyre nor Foot offer adequate solutions.[4] Slote's solution is to build out from a particularist ethic of care in which motivation is central, but there are several difficulties with this. Therefore, any care ethic and any attempt to smooth the bridge between particularism and universalism cannot afford to ignore the principles of liberal justice as set out by Kant, among others. The potential vagueness of virtuism, noted earlier, perhaps implies that we have to choose between the different *political* versions of virtuism on offer.

From justice to politics

I have interpreted MacIntyre's reluctance to grapple with issues of social justice and political economy as a weakness. Similarly, the moral philosophers dominating the virtuism debate have offered surprisingly little discussion of social justice and political economy (Hursthouse, 2001, p 6; also Dagger, 2006, pp 161-9), a strange omission for a perspective concerned with moral education, almost as if our moral instructors (parents, teachers) can be left in a socioeconomic vacuum (cf. Nussbaum, 2001b, pp 311-14).

If we widen our map to include input from political philosophy, we see that some of this vacuum has been filled along two axes. The first concerns the communitarians' allegation that liberalism does not engender the virtues that it itself needs, since individualism fails to inculcate the ethical characteristics required for proper social participation, producing a hollowed out sense of anomie and alienation, and the liberal principle of neutrality (between conceptions of the good) fails to promote those virtues required for social cohesion and the nurturing of public spaces (Etzioni, 1992).

Many contemporary liberals acknowledge some of this (Shklar, 1998, p 15; Beckman, 2001). The idea that the state can and should be strictly neutral between competing conceptions of the good is naïve, since regardless of whether the state intervenes or withdraws from social life there are assumptions about the good underpinning both strategies. Economic liberals who would roll the state back are assuming a conception of the good life different from that of social liberals who demand the equalisation of social conditions.

Yet communitarian warnings about neutrality are themselves somewhat crude. Few liberals have ever embraced an 'anything goes' neutrality (Berkowitz, 1999), as neutrality can also be defined as the attempt to facilitate the largest possible space of acceptable goods (Gutmann, 1989). What do we mean here by 'acceptable'? For some liberals, the relevant principle is 'autonomy', the idea that maintaining the priority of the right over the good demands a non-perfectionist, liberal self capable of doing so (Kymlicka, 2002, pp 244-61). In short, *the main good saluted by liberalism is a recognition that many different goods are desirable*; the main virtue permitted is a willingness to query, reconfigure and, if necessary, reject those virtues that certain moralists and moral philosophers advocate. Communitarians have then either got to accept autonomy as a legitimate liberal virtue or explain why it is not. In the latter case, they either have to nominate some other liberal principle or propose that liberalism and virtuism are incompatible – a position liberals are surely entitled to reject.

It is therefore premature to imagine that liberalism must either give way to communitarianism or merge itself into a new synthesis (Kateb, 1989). As such, the liberal state possesses many more resources than its critics allege, including a welfare state capable of combining 'thin' conceptions of social interaction (rights against coercion) with 'thick' conceptions that many communitarians will support (solidarity and social wellbeing). Holmes (1997), for example, agrees that a liberal state must restrict opportunities for the arbitrary (mis)use of power by those in authority and that strict constitutional procedures are required to ensure this. However, this is not an argument for the minimal state as typically understood, since the point of such restriction is to permit a concentration of effort and resources on addressing social problems that, along with representativeness and the rule of law, should be an additional priority for liberal democracies.

The second 'political' axis concerns a conservative critique that focuses on the particular virtues they associate with authority, custom, family, private property, neighbourhood, nation and (often) the Church. For some conservatives, social morals in general have declined, requiring a society-wide remoralisation (Bloom, 1988); others share aspects of this view but regard the morals of the poorest as being especially problematic (Himmelfarb, 1995).

The former conservatives tend to exude 'Golden Age Syndrome': a rosy view of the past combined with apocalyptic fears of the present. Yet the past has always been a vessel for contemporary fears, and it is not difficult to find accounts that treat the past, particularly the Victorian era, as less of a golden age than conservatives imagine (Pearsall, 1969; Davis, 2001). As far as the present is concerned, Wolfe (2001) reports that most people are responding to an era of 'moral freedom' with thoughtful maturity rather than promiscuous decadence.

The latter type of conservative – those who attribute particular vices to the poorest – can also be challenged. It is hardly 'sociologism' (a phrase of Lawrence Mead's)[5] to propose that the poorest are constructed as a social problem because they possess less economic, political and cultural/symbolic power (Katz, 2002).[6] Despite their supposed vices, evidence suggests that in the UK the poorest proportionally donate four times more of their income to charity than the wealthiest, and are more like to contribute to 'social' charities than those concerned with the arts (Egan, 2001). Further, the cost of benefit fraud is considerably less than that of tax avoidance, despite the poorest already having a higher tax burden (Lansley, 2006: 187-90).[7] The vice conservative allegations of fraud and criminality typically allude to – welfare dependency – is a useful way of normalising the 'market dependencies' to which everyone, especially the non-poor, are subjected. In short, to load moral burdens on the socially excluded is a double standard that only exacerbates their powerlessness; a means by which the affluent attribute their good fortune to virtue.

A more subtle argument is to propose that those resistant to moral reform are harming the very individuals they mean to help. This is because the poorest are, indeed, no less virtuous than the non-poor and would themselves welcome an emphasis on moral reform. But why is moral reform necessary as an anti-poverty instrument if the non-poor are indeed no less virtuous? Conservatives respond to this query with a principle/practice distinction:

> No one has a right to do wrong; in that sense, a moral double standard that demands more of the poor than the rich is obviously unfair. But to the extent that improvidence is more likely to harm the poor than the rich, as a prudential matter the poor really do have a greater stake in avoiding it. (Schwartz, 2000, p 137)

Yet Schwartz never gets around to explaining why this greater vulnerability requires more virtues for the poor instead of more economic resources: higher benefits, more jobs, higher wages, better housing, more teachers and doctors. Schwartz acknowledges that some economic assistance may be appropriate but nowhere supports substantial material redistribution. This is because he does not see inequality per se as a problem (Schwartz, 2000, pp 200-5; 2005, pp 236-7). Yet surely our vulnerability to harm and self-harm are socially dependent. The harm-avoiding value of my resources depends on what others around me possess, so that, for example, £10,000 a year protects me from the vulnerabilities of single parenthood more if median income is £15,000 than if it is £50,000. Therefore, unless significant measures are taken to reduce socioeconomic inequalities, allegations of conservative double standards still apply.

Mead, too, appeals to the virtues of the deserving poor. Claimants should be required to work without any guarantees that 'acceptable jobs' will be available, he says. This is because the expectation that government will create such employment loads too many burdens on it. Whether or not the market delivers acceptable jobs depends not on market conditions but on the amount of effort individuals exert; if claimants 'exploit the available jobs for all they are worth', any job is meaningful and financially beneficial (Mead, 2005b, p 190). Note that Mead's constant reference point is *existing* American public opinion.

Mead's position is based on two premises. First, questions of citizenship are separate from and precede those of justice and equality. Individuals (whatever their wage) only become moral equals once they make an employment contribution, he says. Yet this separation of the person from their socioeconomic environment bizarrely resembles the very hollowing of the self with which communitarians accuse liberalism (Sandel, 1982); for material assets and resources are not only 'external' objects but are also incorporated into our cognitions and perceptions from an early age. Employment contributions are easier to make and opportunities easier to find for some socioeconomic groups than for others. Trying to correct social disadvantage through measures that, attributing too great a role to personal motivation, quickly become punitive and disciplinary is to exacerbate the patterns of privilege and injustice into which we are born. Therefore, the idea that material and moral reward resides within *any* job is equally hollow and patronising.

Second, Mead recognises that different national cultures may see the world differently. Yet cultures change across time as well as across space. Mead, for instance, is willing to acknowledge that marriage tests now have less salience than work tests. But if so, why not continue to press for other social changes that political theorising suggests are desirable? There was nothing inevitable about the eight-hour day, the two-day weekend or the abolition of child labour and conservative opponents at each stage were no doubt articulate in appealing to everyday opinion.

Perhaps we can only salvage conservative approaches to virtue ethics by incorporating them into social democratic frameworks (Deacon, 2002). At their most persuasive, the former complain about the corrosive effects of a modern capitalism that relies so strongly on competitive and possessive instincts. Since this correlates to core elements of leftist thinking, there is a degree of rapprochement here. But the left makes two additional points.

First, White (2003) is clear that the measures conservatives and communitarians associate with virtue – conditional entitlements to welfare services – are justified *only if* the social background conditions are egalitarian. If they are not, charges of hypocrisy are legitimate.[8] This does not necessarily imply delaying virtue-based measures until social justice is in place but certainly suggests avoidance of Mead's citizenship/justice dichotomy. Second, it means applying a virtue ethic consistently across all social groups so that the non-poor 'cannot buy themselves out' of virtue-based socioeconomic reforms.

Even if we go down this road, the virtues to be promoted are not necessarily those advocated by conservatives. Take Tessman (2005; also Lister, 2004), for instance. First, she argues that those who battle against oppressive conditions both require and, indeed, demonstrate certain virtues that embody the goal of human liberation. Second, an ethic of flourishing must be sensitive to the obstacles placed in its way by inequitable distributions of material and cultural resources. Oppressive conditions hamper people's search for the good life by directing their efforts towards short-term activities, for example, consumerist distractions. Those who are oppressed show signs of moral damage, but to attribute this to agents rather than their environments is to blame the victim and reward the perpetrator. Virtue and flourishing therefore depend for their realisation on just social conditions, ones that compensate for bad luck. Correcting 'moral damage', for Tessman, does not mean getting people to eat their greens, obey the boss and go to church; it means encouraging them to resist the sources of social injustice.

Therefore, even if we take the politics of virtue seriously, it might take us in a leftist rather than a rightist direction, with an entirely different set of prescriptions and recommendations. Yet debates by many of the principal moral philosophers dealing with virtuism have barely scratched the surface of these political contestations (O'Neill, 1996, pp 178-83).

Applied ethics

Virtuism might also be accused of avoiding the intricacies of applied ethics. As noted already there are some good reasons for this (Hursthouse, 2003). Ethical dilemmas are often so complex that neither secular nor holy bibles will suffice. The fact that virtuous agents will often disagree with one another is therefore not an argument against virtuism any more than disagreement among Kantians refutes contractualism (Swanton, 2003, Ch 13). The moral agent can be *guided* by principles but rules cannot substitute for judgement. Virtuism performs a service in reminding us of this (van Hooft, 2006). Yet virtuism risks surrendering to its critics if matters are left there and it is Foot above all who has made significant contributions to applied ethics (cf. Oderberg, 2000a, Ch 3; Gould, J., 2002).

Foot (1978, Ch 2; 2002, Ch 5) defends the DDE by endorsing the distinction between intention and foresight (cf. Quinn, 1993, pp 149-74). If I am driving to save five people from a flood and so do not have the time to stop and rescue you as well, I am permitted to ignore your plight in order to save the greater number. I do not intend your death; I merely foresee it. I would not, though, be morally allowed to deliberately run over and kill you if that were the only way of reaching the other five. Yet if you are going to die in both scenarios, what is the difference?

For consequentialists, of course, there is none. Because the outcome is the same, there is no significant difference between allowing you to die (the first scenario) and killing you with my car (the second scenario). By contrast, the DDE normally distinguishes between acts and omissions, since individuals can be held responsible for their actions to a degree not applying to the infinite number of omissions we 'perform' every minute. Foot does not permit herself this escape route, however, since we can imagine instances where omissions are of greater moral significance than actions.

Instead, she distinguishes between those decisions that originate a 'causal sequence of events' and those that do not. In the first scenario, your death would have occurred anyway and there is nothing I can do to prevent it without causing greater harm elsewhere; you are being killed by the flood, not by me. In the second scenario, however, my intervention into one causal sequence (the flood) initiates another (I run you over because you are blocking the way):

> Typically, it takes more to justify an interference than to justify the withholding of goods or services…. So if, in any circumstances, the right to non-interference is the only right that exists … then it may not be permissible to initiate a fatal sequence, but it may be permissible to withhold aid.
> (Foot, 2002, p 83)

Intervention (or interference) initiates a new causal sequence, whereas non-intervention does not.

This distinction can be challenged, though (cf. Kenny, 1995, pp 79–85). First, non-interventions may initiate a new sequence. If we refuse to evacuate some people from a disaster zone because they do not want to leave, we may be transferring a natural disaster into a man-made one. Second, interventions may permit an existing sequence to run its course, so that when we (forcibly) evacuate everyone we prevent the emergence of that man-made contribution to the disaster. With either approach, we elevate the duty to help closer to the duty to avoid harm and so, on Foot's reasoning, make it harder to distinguish between those acts that originate a causal sequence and those that do not. Watson's (2003) point about responsibility may be correct (see p 58), but in reality causal sequences overlap to such an extent that identifying their origins is often difficult. Perhaps it is better, then, to assess our actions on the basis of *effects*, not causes.

In any event, how does Foot's reasoning about the DDE differ from deontologists'? Basically, it centres on the character of the agents involved in these difficult decisions. Both philosophies stress the importance of responsibility but virtuism recommends sensitivity to agents' inclinations and motivations as well. After all, if there is a distinction to be made between intending and foreseeing, surely we have to make some reference to individuals' desires, otherwise we permit the kind of cognitive dissonance whereby we commit horrendous acts by kidding ourselves that these were only foreseen (Chan, 2000, pp 426-8). If I allow you to die, it would be wrong to delight in my non-interference should you be someone I happen to dislike; it would be wrong to rejoice at someone's death even if their organs permit others to live. This point may seem banal but in Chapters Two and Three we charged both consequentialism and Kantianism with being too impersonal in their moral evaluations: the former for not respecting the separateness of persons, the latter for its concern with obedience to universal laws. Virtuism is 'interpersonal' to a degree that those moral philosophies are not. When introducing the personal factor into decision making, however, virtuism also has to ensure that egoism and subjectivism are not part of the equation. The virtue of benevolence, for example, involves the promotion of good actions in oneself and others (Foot, 2002, p 99); not the abandoning of the impersonal for the personal, but a rebalancing of the two.

Virtuists cannot therefore be charged with failing to turn every moral dilemma into a formula of right and wrong because, they say, no such formula is possible. It is instead a *strength* of virtuism that it introduces the character of the actor into the process, although this does not absolve it of the responsibility to engage also with traditional debates like the DDE.

Conclusion

By working with too 'thick' a conception of the good, virtuism potentially underestimates the extent to which we can disentangle ourselves from social contexts. This chapter began by questioning the extent to which Aristotle's ethics can be applied to the modern world and found that contemporary virtuism had gone some way towards updating this ancient philosophy. In doing so, however, it proposed that for a host of different reasons neither MacIntyre, Foot nor Slote had offered a sturdy enough bridge between the particular and the universal, between communal traditions and the extra-contextual standards against which those traditions can be judged. It went on to argue that moral philosophers within the virtuism debate have not yet grappled with the political contestations relating to issues of liberal autonomy or social justice and so risk reifying the (conservative) status quo. Finally, the chapter outlined the distinctive contribution made by virtuism to applied ethics, picking up on a running theme of earlier chapters.

We now go on to summarise those previous chapters, suggest how and why these moral philosophies can be mapped and frame this map in relation to the applied ethics and social policy debates to be considered in Chapters Six to Eleven.

Notes

[1] Some refute this by pointing to the practical syllogism, where the major premise is the equivalent of universal laws, while other defenders of Aristotle argue that one is not a substitute for the other (see McDowell, 1997).

[2] According to UNICEF (*The Guardian*, 15 March 2006).

[3] For an alternative attempt to incorporate Aristotelianism into Kantianism, see Sherman (1997; cf. O'Neill, 1996).

[4] My suspicion therefore is that we need to build out from universalism instead of heading towards universalism from the opposite direction (see the discussion of Banhabib in Chapter One).

[5] Personal correspondence.

[6] What I am hinting at here is the third principle of social humanism, as discussed in Chapters One and Three.

[7] To object to this observation on the grounds that fraud is illegal while some (if not all) tax avoidance is legal is to ignore the inequities of social power, that is, who gets to determine il/legality.

[8] This is a bullet White (2005, p 101) is reluctantly willing to bite, on the grounds that it is still better to help the disadvantaged, although I have noted elsewhere that such differential treatment is only reasonable if it respects the autonomy of all and so emphasises incentives, with sanctions only applying to certain forms of self-harm and only then as a last resort (Fitzpatrick, 2005a).

FIVE

Applications

This chapter begins by summarising our three moral philosophies.

Consequentialism is concerned primarily with acts and judges them according to their effects in promoting some 'pre-moral' property such as happiness or preferences. We do not necessarily have to assess each and every individual action, since we can formulate and apply rules likely to produce beneficial results, but acts *are* the ultimate reference point for consequentialism. And although we should not treat consequentialists as synonymous with utilitarians – the latter recommend the maximisation of utility whereas the former may be less strident about the meaning of utility and whether its maximisation must always outweigh other considerations – there are obvious synergies between the two.

The attractiveness of consequentialism lies in its intuitive appeal: how natural it is to examine and assess acts in terms of their demonstrated outcomes or to weigh possible courses of action according to their anticipated effects. Furthermore, in proposing that it may sometimes be better to perform acts that are beneficial over time, even if they seem objectionable in the short term, consequentialists may demonstrate a better grasp than others of the messiness, ambivalence and practicalities thrown up by moral dilemmas.

That said, there are important objections (notwithstanding that consequentialists have counter-arguments to them, as seen in Chapter Two):

- Consequentialism eliminates good intentions from ethical questions. Kant adds the complaint that consequentialism is too capricious for, as circumstances change, acts that create benefits on Monday may not do so on Tuesday; for Kant, this is no basis for a moral system.
- Consequentialism disrespects the specificities of individuals, perhaps by ignoring the 'separateness of persons' (allowing human integrity to be subsumed within a crude calculus of aggregates) or by requiring us to be selfless saints who must always weigh *every* consequence and act accordingly.
- How can consequences really be measured? The simpler the property to be promoted, the more it crowds out other aspects of human wellbeing. If our aim is to increase pleasure, what about those activities that are meaningful but not necessarily pleasurable? But if

we expand our conception of wellbeing, for example, to encompass freedom and voice, as Sen advocates, we are left with the difficulty of knowing when and how these can be evaluated and enhanced.

When consequentialists have made specific interventions into the field of applied ethics, it has been to challenge the acts/omissions and intending/foreseeing distinctions. If what is important are consequences, my neglecting to act may contain as much moral force as the actions I actually perform. If you are dying of thirst, giving you infected water to drink may be worse than offering you nothing; yet if I allow you to die by not acting at all, you will be just as dead as you would have been after drinking the infected water, in which case my culpability is hardly irrelevant. This allows the claim that consequentialism is rooted in psychological realism: the distinction between intending and merely foreseeing is rarely straightforward and all sorts of atrocities can be justified if we pretend otherwise. Furthermore, if avoiding harm is the good that consequentialism commends, we ought to avoid harm in all cases where it can be experienced. The harm principle will constitute an important element of Chapters Six to Eight.

Deontologists reject the teleology of consequentialism, where the morality of an action derives from its ends. For deontologists, morality resides within the principles *that justify certain actions*. For Kant, this means acting for the sake of the moral law as apprehended by reason. It is not a question of motivations and preferences, since these, at best, generate hypothetical imperatives only; instead, the categorical imperative states that an act is moral if it can be willed rationally in accordance with universal laws, which implies abstracting from the biases and contingencies of the subjective will. This means treating people primarily (if never entirely exclusively) as ends and giving priority to the right over the good, our duty being to embody universally necessary maxims in our actions rather than to chase what is arbitrarily desirable or beneficial at any one time. Kant's philosophy makes room for the virtues *as long as* these have been shorn of the contingencies of the everyday world of time and nature.

Kantianism is one of the most powerful and influential moral theories ever proposed. Used all too often in recent decades as a symbol of the alleged redundancy of enlightenment thought (too universalist, too rationalist, too western), its finest features in fact represent all that is best about that tradition. But there are some standard objections that will not go away:

- Kant ignores the importance of social and natural context, treating nature as a lower form of reality beyond which reason must ascend. Furthermore, it appears insensitive to distributional patterns of social goods, although later contractualists have derived principles of moral and social justice from Kant.
- Like consequentialism, Kantianism erroneously imagines that motives and inclinations can and should be parenthesised. At its worst, Kant's is a system that would require emotionless obedience to rules whose (highly complex) justification could only ever be fully understood by a minority.
- Even if we cannot anticipate all consequences, we can surely identify some, in which case not factoring the latter into our moral calculations seems certain to produce undesirable effects, a worry that no emphasis on universal laws and rational maxims can dispel.

This does not mean, however, that Kantianism is arcane and contemporary Kantians have sought to stem the rise of the anti-enlightenment waters that continue to bubble fiercely. Rawls is one who offers a looser version of Kant's contractualism, one not weighted down by his metaphysics but one that retains reason, universalism, liberty and equality at its core. In Chapter Three, however, I observed that Rawls' grounding of rational consent on actually existing traditions and cultures risks stifling the social imagination, and that he arguably swings too far in an anti-ontological direction.

In terms of applied ethics, Kantianism leaves plenty of room for the judgements of 'moral anthropology', that is, for engagements with the roundedness of human behaviour that are inevitably less systematic than the precepts of pure reason would like. Kant also defends the acts/omissions and intending/foreseeing distinctions. You should never tell a lie, for instance, even when inclination and circumstance urge you to do so. Moral judgement involves judging the extent to which individuals have observed their obligation to obey the dictates of reason. There are millions of possible scenarios that can be foreseen, millions of omissions you are ignoring every second, and since we can hardly be expected to understand and assess each and every potential alternative, surely you can only be responsible for those acts you perform. Furthermore, the Kantian emphasis on a kingdom of ends means that there will always be a presumption in favour of the individual's sovereignty, their inherent moral worth, an important point whenever the actual consent of agents is difficult to obtain.

Finally, virtuists believe it vacuous to expect people to act morally without understanding how to experience the virtuousness of morality.

We therefore have to be concerned not only with our rational capacities but also with the experiential nature of human character, and with our inclinations and habits. For Aristotle, the ends of actions are moral if they fulfil the functions of human nature, the good being a flourishing of human potential that manifests itself in certain behavioural and intellectual virtues. Contemporary virtuists update this basic philosophy to wrestle, with varying degrees of success.

Some of key criticisms include:

- Are virtuists guilty of over-homogenising the human? You do not need an 'anything goes' morality to propose that modern diversity is too valuable an achievement to surrender. Virtuists disagree over the Aristotelian emphasis on function: MacIntyre divests himself of the universal vocabulary needed to delineate human function per se, while Foot talks of humanity as a species. But if what we really need is a continual renegotiation of the universal and the particular, can't this simply be done from within non-virtuist frameworks?
- From where does our sense of virtue derive? If not from Kantian reason, could it be from our communities and traditions? But what is virtuous in space p or time x might not be so in space q or time y. We might, of course, identify certain cross-cultural virtues (candidates include friendship, respect, honour, perseverance, tolerance, fairness, openness and honesty), but their contextual meaning may fluctuate too widely to be of much use. Virtuism does not necessarily result in relativism, but perhaps the renegotiations just invoked demand stronger anchors in a universal frame of reference.
- Virtuists arguably offer unpersuasive accounts of justice. A care ethic is valuable if bolstered by a justice ethic that is not reducible to it. Caring for some might mean harming others, harm that demands the guidance of principles of justice. Also, the communitarian implications of virtuism potentially ignore specifically liberal principles such as autonomy that operate as virtues but prevent the individual from being absorbed into the common good. Finally, the demands of social justice are often set to one side and virtuism risks being associated with the authoritarian moralism of certain (conservative) commentators.

On the plus side, virtuism draws repeated attention to the indeterminacy of the moral field, the matters of judgement and fallibility that the calculus of utilitarians and the moral imperatives of Kantians risk ignoring. This is certainly the case with applied ethics, where knowing the right thing to do is rarely a question of applying formulae and commandments. That said, Foot has defended the distinction between intending and foreseeing, though on the (non-deontological) grounds that applying the distinction in practice will depend in large measure on the characters of the agents in question.

Implications

There are any number of approaches we could now take. We could try to decide which of the above is superior, taking time to justify that decision and rectify any flaws or unanswered questions left hanging in previous chapters. (In my case, this would probably involve an elucidation of post-Kantian contractualism, the moral philosophy to which I am most attracted.) Yet this is not the approach we will be taking.

Quite simply, *each of the above theories offers indispensable insights into ethics while there remain genuine incommensurabilities between them.* Perhaps someday someone will either produce a knockdown argument in favour of one, so that the other philosophies effectively withdraw from the stage, or that a grand synthesis will be effected so brilliant that thinkers will pity the poor idiots of previous generations who could not see it. This seems doubtful, however. The previous chapters aimed to show that when consequentialists defend the desirability of producing beneficial effects, when Kantians argue from first principles to defend autonomous choices that are both rational and reasonable, and when virtuists see morality as springing from habits ingrained in our character, they are each proposing an ethical perspective that is worthwhile and difficult to disregard. Then, when each launches salvos against alternative philosophies, they are not being unwarranted here either. Most consequentialists, Kantians and virtuists do not deny that their rivals' principles are valuable, simply that they are wrong to treat them as essential, wrong to start from where they start.

To take just one example, a modified Kantian may acknowledge that it is sometimes permissible to lie but that lying should be the infrequent exception to a duty of truth telling. A rule-consequentialist may agree, but will maintain that this generic rule must incorporate within it a further rule specifying when deviations from truth telling are warranted. To avoid tying ourselves in circulatory knots, both the generic rule and the rule-permitting deviations must be referred to the overarching aim of promoting the good. The Kantian will respond that orientation to the good makes truth telling too dependent on contingent and rapidly changing circumstances, such that only respect for the inherent moral worth of others will suffice – even if this sometimes means failing to promote beneficial consequences. In other words, *while there are significant points of agreement here, the deontology of the one and the teleology of the other pull in opposing directions.*

As an adjunct (and following on from what was said in the Introduction), it is important to make the point that this is a mapping expedition. The intention is not to offer a comprehensive bird's-eye view, a simplistic chart that neophytes can digest all at once, since this approach frequently distorts the complex realities of an uncertain and accelerating world. Nor is it to excavate just one portion of that landscape. Academic ghettoisation means that all too often intellects parachute quickly to the ground, dig a hole, sit in it for a long time and then proclaim themselves specialists. The premise of this book, then, is that we should be unafraid of loose threads, of provisional conclusions, of tentative patterns, of experimentation, agnosticism and ambivalence. In other words, we need consequentialism, contractualism and virtuism to reflect on applied ethics, but the latter also allows us to reflect further on each of the former. We may decide by the end of Chapter Eleven that, say, contractualism *is* the most convincing theory after all, but that has to be the result of a mapping expedition, a third option with which the hole-sitters often seem uncomfortable.

Contexts

How should we proceed? By contextualising consequentialism, Kantianism/contractualism and virtuism in two senses.

First, there is a certain methodological similarity at work within all three philosophies. Following Sidgwick (1981, Bk. 4), who referred to common sense as 'unconscious utilitarianism', Hare's (1981, p 190) consequentialism embraces what he calls a two-level theory. Reason has its limitations, he observes. We may apply the correct procedures incorrectly or it might be that the very procedures we apply are wrong. Aristotle was one of the most brilliant minds that ever lived and the Bible one of the most influential books, but neither appears to have had a problem with slavery. So how sure can we be that we are right? But this doubt does not mean we should just surrender to it, since we learn and progress precisely by applying prescriptive analysis to the facts of the case. Moral thinking, according to Hare, embraces an intuitive level and a critical one. We cannot help being guided by intuitions, since these make the world manageable, but without critical thinking we may end up repeating our own versions of the mistakes committed by Aristotle and the Bible. That said, critical thinking requires the orientations of the intuitive (the sensible, the obvious, the everyday) if it is to be practical. We therefore need to combine these levels as best we can – although it should be noted that Hare (1981, pp 44-6) did give some priority to the critical.

There are similarities here with the methods of Rawls and MacIntyre (also Scanlon, 1998, pp 197-9). In Chapter Three, we saw that Rawls' reflective equilibrium allows us to reconcile abstract theorising with the shared understandings and communal standards of time and place, bouncing each off the other to throw light on both. And in Chapter Four, we saw MacIntyre observing that a dialogue between traditions is possible, although he thinks that conversation has to proceed from within the interpretative horizons of each tradition rather than from some extra-contextual vocabulary of liberal universalism.

So Hare the consequentialist, Rawls the contractualist and MacIntyre the virtuist all treat the proximate, the consensual, the accepted, the intuitive as indispensable aspects of moral decision making. They each posit social environments as existing in some kind of comparative dynamic with critical reason, even though each offers alternative versions of what this means and what that dynamic implies. Yet the differences are less important than the fact that each is tying into modern conceptions of understanding, knowledge and reasoning as profoundly *social* rather than as, say, that fragment of forgotten eternity that is the soul (Plato, Christianity) or as the complex accumulation of sensory data (Aquinas, Locke).

In the chapters to come, we will therefore draw on the *socially embedded intuitions of common sense* not only when considering certain ethical problems but also as a means of comparing and contrasting consequentialism, Kantianism/contractualism and virtuism.

The second context is that of social *humanism*. The problem with intuitions and common sense is that they can badly lead us astray. They may impel us to initiate a course of action that is ultimately irrational and damaging even though every step in the process seemed, on its own terms, to be unproblematic. Alternatively, they may simply mislead us regarding the reality of the social world, or our moral intuitions may conflict with one another. Philosophy can perhaps protect us from some of these problems but only according to explicit social principles. For philosophers can be as guilty as others of ignoring what Mills (2000) called the sociological imagination, the willingness and ability to dive below social surfaces and appreciate how individuals bear and transmit social structures. We need an orienting framework that can help us to avoid the possible irrationalisms of (in Hare's terms) the intuitive and the critical.

Chapter One referred to 'social humanism'. This was initially defined in terms of two principles. Compatibilism combines freedom and determinism at both a philosophical level (the extent to which we are free) and a political one (how and why we make ourselves freer by intervening in our social environments). Intersubjectivism values universalism as a dialogical process sensitive to social context, such that ethical debate should be seen as a kind of open and participative conversation. An element of this intersubjectivism (its 'creative agnosticism') has been defended above when it was stated that we ought to borrow elements eclectically from diverse and even incommensurable sources without being too worried about the impurities thereby produced.

Chapter Three then alluded to a third principle that was elucidated in Chapter Four when discussing various conservative commentators. This principle resists the idea that what Scanlon calls substantive responsibilities can be divorced from an assessment of sociomaterial circumstances, since doing so both ignores the (compatibilist) limits of human action and attributes to the disadvantaged a degree of agency they may not possess, while perpetuating the injustices with which the disadvantaged already have to deal. Some responsibilities will have little relationship to circumstance – for example, murder is still murder whatever your income level – but many responsibilities will have a closer relationship and contemporary threats come from those conservatives who would blanket everything with an ethic that can be described as an 'uniformity of obligation'. This 'closer relationship' may be articulated along an economic dimension (the prince's theft of some bread is worse than the pauper's) or a cultural one (racism by the white majority is worse than that by a non-white minority since the latter be a regrettable expression of powerlessness) or both (Fitzpatrick, 2005a, pp 46-8).

We will therefore refer to this third principle as *egalitarian* as long as this is understood in such material-cultural terms. (It is not my aim to outline a theory of egalitarian social justice (see Fitzpatrick, 2003: Chs. 2, 5-9), since the focus will remain largely on ethical rather than sociopolitical dimensions.)

Social humanism therefore offers an orientation to guide us in our moral intuitions. Assessing the long-term rationality of a course of action can make reference to the humanist's goal of social justice (egalitarianism); weighing agency and structure, freedom and social/natural determinism, can assist us in developing a sociological imagination and applying this to social problems and ethical issues (compatibilism); and where moral intuitions conflict, a deliberative process of open debate can help dispel inclinations to resolve them through dogmatic canons (intersubjectivism).

In tempering the intuitive, social humanism offers further contextualisation for our three moral philosophies. We saw in Chapter Four that virtuism needs to engage with the kind of political contestations that the social humanist emphasis on egalitarianism embodies. Chapter Three argued that Kant's concept of freedom is less successful than a compatibilist account and Chapter Two proposed that the consequentialist dilemma cannot be resolved by a pseudo-scientific Benthamism and so may necessitate a more intersubjectivist approach – in deciding how to operationalise freedom and voice, for instance.

The map in Figure 5.1 encapsulates these philosophies and the two forms of contextualisation just defended.

Figure 5.1: A map of applied ethics

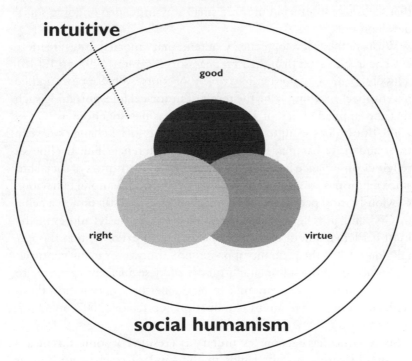

Moral philosophy and social policy

This Figure is a guidebook, not a model, a process of selection and not a blueprint from which a systematic moral architecture can be constructed. It is a series of horizons and contours, a basic compass rather than a global positioning system that offers precise locations. We will make use of it from time to time in the coming chapters, but we must also be prepared to go beyond this map, to travel wherever the relevant literature wishes to lead us.

Is this anything more than an academic exercise, clever but without significance to the real world of policy making? That depends on how seriously you take Keynes' (1964, p 383) famous claim about 'madmen in authority' echoing those voices in the air that originated with academic scribblers. Such analyses as those contained within this book will be one of many millions of voices in the air, most of which are drowned out by noise or by the passage of time. But that does not reduce the value of contributing to an intellectual climate that seeks to capture and in some small way influence ongoing social developments.

What are these developments? Contemporary moral debates are more eclectic in character than their predecessors (Scanlon, 1998, pp 12-13). This observation may be entirely wrong, of course. What appears unified in retrospect may simply be the result of historical foreshortening such that the 'applied ethics' of 1908 really was as heterogenous as that of 2008. But it does seem to be the case that one social change between then and now has made a considerable difference. The decline of religious observance has altered the rhythms and attitudes of social life, since religion is *the* attempt to systematise and codify moral behaviour. Obviously, most people in even secular societies will still profess a belief in God and in religious teachings, however tenuously; and even the most hardened atheist cannot escape this culture. For all this, though, religion *has* lost the centrality it possessed for however many centuries – a timescale those advancing a model of 'desecularisation' prefer to ignore (although for an attempt to reconcile the secularisation thesis with an account of religious pluralisation, see Taylor (2007, pp 431-7, 514-22)).

Social ethics has become less unitary as a result. For some, this means we should throw up our hands in the kind of celebratory despair characterised by postmodernism and its tributaries. For others, this should impel us to reinvent communal allegiances, the process of identification perhaps being less important than the precise content of the community identified with. As long as people have a strong sense of right and wrong, it might be proposed, it is less important whether they derive this from religious communities, ideological communities, national communities or any of a range of alternatives. Most commentators on applied ethics navigate between these extremes, content neither with a thoroughgoing scepticism nor with the givenness of existing moral orientations, seeking instead conclusions that are open and reflective, directions for travel that never consist of one-way traffic.

This book's approach is such an eclectic, mapping expedition. Sometimes the tools with which we journey may need to be rethought and sometimes a complex world simply cannot fit our philosophical abstractions and we risk losing our bearings. But better these risks than those that come from hiding in a hole. The map is not just an academic exercise, but one that mirrors and hopefully assists the process of heterogeneous, cautious and deliberative decision making now needed in what was earlier referred to as an uncertain and accelerating world.

We are now ready to discuss some applied ethics.

SIX

Protecting

Chapters Six to Ten deal with the boundaries of free choice. Self-determination and self-ownership are crucial to modern conceptions of the person, but what these terms mean, and what kind of social organisation they imply, is obviously contentious. The idea that liberty requires a cloak of paternalism is accepted by all but the most uncompromising libertarians and anarchists, and is a crucial principle of social welfare. But how thick should that cloak be and what is its appropriate design? How self-determining and self-owning are we really? How should we balance paternalism with liberty, security with autonomy? How far should we tip the balance in one direction or the other? When is autonomy enhanced by paternalism and when is it hindered?

We will tackle these questions repeatedly from a number of angles over this and the next four chapters. Since autonomy is central to our approach, we begin with one of its most celebrated defences and so on three issues dealing with harm to others and harm to oneself. It is Mill's utilitarian liberalism that offers a perennial starting point for such discussions and so provides the framework for this chapter.

The harm principle

For a century and a half, Mill has been crucial to any discussion of choice and paternalism, his 'harm principle' being one of the central tenets of liberalism – for recent critiques, see Jacobson (2000) and Holtug (2002).

According to Mill (1962, pp 135-8), we are entitled to interfere with the actions of individuals for reasons of self-protection only. If someone is harming another, we may take steps to prevent them, whether by impeding their actions or compelling them to perform actions whose non-performance would otherwise be harmful. But if someone is acting, or neglecting to act, in ways that create harm or diswelfare for *himself alone*, we are *not* entitled to force him to behave differently. We may entreat that person, but we cannot *compel* them without violating their personal sovereignty, a violation impermissible on utilitarian grounds since Mill regards the freedom of individuals to live as they see best, so long as they do not harm others, as the basis of a good society (Berlin, 1991;Ten, 1991).[1] Someone can be compelled when the wellbeing of others is at stake but should otherwise be free to determine the meaning, purpose and degree of their own welfare as an autonomous being:

> The only freedom that deserves the name is that of pursuing our own good in our own way, so long as we do not attempt to deprive others of theirs, or impede their efforts to obtain it. Each is the proper guardian of his own health, whether bodily *or* mental or spiritual. Mankind are greater gainers by suffering each other to live as seems good to themselves, than by compelling each to live as seems good to the rest. (Mill, 1962, p 138)

Mill is aware that this is not unproblematic. Five points stand out. First, since we *are* entitled to compel those who might harm themselves because they lack the requisite sovereignty, that is, the competence to anticipate the consequences of their actions, there is a question mark over when such sovereignty is attained. In the case of children, we are not only entitled but also obligated to intervene if the child is harming or likely to harm herself (LaFollette, 2007, Ch 10). Here, Mill assumes that a line can be drawn between childhood and adulthood.

Is there such a hard–and–fast division? When, morally speaking, does a child become an adult? The idea that protection against self-harm[2] should end once adulthood commences might be rejected by those claiming that Mill is insufficiently paternalist (see below). We might go further and observe that the boundaries of the self are so fuzzy as to be meaningless. Because practically everything we do has an impact on others it might be doubted whether a self/other distinction carries *any* weight, undermining the very core of Mill's principle (cf. Rees, 1991). Furthermore, what about other forms of dependency, such as those created by mental illness or incapacity? How easy is it, really, to distinguish between independence and dependency, sovereignty and its lack?

Second, if the dependent/independent line is blurred, so perhaps is that between compulsion and persuasion. It is not always clear when pains/penalties are being deliberately inflicted to prevent self-harm (which Mill does not permit since it implies compulsion) in contrast to when they are merely side-effects of previous actions the individual has performed. Mill's distinction between compelling and entreating is based on a dichotomy between the involuntary and the voluntary that more recent advances in psychology and social science have undermined.

Third, Mill is aware of the need to define harm robustly. While he believes it essential for social interaction and inquiry that 'unnecessary offence' be avoided (Mill, 1962, pp 181-3), he is also aware that some may simply be too quick to take offence, while others may be trying to ban something they dislike by falsely claiming that it harms them. To take a ridiculous example, I announce that I feel harmed whenever I hear the word 'rabbit'. Does this mean that you should be prevented from saying 'rabbit' in my presence? How are you to know whether or not my harm is genuine? Perhaps I am actually imposing a religious or ideological doctrine on the speech of others. And even if it is a genuine harm, is it perhaps too trivial to bother about? Now take some actual examples. Should I be allowed to shout 'fuck', even though it harms your sensibility? What if I paint my face black and dance in a minstrel show? What if I make fun of Jesus or Mohammed in ways you consider to be sacrilegious? At what point, in short, does illegitimate harm to others give way to *legitimate* or permissible harm?

Mill (1962, pp 215-16) does not rule out the permissibility of harming others when they are so thin-skinned or tempestuous that they are simply too easily offended. Unless we resist applying the harm principle to each and every case of possible harm, we risk a society where the 'moral police' and 'language police' seek to prevent anything that those suffering from 'imaginary evils' might be distressed by. Yet, and this is the fourth point, Mill relies on a key distinction that may not always hold. The touchiness of the religious believer may be something they just need to get over, not something that should influence public policy; but it is also possible to think of examples where desirable social progress has come from redefining as harmful that which had been previously taken for granted. The minstrel example falls into this category. Therefore, which 'evils' are imaginary and which are not is a matter of social, cultural and ultimately political contestation. What I call respectful language is what you call political correctness.

Despite all of these questions and potential difficulties, we should not get too carried away, since the harm principle has stood the test of time and is a key reference point in liberal democracies. We will invoke the above critiques as we proceed, but there is a fifth and final issue that has more direct implications for our discussion.

Mill (1962, pp 128-30) is famous for proposing that any society has to protect itself not simply from the tyranny of the ruler but also from the tyranny of majority opinions, communities and customs. This is particularly the case with liberal societies, precisely because it is here, with the rule of law and democratic procedures, that the majority might be thought to be right *simply because it is a majority*. Inspired by Tocqueville and Carlyle, Mill is obviously aware that liberalism cannot imply simple majority rule since the demos is capable of becoming a new form of despotism. The minority always needs protection for those opinions, habits and lifestyles that the majority may not care for. But if the majority can act tyrannically and if tyranny is something we should resist, are we not sometimes *obliged to harm the majority* if that is what resistance demands? We are not only talking here about harm as a regrettable but unavoidable side-effect of social interaction (as when we harm the thin-skinned), but harm as deliberately and directly inflicted on others and so presumably ruled out by the very harm principle Mill is defending.

Mill would no doubt dispute there being any contradiction here. For when a majority is tyrannical, and because tyranny is opposed to freedom, we may indeed be allowed to harm them, since it is they who are preventing a free society. Yet this counter-argument depends on too severe a contrast between freedom and non-freedom. What the majority may display is not 'tyranny' per se but another characteristic that is oppressive towards a minority without being entirely inimical to a free society. It might therefore be better to talk not of the tyranny but of the intolerance or prejudice of the majority. However, it seems that Mill does not bring his discussions of the tyranny of the majority and the harm principle together systematically, since if we are sometimes *obliged to harm others as a means of maintaining social freedom*, the apparent simplicity of the harm principle has been compromised at the conceptual level.

Having reviewed the above critiques, we are now ready to explore three issues drawn from contemporary debates about choice, harm and the paternalism that may be required to ensure that choice and harm can coexist effectively.

Drug taking

Should smoking be banned in public places?

Smoking has quite rapidly become deeply antisocial in the UK, despite previously being regarded as cool and sophisticated. Its antisocial signature has spread quickly, first on public transport and in cinemas, theatres and offices and more recently in pubs, bars, clubs and restaurants. This cultural and legislative shift is an evolution of the harm principle.

You can do what you like as long as you do not harm others; passive smoking harms others and therefore smoking should be banned from places where unwanted inhalation is likely. Much of this has therefore concerned *enclosed* public spaces, but as bans have become more common, this proviso has fallen away so that any possible public space becomes a site for potential prohibition. For non-smokers like myself, it is tempting to leave this trend alone, if only as revenge against the many hypocrites who happily share their smoke but would react aggressively if I tried to drink their beer. Besides, many smokers want help in quitting and society has a financial interest in discouraging children from ever starting. But we do need to pause before going too far or too casually down this road.

As discussed earlier, Mill's harm principle may sometimes allow us to harm others if they are too thin-skinned or if their intolerance is unreasonably oppressive to a minority. We may now add a third caveat, where your harm, though ostensibly the effect of another person's action, is really caused by your placing yourself in a dangerous position. If I shout 'fore' before swinging a golf club, but out of my line of sight you step closer and get knocked unconscious, that is presumably your fault rather than mine. Do these three qualifications to the basic harm principle prescribe limits on smoking bans?

First, are non-smokers too thin-skinned? The obvious answer is 'no', since health considerations surely apply. Even for those of us who do not suffer from respiratory problems, the potential effects of passive smoking are now well documented (Vineis et al, 2005) so that although the harm caused by any single intake of breath may be negligible, repeated exposure to a toxin means that considerable harm accumulates over time. It is this cumulative harm that is relevant and so imposing your smoke on others would indeed seem wrong according to Mill's harm principle.

Second, should we permit smoking because non-smokers are simply being intolerant towards a minority activity? Such intolerance is certainly in evidence on 'moralistic' grounds. How often have you heard the phrase that smoking is a 'disgusting habit'? Disgusting it may be, but such pronouncements easily cross the line from judgements about what is bad for the non-smoker to judgements about what is bad for the smoker, a transition that the harm principle does *not* allow us to make. Were it not for its ill effects, the simple act of breathing in someone else's cigarette smoke would not be enough reason for prohibition *unless*, perhaps, we were also willing to ban *all other* man-made substances that we unwittingly inhale. The smoker is therefore correct: such intolerance is not grounds for prohibition.

However, health considerations still have to be paramount. Taking offence at someone smoking perhaps qualifies as – in Mill's phrase – an imaginary evil, distinct from harms that, based on evidence, reasonableness and rationality, can legitimately be subject to policy interventions. A claim to have been harmed is not enough. Such claims must be amenable to scientific proof and to – in Kant's (2001, pp 135-41) phrase – standards of 'public reason' that cannot be based on mere dislike of the action, belief or lifestyle in question. In other words, public reason must assume the moral equality of all agents. Therefore, if we ban smoking from intolerance of the smoker's lifestyle, this is illegitimate, but demonstrable harm to health (through passive smoking, for instance) *is* sufficient grounds.

Finally, should smoking be banned when it is non-smokers who are placing themselves in harm's way? This question affects what we mean by public space and presumably depends on the extent to which non-smokers can realistically avoid placing themselves in harm's way. The argument that they can *always* do so is too severe. Consider the proposition that smoking should be permitted on public transport because non-smokers always have alternative means of transportation; 'if you choose to share a plane with me, you are implicitly accepting my right to smoke'. This is true almost in the same way that you always have a choice whether to hand over your wallet or get shot, but can hardly be called a 'realistic' choice. So why not simply provide both smoking and non-smoking areas in public places, as used to be the norm? This would seem to define public space as 'spaces for publics', that is, for plural, heterogeneous ways of occupying space with others. While this conception of public space is admirable, however, the compromise described fell out of fashion because the spatial boundaries between smoking and non-smoking areas have to be real and substantial if the effects of the former are not to drift into the latter. This is why in enclosed public places, such as on planes and trains, total bans on smoking came to be the preferred option, while in non-enclosed public places the gap between smoking and non-smoking areas has generally been widened.

The real controversy has centred on those places that are neither entirely enclosed nor non-enclosed, such as pubs and bars. They are enclosed in one respect but, then again, those within them have greater freedom to enter and leave than is the case with, say, public transport. This is perhaps also true of those for whom such bans have been widely justified, for instance, bar staff and waiters. Health and safety rules certainly stress the obligations of employers, but also those of employees. If I throw myself out of a window, my employer might be liable if they helped cause my depression but not if they neglected to paint the windows shut. Occupational hazards can never be entirely eliminated and individuals have a responsibility to choose when and where they will occasionally place themselves in harm's way. So although people may have restricted options when it comes to enclosed public places, there are arguably limits on the extent to which they need or require protection when it comes to non-enclosed and semi-enclosed places. We should not ban smoking in the street because a non-smoker 30 metres away might be harmed.[3]

In short, it seems difficult to justify generalised bans on smoking in non-enclosed and some semi-enclosed public spaces and it is worrying that such trends represent a move towards a sanitised, homogenous conception of public space that is not only concerned with eradicating harms — acceptable, so long as the harms are not so trivial that even more damage is done by eliminating them — but no longer trusts adults to judge risks and choose sometimes to place themselves in potentially harmful situations (Schaler, 2002). The medical expert who wants smoking banned from *all* public places (for example, Eisner, 2006) has crossed the line from doctor to nanny.

Should bad habits be taxed?

Mill's harm principle prohibits harm to others. But what of harm to oneself? Are we never entitled to intervene when someone is harming, or likely to harm, themselves? There is a debate within applied ethics over whether and, if so, when we are allowed to intervene on the grounds of paternalism and it is to this debate that we now turn.

Robert Goodin (1989, 2002a, 2002b) has defended paternalism from a utilitarian stance inspired by Mill's harm principle. When individual autonomy is interpreted in terms of choice and rights, it is all too easy to imagine that it and paternalism are diametric opposites. However, because Goodin is one who prefers to base consequentialist ethics on 'interests' (see Chapter Two) he asserts that autonomy and paternalism may not be so opposed after all (see Gray, 1983). This is because individuals may not always realise or appreciate what their best interests are, in which case paternalistic intervention may enhance rather than diminish their autonomy. There are two respects in which this is true, he says.

First, I may not be the best judge of my interests when I have insufficient information. Let's say that I am about to walk on to a bridge that you know may collapse but I do not. Would you infer that I am not acting with full information and so warn me about the danger and, if necessary, physically prevent me from crossing the bridge? Most people would, presumably. The harm principle therefore permits you to interfere with my autonomy, when it is exercised without sufficient information, in order to ensure my autonomy's preservation.[4] Second, even when I do possess full information, an intervention may still be justified in order to protect my *future* interests. Let's say I have researched heroin thoroughly. I know the difficulties involved in withdrawing from it. However, I am also intending to begin taking heroin because I have decided it is something I would like to try. Are you morally allowed to prevent me from doing so? Goodin believes you are because the *choices* exercised by my present-day self rank lower than the *interests* of my future self and if those interests are to be damaged or restricted, interfering with my current choice is warranted. When a course of action will lead to an 'irreversible' state of affairs (which, for Goodin, implies addictive behaviour), we should either be prevented from taking it or there should at least be considerable obstacles placed in the way that force us to think again.

Goodin therefore distinguishes between 'surface preferences' and 'deep preferences'. It is a presumption of liberalism that the two often correspond but we should not imagine that they *always* do so, in which case it is the job of policies to guide individuals towards those choices that reflect preferences that are genuinely informed, non-impulsive and self-directed, sometimes by persuasion and education, sometimes through cultural pressures, sometimes by a system of dis/incentives (including taxation) and regulation, and sometimes by outright compulsion and/or prohibition. So although Goodin might not ban cigarettes, he would place considerable restrictions on their advertisement, sale and use in public places, while also making them considerably more expensive. And as the addictive, harmful properties of a substance increase, the more compelling the case for simply banning it becomes.

Much of the above corresponds to what Mill (1962, p 229) proposed – the bridge example comes from him. But note that Mill also distinguishes between the *certainty* and the *danger* of mischief. Certainty does indeed justify paternalistic interference. But when there is only a danger of mischief, paternalism should go no further than warning someone of that danger; once warned, no additional intervention is permissible to prevent self-harm. You may be convinced that my weak heart could not bear the exertion of walking up a hill, but the 'danger of mischief' only gives you a right to voice your concern and then step back and let me make my own decision. To prevent me from doing so is to treat me like a child. The fact that the line between childhood and adulthood is blurred (see above) does not mean the line is non-existent. Goodin's paternalism, however, risks collapsing certainty and danger together.[5] His favoured policies arguably resemble the cultural pressures he elsewhere criticises the tobacco industry for exerting (R. Goodin, 2002b, pp 310-11). Mill (1962, pp 233-5) therefore presumes against the kind of measures Goodin advances; he does, it is true, support the taxation of stimulants but only because 'taxation for fiscal purposes is absolutely inevitable' (see below) and not in order to compel behaviour. Mill's is at best a 'soft paternalism' (Feinberg, 1986).

Goodin's second argument – regarding future interests – also tallies with Mill's (1962, p 236) view that we should not be free to alienate our freedom. But Mill's example is the extreme one of somebody selling himself into slavery and so it is not clear that he would welcome any more paternalism here than in the case of Goodin's first argument. Goodin stresses the possible divergences between your current choices and your future interests but, of course, what links these two timeframes is the fact that they are both *you* and so allowing others too much licence in deciding what is best for the 'future you' is to invoke what is worst (and least popular) about paternalism (Scanlon, 1998, p 31). Few decisions are completely irreversible (Shapiro, 2005, p 657) and even those that are may be hindered, but ultimately not prohibited, without disrespecting the autonomy of the individual (see Chapter Ten). So the future interests argument seems reasonable, but might not warrant the scope that Goodin attributes to it.

Therefore, Goodin's attempt to paint the harm principle with a glossier coat of paternalism either provides little beyond what Mill had already established or advances additional arguments that Mill had already anticipated and disallowed. There is, though, a third possible argument in favour of paternalism that Mill somewhat fumbles.

Mill's view that taxes on stimulants are permitted because fiscal taxation is inevitable is one of *On Liberty*'s weakest parts (Mill, 1991). But what if for 'fiscal' we substitute 'health'? We then have a point made often in contemporary debates, namely, that the costs of indulging in activities potentially damaging to health should be passed on to the individual at the point of consumption in the form of a sales tax (Veatch, 1974; cf. Smurl, 1980). We cannot pass those costs on at the point of *treatment* (even assuming that costs for past indulgences could be efficiently assigned)[6] without compromising the principle of offering free care at the time of need. But, if personal responsibility is important, those costs might take the form of a hypothecated health tax on consumables. Such a tax is not only a matter of society protecting itself against the burden of excessive health spending in the future, but is also a means of encouraging individuals to reflect on their current impulses, to act with what might be called 'self-paternalism' by weighing current desires over a longer timeframe than would otherwise affect consumption habits. A health tax therefore satisfies Mill's distinction between certainty and danger – it is a signal similar to issuing a health warning on cigarette packets – but might also satisfy Goodin because surely we must make a further distinction between those dangers where the risk is infrequent and minimal and those long-term dangers more likely to be frequent and severe. In the case of the latter, something additional to a mere warning could be justified.

Health taxes have crept on to the agenda in recent years and seem certain to stay.[7] In the UK, and no doubt elsewhere, suggestions are increasingly made about the need for a 'fat tax', that is, a health tax on foods with a high fat content, on the grounds that with rising obesity and incidents of heart disease such foods are becoming as potentially ruinous to lives (and healthcare costs) as tobacco and alcohol (but see Reiter, 1996; Kuchler et al, 2005). Health taxes are designed to alter the behaviour of consumers and producers, encouraging the former to cut down and the latter to design healthier alternatives to their products. If there is a Mill/Goodin consensus here, it presents a formidable case for paternalistic intervention to prevent self-harm that nevertheless respects and remains within the harm principle's basic framework. Objections to it do occur, however, once we question their utilitarian assumptions (see for instance, Dworkin, 2000).

The utilitarians' aim is to promote a conception of the good (happiness, preference-satisfaction, interest-fulfilment) as measured through the effects of actions. A strict utilitarian society would measure every effect to assess the extent to which it promotes the good and, presumably, take steps to prevent those acts whose effects do so inadequately. If avoiding harm to one's future health is a good, health taxes on tobacco, alcohol and fatty foods are indeed justified. But a strict utilitarian society could not stop there. Most of the things we do have potentially harmful consequences. Applying utilitarian paternalism consistently demands that we root out and tax, or if necessary ban, all of them. Your preference for reading tabloids is ruining your intelligence, for example; therefore we should impose a 'stupid tax' on tabloids. Over-working takes time away from family life; therefore we should impose a 'family tax' on it. The list could go on forever, but the point is a simple one. Either utilitarianism requires us to apply the Mill/Goodin defence of paternalism to *every* harmful activity or we should adopt a less strict version of the defence and of the utilitarianism from which it springs. The latter need not rule out health taxes on tobacco, alcohol and fatty foods (and perhaps other activities too) if these do indeed qualify as dangers 'more frequent and severe in their effects', but only as long as a considerable degree of autonomy is respected.

Kant has no more liking for addiction and excess than Goodin, but on the grounds that these violate one's duty to oneself (Smith, 2002). Sovereignty and autonomy nevertheless constitute principles that warn us against imposing paternalistic taxes or bans on anything potentially harmful. In the present context, this might mean objecting to forcing the many who consume tobacco, alcohol and fatty foods in moderation to pay for the over-indulgence of the few. Why should the consequences of your abusive intake restrict my freedom to consume those substances responsibly without the monetary constraints that a health tax would impose? We should not succumb to contingent, dependent desires, but your failing does not mean that I will succumb too. As an inalienable characteristic of what it means to be a sovereign 'end', my autonomy should not be limited because you have misused yours. The fact that many people lie does not mean that we should impose taxes on lies, as this might lead people to tell the truth for reasons that are self-interested and ephemeral and so unrelated to the categorical imperative. For Kant (1996, pp 550-1), doing the right thing cannot be a matter of avoiding penalties:

> ... the reason for considering this kind of excess a vice is not the harm or bodily pain (diseases) that a human being brings on himself by it; for then the principle by which it is to be counteracted would be one of well-being and comfort (and so of happiness), and such a principle can establish only a rule of prudence, never a duty ...

Virtuism, too, encourages people to be moderate in their indulgences without blanketing everything in a generalised harm principle. In its more conservative form, virtuism might well justify a degree of social constraint that goes way beyond paternalism, as when Aristotle (1955, pp 336-8) states that because 'the many' are ruled by fear and a desire to avoid punishment the law should proscribe certain impulses. But a more liberal politics might involve trusting the individual to find their own 'mean' between the excesses of frugality and profligacy. Those who are being educated in the virtues certainly require the guidance of those who are more experienced and this will involve prohibitions and restrictions of one kind or another. But if social policies are shaped so that they treat virtuous adults like mice in a maze – with doors continually opening and closing to channel subjects along what policy makers define as the correct track – what we are left with is less virtue and more blind obedience to disciplinary imperatives. When we err, as we all do occasionally, what brings us back to the path of moderation is a moral compass plus the compassion of others, a compassion that might be undermined if people are thought to have paid for their care entitlements already through a health tax. Measures like health taxes risk promoting distrust and indifference in public life: 'You chose to purchase health-taxed cigarettes, so why should I care about your lung cancer?'.

None of this is to claim that either Kantianism or virtuism are anti-paternalist. Virulent opposition to paternalism is associated with libertarian thinking (see Danley, 1979) and you are unlikely to find too many Kantians or Aristotelians who are also libertarians. Instead, they are more valuable as correctives to the utilitarian impulse to hunt down and restrict every example of harmful activity. A moderate utilitarianism must therefore be consistent with principles that emphasise the rational and virtuous capacities of individuals. So *while there is a prima facie case for attaching hypothecated health taxes to those activities where harm is not certain but there is a high probability of danger, as with the ban on smoking in public places we must be careful to respect individuals' autonomy and sense of responsibility and to protect a diversity of activities and conceptions of the good life.* Individuals might be *partly* subject to paying for the consequences of harmful activities but perhaps not *totally* subject if freedom of choice, compassion for others and public pluralism are social values worth preserving. Any health taxes, in short, should fund only part of the future health expenditure related to the activity in question.[8] They would signal a potential for future harm by encouraging people to think twice before consuming the product.

Should some drugs be legalised?

Should we permit the consumption of those substances that, like tobacco, alcohol and fatty foods, are potentially addictive but where there is only the danger and not the certainty of mischief?

Shapiro (2003) is among those who have called for a 'social libertarian' approach to drugs policy (see Thornton, 1995). He argues that the medical model of addiction is misleading, citing research regarding the symptoms of addiction (recurrent cravings, an ever-increasing tolerance that demands more of the drug, a fear of withdrawal symptoms) that suggests that these are less substantial than both expert and mainstream opinions imagine. His principal argument is that social and cultural norms shape behaviour as much as, and perhaps more than, biochemical ones. Therefore, a substance's addictive properties differ from person to person and sociocultural setting to sociocultural setting. Those with a predisposition to destructive behaviour will find an outlet for their addictive needs even if you remove every last drop of heroin, cocaine and so on from the planet, while those whose lives are rewarding will be more able to use drugs with caution. Rather than treating addictive and dependent properties as inherent to a drug, we should therefore attend to 'set and setting', that is, the interaction of the drug's pharmacology with the social environment within which it is taken. Shapiro therefore calls for the legalisation of heroin and cocaine.

Much of this is echoed by Oddie (2005), who rejects the World Health Organization's definition of dependency (wanting and trying to quit x but tending to fail because of x's addictive properties).[9] The problem with the definition, according to Oddie, is its reliance on 'wanting and trying'. If I never want to quit heroin, ipso facto I cannot be addicted to it; nor can your watching television be counted as a dependency if you never want to quit, even though it might be more of a problem for you than your neighbour's cocaine intake is for him. Oddie's alternative, like Shapiro's, is to introduce personal and social circumstances into the picture. To generalise about addiction from the inevitable 'bad cases' is as distorting as generalisation from the inevitable 'good cases'. If we treat pro-drug gurus like the 1960s American writer Timothy Leary with scepticism, why not also doubt the official line that dependency and addiction are inherently bad? By becoming dependent on x, I may miss out on the joys of y, but by not becoming dependent, I may miss out on those experiences, making x superior to y.[10] Addiction might reduce the quantity of options I can choose, but may enhance the quality of the ones I am left with. The point of drugs policy should be to respect autonomy rather than fear dependency.

There are, of course, additional arguments for legalisation that are less libertarian. First, the pragmatic one that because drug use can never be eliminated the best we can do is to detach it from the criminal empires it feeds (Buckley, 2002; cf. Wilson, 2002). Similar arguments are advanced for smaller-scale initiatives, such as needle exchange programmes designed to impede the spread of HIV. Second, there is the regulative idea that by managing the drugs market government can have a greater influence than at present on supply and demand (Polsby, 1998). Permitting and taxing soft drugs like cannabis would raise the revenue needed to tackle the detrimental effects of harder drugs. Making heroin available through GPs or other practitioners makes it easier to implement and monitor programmes of withdrawal.

The problem with the libertarian position is one of wishful thinking (Macleod, 2003). The conclusion that all currently illegal substances should be legalised does not necessarily follow from the premise that dependency and addiction are social constructions. It is common to insert the 'bridging premise' of personal autonomy in order to supply the missing link and yield the above conclusion, but, as we saw earlier, autonomy does not necessarily rule out paternalism. Szasz (2003, p 388) asks,

> ... how long can we live with the inconsistency of being expected to be responsible for operating cars and computers, but not for operating our own bodies?

Yet the analogy is conveniently facile. It would be equally cogent to assert that because we do not allow people to make bombs in their garage, they should have *no* control over their bodies. Indeed, if 'society' is important, in those countries where social pressures, expectations and stresses are high there may be even more reason to restrict certain substances and activities.

More reasonably, Cohen (1995, Ch 4) argues that the principle of 'self-ownership' must mean *partial* ownership. This is on the Rawlsian grounds that because the talents we are born with are, to whatever extent, matters of luck, they are arbitrary from a moral point of view (Kymlicka, 2002, pp 107-27; Taylor, 2005). Therefore, I have some claim on the goods generated from you exercising your talents, just as you have a claim on mine.

This parallels the Mill/Goodin defence of paternalism, which, to summarise, is based on a threefold distinction:

(1) the certainty of harming oneself;
(2) the strong danger of harming oneself;
(3) the weak danger of harming oneself.

For libertarians, autonomy implies full self-ownership, that is, full control over oneself and the resources generated by your talents, such that interference is only warranted when a person is harming others (Nozick, 1974, pp 58-9). But as noted earlier, Mill would allow interference with autonomy in the case of the first scenario (1), for example, stopping you walking over a bridge about to collapse. Allowance was also made for the possibility of a Mill/Goodin consensus in the event of the second scenario (2), which was the possible justification for health taxes; though less so as we near the third scenario if we are to avoid the excessive paternalism of Goodin's anti-smoking arguments (3). Because you do not 'own yourself' completely the *strong danger* of self-harm could warrant paternalistic interference with your freedom of action – perhaps because your future self shares ownership of the person you are now and so needs protecting against your present-day recklessness.

The Mill/Goodin defence therefore involves basing autonomy on a 'principle of majority self-ownership', where you have a large degree of ownership, but not total ownership, over your body, its talents and the resources it generates (cf. George, 2004, pp 26-31). This fleshes out the compatibilist account of freedom advanced in Chapter One, which attempts to avoid absolutist conceptions of freedom, such as that of the libertarian's. On these grounds, the libertarian defence of drug legalisation is probably less convincing than the government regulation, restricted distribution and perhaps health taxing of drugs.[11]

Therefore, the pragmatic and regulatory arguments for limited legalisation are more convincing. Conservatives of left and right will warn about the dangers here of moral hazard – the suspicion that if drug taking is sanctioned, the number of drug users will increase – and complain about the state becoming a pusher rather than a prohibitor. Yet unless we are content with the social consequences of the drug policies that currently prevail in most countries, those warnings should motivate us to move cautiously and experientially. They should not motivate us to remain where we are. Fighting a war on the supply of drugs is less effectual than influencing the demand for drugs through policies designed to improve the social environment.

The social context

I have argued that smoking in public places should be banned except when, within non-enclosed and semi-enclosed spaces, non-smokers can be trusted to choose whether to place themselves in harm's way or not. I also indicated health taxes may be justified in the case of activities hovering around category (2) but that individuals also have a right to take risks without society making these prohibitively expensive. While health taxes stress the responsibilities attached to this 'right of self-harm', the values of personal choice and social pluralism mean we should not expect health taxes to fund each and every health cost that risk taking invites. We are similarly entitled to take a regulatory and pragmatic approach to the legalisation of those drugs approximating in their effects to alcohol, tobacco and fatty foods.

These views are partly in line with some recent developments in public policies, but not all. We hypothesised earlier about a drift towards a sanitised, standardised conception of public space that is not only concerned to eradicate harms but no longer trusts adults to make their own judgements (Bauman, 2001; 2005, pp 71-86; Hier, 2003; Kenny, 2005). Some theorists have highlighted a distinction between risk avoidance and risk taking (or risk navigating) and the mistake made in applying one category to those contexts where the other is most appropriate (Lupton and Tulloch, 2002). For instance, some argue that we have been over-protecting children, thus making them *more* vulnerable to harm by not allowing their skills of risk assessment and negotiation to develop fully (Furedi, 2001). If this hypothesis is correct, why might such category mistakes, such miscalibrations of avoidance and taking/navigating, occur? There are several currents at work, at least.

In one respect, these developments represent a regrettable shift away from the economic regulation and social liberalisation of post-Second World War socioeconomic policies towards one where gluing together the fragmentations and inequalities produced by market deregulation, individualisation, privatisation and globalisation is thought to need increased social regulation, surveillance and supervision (Fitzpatrick, 2002b). We have arguably been over-exposed to risk taking in those marketised areas of society from which government has withdrawn and been under-exposed to it in those areas where government has rolled itself forward in finding an outlet for its managerial and legislative impulses. The more we have become defined as consumers, the more non-market areas of life have been bounded to contain the possessive individualism to which consumption all too easily gives rise. The repeated panics surrounding employment obligations, antisocial behaviour, family breakdown, feral teenagers, identity checks, ethnic/cultural separatism, immigration and asylum, criminal justice and so on may all be taken as evidence of those new disciplinary mechanisms (Fitzpatrick, 2003, Ch 3; 2005a: Ch 8).

The recent fashion for wellbeing constitutes another current. This is the idea that personal and social welfare requires not only the evading of 'bads' but also the promotion of 'goods' and of the opportunities to realise them. To some extent, this offers a welcome attempt to redefine social and public policies as concerning more than social problems (Dean, 2006). But when allied to overly paternalistic, top-down assumptions of what those goods are, a politics of wellbeing can also engender the disempowerment of individuals. For example, Layard's (2005) Benthamite treatment of happiness makes little room for subjectivism, being highly positivistic and elitist in its policy implications. Chapter Four similarly argued that when the care ethic, which is presumably implicit within this notion of wellbeing, is given an anti-liberal tenor, the ethic threatens to detach from considerations of individual rights. What this does is emphasise the pre-emptiveness of social policies that, in a neoliberal, globalising context, are concerned increasingly with conducting and constraining the meaning and scope of agency. Governance operates through our freedoms (Fitzpatrick, 2005a, pp 158-64), our job being to realise the goods and avoid the bads that have been defined as such elsewhere.

So while the goal of social justice has been retained within social democratic politics, with no substantial redistributions of income and wealth having been either attempted or effected, social democrats have turned to other mechanisms. New Labour, for instance, has been criticised for not attending to socioeconomic inequalities per se, preferring to interpret health inequalities as manifestations of personal behaviour and poor management rather than as sociostructural determinants (Davey Smith et al, 2005). And with worries that ageing populations will place unsustainable pressures on health and long-term care budgets there are perhaps financial reasons why social democrats have emphasised personal behaviour. Battin (2005, pp 269-76) observes that ageing populations only increase public expenditures unless accompanied by 'longer-health scenarios'. In short, with rising life expectancy, the period of pre-terminal decline has to remain stable if the additional social costs of ageing are to be minimised. The emphasis on lifestyle regulation must at least partly reflect a fear that without longer health ageing populations will make public services unaffordable.

To put it crudely, if most of us are going to have to work longer to earn our pensions, we can't have socially excluded people falling out of the labour market prematurely due to unhealthy behaviour. Some who would restrict the right to indulge in potentially unhealthy activities are concerned with the detrimental effects of smoking on disadvantaged people (Arneson, 1989), but others are probably more concerned with the health of the labour market in a globally competitive economy. Egalitarians must continually ask themselves when excessive paternalism becomes too high a price to pay for equality. Information about un/healthy lifestyles is one thing, but the poorest ultimately need more income, wealth, quality jobs, meaningful free time and political participation rather than more prohibitions and lectures from middle-class therapists.

For all of these reasons – what we might call respectively the marketisation, welfarisation and medicalisation of risk – there has been a tendency to stress risk avoidance at the expense of risk taking and navigation, and to re-regulate public space due to a lack of trust that individuals can recognise, gauge and traverse harms themselves. The notion that we can sometimes choose harmful acts has become more alien to policy makers; taken as a failure of reason rather than reason's manifestation. We are often prevented from walking on to the bridge even when the dangers are weak (category 3). Therefore, while agreeing with some public health measures introduced recently, this chapter suggests that there are deeper currents below the social surface drifting us towards infantilisation (Barber, 2007) that need to be captured by traditional debates regarding harm and paternalism. This is not to suggest it has been all one-way traffic. The growth in information about risks and harms can represent genuine forms of empowerment and progress. Overall, though, I am hypothesising a contemporary tendency to miscalibrate risks, by imaging that harms are nearer to category (1) than they in fact are, and to distrust individuals' capacity to accept harm rationally and reasonably. These social currents will be discussed further in Chapter Seven.

Conclusion

For all its potential difficulties, Mill's harm principle has stood the test of time remarkably well. It is one of the most welcome legacies of utilitarianism's influence. But if I am right about recent trends, we are currently being too sensitive where harm to others is concerned and too protective where individuals make decisions about possible harms to themselves. In both senses, harming is entwined with our social freedoms such that eradicating all instances of the former also threatens the latter.

So, in answering the questions with which we started, it would indeed be simplistic to regard paternalism and autonomy as a zero-sum game. Yet this should not fool us into believing they are therefore always mutually reinforcing. The character and scope of each can sometimes threaten the other. In the 1970s, Conservatives worried that welfare state paternalism was undermining capitalist freedoms. Thirty years later it is the paternalism of a marketised and disciplinary state that possibly represents the greatest threat to our 'social freedoms'.

Notes
[1] Of course, utilitarianism can be accused of leaving the door open to legitimations of harm if this could be shown to serve the greatest good of the greatest number. That is not Mill's take on the principle,

given the strong post–Benthamite flavour of his liberalism, but some have questioned the extent to which his utilitarianism is consistent with his liberalism.

[2] By 'self-harm' is simply meant 'any form of harm to oneself committed by oneself'.

[3] To allow smoking areas outside a bar may seem a reinvention of the smoking/no-smoking areas that had previously been located inside the bar. But if the health of bar workers always predominates over their freedom of choice, because some smoke (and, incidentally, carbon monoxide from the road) will no doubt drift back into the bar, presumably we should widen the no-smoking zone – to the point where workers in next door's shop start complaining, perhaps? But if we widen it too far, of course, then we risk introducing a de facto blanket ban on smoking.

[4] I am setting aside the question of what constitutes 'sufficient information'.

[5] By 'danger', we therefore mean 'degree of probability'. Some probabilities are so high risk that they come close to certainty, while others are lower risk. The threefold distinction proposed on p 110 only captures the staging posts on a spectrum along which degrees of probability are admittedly difficult to assess. Nevertheless, we need this spectrum if we are to avoid collapsing 'weak dangers' and certainties together, as Goodin arguably does. Even if each cigarette I smoke pushes me incrementally across the spectrum towards the certainty of harm (although even this can be disputed), a puritanical opposition to smoking per se, demonstrated by many within the medical profession, is unwarranted.

[6] It is for this reason that we should not distribute transplant organs to the patients who need them on the basis of past behaviour alone. You may need a new kidney because of cirrhosis but to what should we attribute your alcoholism? A lack of virtue? Parental example? Damaged relationship? Deprived childhood? If past behaviour alone is the criterion, transplantation policy is biased against those groups most likely to experience debilitating conditions; another health inequality to mirror unjust social inequalities (Wilkinson, 2005). At best, past behaviour should, where possible, shape an agreed programme of pre-transplantation behaviour but only on the principle that when it

comes to treatment all patients start off with a blank sheet of paper (Ubel et al, 1999).

[7] Obviously, products like alcohol and tobacco already attract sales taxes but justifying these in terms of health effects is relatively recent.

[8] We might also oppose placing too much emphasis on sales taxes because of their regressive effects (Wilson and Thomson, 2005), but the point is that even in an egalitarian context, where the regressive effects are modest, there would be good reason to avoid weeding out and taxing every form of harmful consumption.

[9] However, Oddie's is more of a critique and he is not necessarily advocating a libertarian policy on drugs.

[10] If you doubt this possibility, imagine that x = 'the works of Shakespeare' and y = 'the speeches of Rupert Murdoch'.

[11] It was never the intention to prescribe a list as there are potentially many substances that hover from (1) to (2) to (3). A combination of scientific determination and public debate is needed to establish which substances apply to which part of the scale, and so where bans and health taxes (at varying levels) should be imposed. In most countries, getting governments, media and other agencies to engage in such open, honest and scientific debates is regrettably infrequent.

SEVEN

Choosing

We have now introduced a social critique into our discussion of autonomy and paternalism.

So far it has been proposed that the marketisation of society and social risks is important because, by engendering economic and cultural fragmentation, contemporary social policies are characterised less by interventions intended to reduce structural inequalities and more by a pre-emptive management of agency, the latter being a kind of 'situational engineering' through which the environmental possibilities of action are manipulated. According to this prevailing logic, if we can neither eliminate those fragments (there supposedly being 'no alternative' to free markets), nor pacify them, the best we can do is to limit the ground over which they are scattered. The freedom to earn, consume, possess and exchange must therefore be accompanied by the enforceable obligation to do so responsibly. Thus we have experienced the simultaneous and often paradoxical expansion of autonomy and governance, active citizenship and prohibitive paternalism, mobility and surveillance, information highways and identity scans, market competition and social re-regulation, individualism and legislative hyperactivity, decentralisation and micro-management (Dean, 2007). This has led not only to a punitiveness directed towards those who will not or cannot 'play by the rules' but also to social spaces that are more regulated, scrutinised and distrustful than before. Paternalism becomes less about respecting individuals' freedom to choose from a plurality of goods, even at the risk of self-harm, and more about ensuring that they do not make the wrong choice in the first place. The freer we are to wander the aisles of the internet, the naves of supermarkets and malls, and the arterial transits of airport hubs, the greater the need to emphasise common roots, boundaries and understandings, no longer through socioeconomic position (class) but in terms of certain values, codes, laws, norms and identities. Social institutions must remoralise if market liberations are to be tamed.

We will now explore some of the ethical dimensions of this 'social politics' as it plays out across the traditional sectors of policy analysis. In this chapter, we look at the increased use of market principles and assumptions in welfare institutions. In Chapter Eight, we turn to relations of family and intimacy. As before, we use specific questions to focus and organise our journey. Later, we interrogate the extent to which welfare services should be delivered through regulated markets; beforehand, we explore the role parental choice should play in schools' admissions. But, to get to these questions, we first need to develop the framework already sketched.

Environmental paternalism[1]

Chapter Six presumed in favour of autonomy as long as the harm principle is respected and we can be reasonably sure that the autonomy exercised is authentic. Should the same presumption apply to issues of *market* choice too? For, whatever the additional roles played by the economically powerful and by social structures, markets are to some extent the product of individuals' free actions. So surely, according to the harm principle, though interference with my transactions is legitimate where harm to others is concerned, to either prevent or restrict me from exercising my autonomy because I may lose from an exchange is excessively paternalistic. Is this the correct application of the harm principle? When is interference with market choice permissible, either because harm to others is being or likely to be committed or because I self-harm through transactions that are not genuinely autonomous?

Much depends, first, on whether we apply the DDE. It may be impermissible to deliberately hurt others, but what happens when that harm is merely foreseen rather than intended? A course of action leads to the closure of a factory and the loss of 500 jobs, but if my aim was to avoid bankrupting a firm in which a total of 20,500 employees work, is that not a regrettable but nonetheless acceptable side-effect?[2] For Kantians, the redundancies would have to be consistent with rational and reasonable principles (Ballet and Jolivet, 2003). To Kant (1996, p 468), this implies a doctrine opposed to self-interest, since, he says, only by observing obligations *to* the commonwealth can the affluence *of* the commonwealth be preserved. Rawls might argue that the action is acceptable as long as those made redundant are better off as a result.[3] Virtuists would presumably be concerned with whether I was acting responsibly, with concern not only for the firm per se but also for the potentially unemployed. This implies that my obligation is not merely an ephemeral one but extends beyond the immediate decision to one of enduring care motivated by an ethic of compassion and empathy. The DDE does not allow us to be indifferent to those whose harm is foreseen, perhaps offering a prima facie reason why interference with markets is warranted when harm to others is at stake.

By contrast, if we are consequentialists who ignore or downplay the DDE, this might imply we are dealing with a straightforward trade-off. In the above scenario, the continued employment of 20,000 workers trumps the redundancy of 500. If it can be demonstrated that free markets produce better consequences, interference is impermissible (Narveson, 1984). But of course consequentialism is rarely as neat as this (Jackson, 2004, pp 528–35). It might well be that the diswelfare of the 500, given the documented effects of unemployment, will exceed the welfare of the 20,000 for whom daily life continues as usual (even if they are initially grateful for keeping their jobs). In this scenario, interference *is* warranted, if not to prevent the redundancy, at least to assist the 500. Therefore, interference with the market is permissible unless we prefer *an ethos of laissez faire individualism that cannot be generated by consequentialism alone.*

Whether we apply the DDE or not, it seems that some interference with individuals' transactions can be justified where harm to others is concerned. (Some free market advocates might argue that the apparent harm to B committed by A is really self-harm if and when B has failed to act as a free agent, for example, if B has thoughtlessly bought a house from A that is experiencing subsidence. But we will see below why that is too severe a conception of individual freedom.) This does not determine the details of any interference, of course, and much depends on the degree and the nature of the harm in question.[4] The point is simply that we cannot be indifferent to the harm to others committed through market exchanges, *even if* markets were purely the result of free choice.

What about harm to oneself, though? Is a market transaction analogous to the freedom to smoke? Chapter Six distinguished between the certainty, the strong danger and the weak danger of self-harm along a sliding scale. In the case of certain self-harm, we permitted interference when a person is about to walk on to a bridge they do not know to be unsafe. But what if they decide to walk on to it anyway once informed of the danger? Do we assume that they have not heard us properly or are experiencing some kind of delusion? Are some actions so personally reckless that we must prohibit them even though that person is fully informed and apparently behaving rationally? The 'future interests' defence suggests so, but although we acknowledged the relevance of this, we also found reasons for questioning the degree of paternalism it actually permits. Basically, where we can be reasonably certain that someone is acting with foresight, as the best judge of their own future interests, we ought to allow them to proceed. This is not a libertarian argument where we step back completely. Instead, courses of actions that are irreversible or difficult to reverse should be discouraged but nevertheless permitted, according to specific regulations, if good reasons for taking them can be advanced (see Chapter Ten). We should not make walking on to the bridge an easy option, but nor should we prohibit it entirely. This means that market transactions should be difficult but not necessarily impossible to perform where there is a certainty of self-harm.

In the case of strong and weak *dangers* of self-harm, the paternalism that is appropriate presumably becomes less restrictive. We may still issue warning signals (such as those on cigarette packets) and/or taxes that require people to think twice, while enabling society to cover the costs of bad decisions, but 'stepping back' is ultimately more of a responsibility if we wish to respect that person's autonomy. Take the house-buying example. One of the reasons why market interference is justified is because some parties will possess more information than others (O'Neill, 1998, Ch 10). Where that inequality is likely to produce a distortion in the exchange, we are justified in interfering to ensure that relevant information is made available. We should therefore require A to declare important information about his property for, to be a genuinely free exchange, government must equalise the information possessed by the relevant parties. It is the equivalent of a warning signal. And yet, according to the argument just advanced, this does not mean we should prevent B from making the purchase if he nevertheless feels it is worth the risk.

Yet unregulated markets not only imply inequalities of information but also inequalities of resources and capabilities. Why should that matter? If my resources and capabilities are purely the product of my own efforts, there is no problem here. We should not be restricting freedoms because of the unequal outcomes of free decisions and actions previously taken. But throughout this book we have questioned the validity of such reasoning. Social humanism assumes that our agency is not entirely free, that free will is a cultural as much as a psychological phenomenon that increases or diminishes along an evolutionary trajectory and so can only be understood against the background of certain natural and social determinisms. Social structures, situations and circumstances both enable and constrain who we are and what we think and do. Where structures are inegalitarian, and where inequalities are the result not of effort but of luck, socioeconomic power, inheritance or exploitation, freedom too is skewed away from the disadvantaged and powerless, not only in terms of their political and economic liberty but also as a fundamental undermining of agency and self. Market transactions between unequals therefore perpetuate injustice when the unequal resources and capabilities in question are the product of factors beyond individuals' control (MacLeod, 2003).

This is, obviously, the beginning of an argument for egalitarian justice on which, as noted in Chapter Five, we will not be dwelling. This means that various questions have to be sidelined. How much equalisation is desirable? How should it be effected? It is clear, however, that the equalisation of resources implies the redistribution of primary goods like income and wealth, as well as many cultural and ecological resources additionally important to wellbeing (Nussbaum, 2006, pp 165-8). By 'capabilities' is meant the opportunity and ability both to make best use of existing resources and to maximise future ones.[5] Real freedom and choice therefore requires that information, resources and capabilities be distributed relatively equally in order to allow individuals the greatest possible amount of control over themselves and their environments. Which of our moral philosophies captures this view the best?

In fact none can provide us with an exact calibration. A virtuist such as Held (2002, pp 28-32) believes that liberal individualism cannot draw adequate boundaries for market activity (see also Macdonald and Merrill, 2002). Kantianism, she says, is concerned with rights, resources and autonomy, and so is neutral over whether markets can and should deliver these; utilitarianism is concerned with the maximisation of utility and so is also neutral between market and non-market forms of provision (Corson, 2002). What neither can do, she believes, is recognise our need for the shared enjoyment, social responsibility and collective caring that markets tend to inhibit. For Held, only an ethic of care can properly show us where to limit markets and what kind of markets to limit.

But while care may indeed enable us to question the ethos of market competition, it is not clear that virtuism really is that superior. Aristotle argued for private property and so it is no great leap to see that such arguments can also be used to defend the private acquisitions and exchanges of a market system.

Does consequentialism therefore offer a better alternative (Arneson, 2003)? As we saw in Chapter Six, Mill defined utility in terms of liberty and obviously liberty refers not only to existing pleasures, interests and preferences but also to the capacity to form new ones in the future. He therefore seems to have supported the notion that markets and economic imperatives have little role to play in public services like education in order that students can be exposed to the widest possible range of values, beliefs, traditions and so on (Baum, 2003; Tarrant and Tarrant, 2004, p 113). Yet Mill's objections to market principles are not firm. In *Principles of Political Economy*, he makes considerable room for private and voluntary schools and if his arguments for government intervention into the market are shaky or no longer apply[6], his utilitarianism makes greater room for market choice than is being proposed here (Mill, 1985, pp 371-21).

Finally, it is possible to construct a broadly Kantian and contractualist argument that says that the autonomy of all is most enhanced when social conditions are fair (Dodson, 2003). For instance, Kant (1996, p 593) seems to agree with Mill that the marketplace and the schoolroom must be kept distinct. In Kant's case, this is due to the need to orientate public interaction to the moral law, though more recent contractualists like Rawls and Dworkin defend market regulation without as stringent a requirement (Olssen and Peters, 2005, p326). That said, it is also possible to construct free market defences of capitalism on Kantian principles (Muller, 2006; also White, 2004) on the basis that personal autonomy and sovereignty require the kind of 'sociable self-interest' that some defend capitalism as embodying: pride at one's personal property engendering a mutual respect for that of others.

So none of the above can offer a conclusive foundation for a politics of distributive justice. This is partly why Chapter Five argued for a pragmatic, eclectic approach that draws on multiple perspectives. This basic point can therefore be restated, even in the absence of a more thoroughgoing account. The principle of autonomy demands that we respect individuals' choices even when they reasonably risk self-harm, though not when harm to others is concerned. However, we cannot infer from this that market choice should be unrestricted (even when the harm principle is being observed). Inequalities in information, resources and capabilities tend to adversely affect the freedoms of the least advantaged, an injustice given the role played in human affairs by luck, inheritance and exploitation. Therefore, we need to apply a politics of distributive justice whose aim is to equalise social conditions. Autonomy is only real and meaningful depending on the extent to which such conditions are in place. So while we must respect choice, we should not automatically equate this with 'market choice', the latter being permissible only in so far as it is consistent with just social conditions. This may, of course, still leave a considerable role for markets if it can be demonstrated that they contribute to such distributive equality; the purpose of the discussion below is to test how far this is so by addressing two specific questions.

What this argument does, in addition, is require us to rethink what we mean by paternalism. In Chapter Six, paternalism took a fairly prohibitive form. When, we asked, should bad habits be proscribed? But the more 'environmental paternalism' sketched above suggests that by addressing unjust circumstances autonomy can be enhanced by decreasing the inequities to which free choice can give rise in unequal societies.[7] It is easy to confuse prohibitive and environmental paternalism, especially when marketisation appears inexorable. For if you are worried by the cultural and economic fragmentations mentioned earlier, but sceptical that an egalitarian politics can succeed, how tempting it is, especially for puritans on the left, to prefer interference with individuals' privacies and freedoms. But my position suggests that it is better to discourage bad habits by addressing the social stresses, anxieties and inducements that drive people to them, than to try and create equality by banning bad habits.

Therefore, the conclusion arrived at here is consistent with and builds on that of Chapter Six. What has shifted is the context. We are no longer talking simply of prohibiting, restricting or barring but of arming, equipping and enabling. The choice of those who do not possess sufficient information, resources and capacities is hampered. What constitutes 'sufficiency' in each case partly depends on the holdings of those with whom we share social space. If my wealth is bought at the cost of social injustice, I harm the disadvantaged by undermining their freedom to decide for themselves how best to live. We can therefore rely on markets the most when markets are not allowed to dominate social interactions. As Schwartz (2004, p 104) notes, what we prefer above all is the choice of *when* to choose, a capacity that market ubiquity undermines. So in addressing the following questions, we explore the extent to which 'choice' is enhanced by association with distributive justice and so does not necessarily translate into 'market choice'.

Choice and equity

> *To what extent should parents be able to choose their child's school?*

There are many reasons why choice became central to social policy debates. Some fear that unless public services at least approximate to the demand-led individualism of consumer societies, people's expectations will exceed what the public sector can deliver and the latter will lose political support (Hutton, 2003). Others *hope* that a consumerist ethos will infiltrate public services so that these become characterised either by full-blown market competition and profit motives (Seldon, 2005) or at least by more quasi-markets and state–market partnerships (Le Grand and Bartlett, 1993; Bartlett et al, 1998; Le Grand, 2007). So what, first, does choice mean in the context of public services (see Dowding and John, forthcoming)?

It cannot simply mean greater quantity. On the face of it, having a choice of three schools is better than a choice of two; but if the additional school is identical to the others, we may have increased supply without increasing choice in any meaningful way. It may sometimes be better to have a choice between an x school and a y school than to have three schools that are all x. But if quantity per se does not get the job done, neither does diversity per se. If three schools each teach extreme versions of different religious faiths, we may prefer three other schools that resemble one another but are moderate towards religion. Nor does invoking 'quality' provide a solution because, even before we arrive at the problem of how to measure it, parents will disagree over what quality means. For some it will imply high test scores, some will be interested in a school's specialisms, others will be more interested in creative and non-pressurised learning environments. In short, quality is a sub-set of diversity and returns us to the difficulty of squaring diversity with quantity (van Hees, 2004, p 265). Should we prefer fewer, more diverse schools or numerous schools that are similar to one another? And if your answer is 'lots of schools exhibiting reasonable diversity', how do we know what this is and how to achieve it?

The ultimate problem is one of scarcity, of course. If the education system could be run at excess capacity, if a 'reasonable diversity' were achieved and if the highest possible quality (however defined) were attained everywhere, the question of choice would be muted. Choice becomes an issue when not everyone can receive their ideal, when there is not enough of a given resource to go round. At this point, choice relates as much to distributive justice as to individuals' freedom because scarcity means that your choice affects mine far more than if opportunities are abundant. It matters less to me if you appropriate a piece of land in a large, fertile valley than it would if we were sharing a small, barren island. The meaning and implications of choice differ from setting to setting.

Within social choice theory,[8] envy-freeness is the point at which no person would prefer the goods of anyone else because they were free and able to acquire those goods themselves (Dworkin, 2000, pp 139-47; Heath, 2004). Scarcity, though, means that this ideal is unlikely to be achieved. As such, equity is here defined as the second-best distribution we can achieve. It implies not total envy-freeness but its greatest possible approximation, that is, through the maximisation of capacity, diversity and quality, combined with the principle that the envy-level of those with the fewest resources should be broadly equivalent to those with the most. In other words, at $t + 1$ the satisfaction of those with the smallest holdings should approximate to that of those with the greatest since, at t, both had access to roughly equivalent opportunity sets and roughly equivalent amounts of resources with which to bid. So this is not to assume strict equality but certainly a greater equalisation of conditions than currently prevails, redistribution being justified as the reduction of scarcity through the expansion of public goods and services, and compensation provided to the poorest for the disadvantages they face due to any remaining scarcity. The aim of social policy should be to approximate as closely to this principle of equity as possible – though this formulation does not take full account of the role always played by adaptive preferences (Elster, 1985; see below). Equity and equality are therefore related without being identical.[9] What moral philosophy might therefore guide the attempt to combine choice with equity when it comes to school admissions?

Consequentialism does not quite get us there. On the face of it, the goal of maximising individuals' satisfaction with their goods provides consequentialism with a clear principle of allocation, since it presumably implies an increase in happiness, the elimination of unfulfilled preferences and a concern for welfare (Reeve, 1990). But as noted in previous chapters, consequentialism is not always sensitive to individuals' sovereignty; if might, for instance, allow skewed forms of choice so that satisfaction is merely a result of people adapting to given circumstances. A society of happy slaves would be consistent with consequentialist principles such that these may underestimate the degree of resource redistribution that equity requires (Nussbaum, 2001a, pp 78-81). In the context of education (and welfare systems more generally), it is easy to increase choice for the disadvantaged in a quantitative sense without having altered their position in the queue – that is, their bargaining power compared with others' – and insist that this is all that justice requires. This is potentially the case with proposals for voucher schemes (see below).

Kantianism does not quite get us there either (also Brighouse, 2000, Chs 4 and 5). The principle of equal autonomy respects choice, as long as this accords with rational and reasonable criteria, while acknowledging that my autonomy is in some way linked to yours (van Hees, 2003). However, Kant himself was more concerned with charity than equity (see p 52) and while theorists like Rawls and Scanlon have modified Kantianism, a frustrating indeterminacy remains. For instance, when Kant enjoins us never to treat others 'only' as a means to our ends, what pattern of social distribution is this consistent with? Are p and q allowed to treat each other as a means so long as the one balances out the other, or is *p* allowed more latitude to correct a disadvantage for which *q* can be held responsible? Should schools' admissions systems be based on an instrumentalist individualism (I am happy for your child to prosper in order to help my child prosper) or a form of social engineering that addresses socioeconomic disadvantages?

Finally, while not valorising choice, virtuists, too, may make room for it so long as it promotes principles of virtue (care, eudaimonia, 'internal goods', communal values, good citizenship, excellences and so on [Carr, 2003]). But, again, where does this get us? Aristotle (1955, p 65) recommended a well-rounded education, but to what extent would this permit us to frustrate pupils' development when they demonstrate certain abilities and aptitudes? To what extent should we do so in order to equalise social conditions? Virtuists see education as simply one site for the promotion of virtue, but how, then, do we actually assign responsibilities? Can parents be sanctioned for not contributing to their child's well-roundedness, for example? Modern governments are certainly not above recommending that parents observe good habits at home. At its most conservative, virtuism treats education as instruction into the canons of a tradition, rejecting choice as a sign of the self's hollowness and equity as the engineering of the self's social practices (MacIntyre, 1981, pp 190, 247-55).

Perhaps, therefore, in thinking about how to frame choice and equity we have to be more down to earth than the above '-isms' permit. What if we based school admissions on proximity? Perhaps only those within a particular catchment area should be permitted to send their children to that school, with the nearest coming head of the queue. This has the virtue of simplicity, but what if the local school is a poor one? We might solve that problem by widening the catchment area to include several schools, so giving parents within it a menu of options to select from. The problem is that if those schools vary in quality, affluent households will probably dominate the better ones as a result of 'push' factors (home life more conducive to learning, sharper elbows) and 'pull' factors (schools cream-skimming the best pupils).

We might alleviate that concern by requiring each school to take pupils from a diversity of socioeconomic, cultural and mixed ability backgrounds through some kind of banding method, although this means we lose the simplicity with which we began. It is also the case that those with the money can 'buy proximity' to the best schools by purchasing houses within desirable catchment areas ('selection by estate agent') (Leech and Campos, 2003). Banding might counteract those effects, too, but in any event for proximity to work we would need to restrict the freedom of schools to decide their own admissions policies, increasing complexity, with knock-on effects for parental choice.

An alternative is to allocate by lottery so that chance becomes the distributive principle. However, this eliminates any kind of choice from the equation and may not reduce the inequity identified above. Since there would have to be a maximum distance across which it is reasonable to expect a child to travel to school, this will severely limit the area within which lotteries could occur. And if lotteries are in some way restricted[10] (geographically or otherwise), we again retain the likelihood of richer households buying themselves into the best catchment areas.

Perhaps we should simply allow a free market, where parents choose schools and schools choose pupils, with demonstrable ability and/or aptitude likely to predominate – 'aptitude' could be religious, academic, creative or athletic in nature. Evidence suggests that free markets in education advantage those who are already advantaged (Foster et al, 1996; West and Pennell, 1997; Apple, 2001; Barry, 2005, pp 64-6; cf. Gibbons et al, 2006), but why is this necessarily a problem?

It is tempting to treat 'choice' and 'markets' as coterminous. Choice is a means by which we signal our needs and wants to others. In a market environment, consumers signal what they want and are willing to pay, while producers signal what they can offer at a price that covers their costs and generates profits. Ideally, markets recognise both types of signal, enabling both consumers and producers to gain. By contrast, where needs and wants are determined centrally, fallibility and an absence of incentives ensure that signals become deformed and misread.

Yet we saw above why this 'ideal' should be treated with suspicion. Agents do not enter the marketplace on equal terms. Some consumers will have a tendency to be at the head of queue more often than others, not because of personal desert but because of social advantages. Also, producers and vendors may have an interest in concealing or misrepresenting information. The 'neutral' signals that circulate within markets may therefore be distorted and lead to unfair outcomes for the unjustly disadvantaged. Regulation and redistribution is therefore needed to level the conditions of agents, to 'smooth out' those signals and enable outcomes to reflect individuals' efforts rather than their unchosen backgrounds (Brighouse, 2000, pp 201-2). Choice and markets are more aligned when those markets are managed and equalised.

And if this is the case with microwaves or televisions, how much more so with goods essential to autonomy and wellbeing, such as health, education, income, shelter and care (Copp, 1992)? Inequalities in televisions can matter,[11] but it is harder to justify government interventions here than it is with more essential goods. Inequalities in essential goods strike at the root of agency. Not only are health, education, income, shelter and care fundamental needs that, shaping the resources I can access and the capacities I possess, determine the degree of choice I can exercise, but your holdings affect the quality and value of my holdings much more so than in the case of non-essentials.[12] It is not only a case of public goods being 'positional' but of them being basic to individuals' agency, to the resources and capabilities that underpin and set our varying freedoms to choice.[13]

To what extent should we allocate public goods through regulated markets?

Given how difficult it is to reconcile choice and equity in schools' admissions, we cannot properly answer the first question until we have explored a second. One rejoinder is to insist that because markets enable allocative efficiency, public services like education require at least quasi-markets where risks and decision making are decentralised but competition is regulated and choice structured (Le Grand and Bartlett, 1993; Bartlett et al, 1998; Galston, 2003, pp 218-22, Perri 6, 2003). This means schools becoming the providers of education to purchasers (parents), perhaps financed directly by central government according to input – for example, the number of students enrolled – and/or output – for instance, qualifications achieved, with some regulative role for a local authority to ensure fairness (Le Grand, 2003, pp 109-15). Providers are thereby required to improve their efficiency and purchasers are given enhanced choice, while government ensures that principles of justice are observed by keeping the reins of control tighter than in a free market arena.

Are regulated markets therefore superior to the above measures (proximity, banding, lotteries, market competition) when it comes to reconciling choice and equity in public services?

Many additional claims have been made in favour of quasi-markets. They arguably offer one way of reducing scarcity by enabling both the quantity and diversity of providers to expand (but see below) (Le Grand, 2007, pp 106-9). They potentially keep the middle classes on side by offering opportunities, choices and advantages that they will otherwise seek in the private sector (Adonis and Pollard, 1998, pp xv-xxi). Quasi-markets may benefit the already advantaged, but, while allowing a degree of meritocratic elitism within the public sector may appear inegalitarian, by securing the commitment of the middle classes to the state system it will enable all boats to rise higher and quicker than if a public–private divide is allowed to solidify (cf. Davies, 2000). Finally, Le Grand (2003, pp 163-8) believes that quasi-markets enable welfare 'pawns' to become welfare 'queens' by facilitating mutuality of respect, empowering service users and reducing the exploitation characteristic of state monopolies.

There are at least five counter-arguments to this (Taylor-Gooby, 1998; van den Brink et al, 2002; Considine, 2003; Kahkonen, 2005; Stuyven and Steurs, 2005; see also the addendum on Le Grand later in this chapter). First, the quasi-markets of the public sector may only offer a limited number of providers, undercutting claims regarding choice and efficiency, for example, where an area is serviced by only a couple of schools and hospitals. One remedy is to invite private providers into that quasi-market, although this may only siphon public funds off into commercial firms. Besides, it contradicts one reason for keeping markets *quasi* in the first place: to avoid privatisation.[14]

Second, as in any market setting, the least advantaged will have relatively less purchasing power and providers may acquire the familiar incentives to conceal and distort in order to simulate efficiency. In education terms, schools may 'teach to the test', emphasising values of acquisitive individualism, instrumentalism and game playing rather than those stressing the fun and mutuality of learning, characteristics that are not easy to measure.

Third, the arm's-length regulation of quasi-markets has accompanied, and arguably driven, the 'new public managerialism' that seeks to 'reach over' the intermediate layers of civil society to manage from afar (Fitzpatrick, 2005a, pp 158-64). Methods such as performance-related pay, targets, auditing and market-type ranking bureaucratise at a distance without also offering the mechanisms of support and accountability that traditional bureaucracies at least theoretically embodied. Public sector motivation, cooperation, trust and professionalism risk being undermined as a result. As such, public sector workers are expected to demonstrate a cognitive dissonance: required to act like economic agents whose performance is quantified in a tick-box culture, while still expected to offer care and emotional labour. They are treated, in Le Grand's (2003) terminology, as knaves *and* knights *and* pawns.

Fourth, where public services are broken up and functions contracted out, a more rigid division of labour may result that is inimical to care. Toynbee (2003, pp 64-7) reports how the contracting out of UK hospital cleaning and portering has adversely affected patient care. This new managerialism may also lead to increased administrative costs and more bureaucracy at local level, as providers have to perpetually negotiate, contract and invoice purchasers and other providers, taking money away from front-line services.

Finally, because productivity and efficiency in allocation is only one of the criteria against which public services should be judged, giving them too much priority may disguise the extent to which 'waste' is sometimes a *useful and necessary part of the allocative process* rather than an embarrassing and regrettable side-product. Earlier mention was made of the complexity of adding socioeconomic diversity into school admissions policies, but such complexity may well be valuable if the social consequences are demonstrably more desirable than treating complexity as a clumsy relative one tries to avoid.

These points do not necessarily provide knockdown arguments against quasi-markets per se. Some research evidence suggests that, ultimately, quasi-markets cannot be treated monolithically, any more than it makes sense to speak of 'the state' or 'the voluntary sector' (McMaster, 2002; Adnett and Davies, 2003; Powell, 2003). Diversity within and between sectors always makes generalisation difficult. In short, whether we should allocate public goods through regulated markets depends on the institutional context, on how and why such markets are bordered and sustained.

Let us take as an example the long-running proposal to introduce education vouchers (Friedman, 1962, pp 89-95; West, 1997). Although much depends on their design, vouchers have been offered as a means of introducing consumer-like choice into educational provision without dismantling public services. Distributing all or most of a nation's education budget via parental choice, so that money follows the pupil to the school, has been argued to place greater power in their hands and means that schools must become more responsive to parents if they wish to attract the latter's income. This neoliberal version of voucher reform is something at which left-wingers often blanch for familiar reasons (Gutmann, 2000; Prasch and Sheth, 2000).

If vouchers can be topped up by personal income, they effectively represent a state subsidy for the already advantaged, maintaining the cherry picking that already occurs and ensuring that it is schools (or at least the most prestigious ones) that pick parents (see Le Grand, 2007, pp 92-3, 147-51). Also, they introduce a competitive ethos into public provision, one that arguably contradicts the motivations of public sector workers – not generally defined by monetary incentives (Sennett, 2003, pp 200-4) – and transforms relations between schools, parents and pupils into contractual and impersonal ones rather than relationships of trust and mutuality. Cash and care can sometimes accompany one another, but the more interactions are defined as commodified exchanges between customer and producer, the more likely it is that characteristics such as attentiveness, cooperation and selflessness are either simulated or get squeezed out of the picture altogether. Teachers may be focused on performance targets to the point where they neglect the time-consuming but valuable pastoral care that pupils often require. Why? Because such care may detract from productivity, so giving an impression of inefficiency and poor service – risky when it comes time for grading, promotions and league tables.[15]

However, some have argued for modified vouchers (Bowles and Gintis, 1998, pp 41-4; Brighouse, 2000, pp 196-202; Le Grand, 2003, pp 115-16). After all, social democratic Sweden has operated a universal voucher scheme since 1992 (Lundahl, 2002; cf. Blom, 2001). Perhaps only some of the education budget could be turned into vouchers; perhaps a culture of cooperation between parents and schools needs to be maintained (rather than a strict purchaser/provider split); perhaps no parental top-ups should be allowed and perhaps the lowest-earning households could receive more expensive vouchers to compensate for their lower incomes and make them more attractive to schools.[16]

Problems remain, however, even with modified schemes. For instance, if vouchers are weighted towards the lower end of the income scale (or even simply given to families in poor areas), we are, as so often before, offering something that is withdrawn as income rises, so exacerbating poverty traps. Further, modified vouchers may still erode the ethos of public service, leading teachers, parents and pupils to see themselves as customers and vendors rather than as co-participants. (As noted in Fitzpatrick (2005a, p 53) Le Grand does not specify how quasi-markets are to facilitate the knightish behaviour he lauds.) More generally, there is a question mark over whether a choice agenda really necessitates such 'big bang' reforms rather than more modest adjustments to the current system.

Take the 'Choose and Book' scheme announced in 2002 and estimated to cost £1.5 billion in its first 10 years (Craig, 2006, pp 215-20), the idea being to give patients more choice over which hospital they attend and over the date/time of their appointments. This reform is both controversial and uncontroversial. It is uncontroversial in so far as patients most certainly have a right to control their healthcare as best they can. The 'yes doctor' passivity of old has been eroded. Yet it is controversial to the extent that its champions imagine that large-scale changes are thereby needed. The number of patients who want a good local hospital, rather than the equivalent of a supermarket trolley, is probably higher than the government assumes (Burgess et al, 2005, pp 29-30), nor is it clear that competition is positively correlated with healthcare quality (Gaynor, 2006). We are not at the point where hospitals and other healthcare providers are competing for your business, but if the threat of censure, loss of income, ward and unit closures becomes endemic, this may well follow. And in conditions of scarcity, choice will always benefit those most able to understand and play the system.

In short, choice can only be represented as a revolutionary concept if, first, you misconceive of state welfare as inherently consisting of bloated, anti-choice, producer-driven bureaucracies, and second, imagine the solution to this is the introduction of market competition and consumerist ethics, that is, choice as *market choice*.

School league tables have long illustrated the deficiencies of this logic. Ranking schools into tables has proved popular with many parents, since they allow information from different schools to be easily compared. But what does the information actually represent? For what league tables have done is confirm that schools' performance corresponds largely to the wealth of their pupils' parents (Herbert, 2004; cf. Noden, 2001). The result is a continued mirroring of class stratification, neglecting both the principle of equity set out above *and* the goal of social mobility and meritocracy beloved of politicians. Parents' understandable desire for more information is wrapped in a system that colludes in the pretence that what matters are 'standards' while verifying that what actually matters is wealth. New Labour came to accept this and recognise that broader (value-added) criteria, sensitive to schools' socioeconomic intake, was needed. But of course the richer the information available, the more artificial any ordinal ranking of performance becomes. The improved data required for informed choice sit uneasily alongside choice defined as competition for prestige and position (see West et al, 2004).

The case for quasi-markets, vouchers and other large-scale, market-type reforms therefore seems unproven at best and ideologically driven at worst. This is not to suggest that market choice is everywhere and always inconsistent with the principle of equity, but any association seems less likely the more conditions of scarcity and social inequality pertain. Quasi-markets may help reduce scarcity (by inviting commercial and non-profit organisations into the public sector), but it is not obvious that they are the best way of doing so, especially given the disadvantages to which quasi-markets may lead. Choice can sometimes help to empower the disadvantaged, but even regulated markets do not avoid problems of queue jumping, cherry picking and so on. When individuals' choices conflict with one another, those with the greater amount of information, resources and capabilities usually prevail. Against such social backgrounds, regulated markets have at best a minor role to play in essential public and welfare services.

Addendum

At the time of writing, Le Grand (2007) has provided the most vociferous defence of regulated, public sector markets. Here, he does not rule out reliance on other principles of public sector organisation (trust, control and command, voice), but maintains that for various reasons they are inadequate without thorough grounding in a fourth principle: choice and competition. The latter is alleged to be superior for the kind of reasons reviewed above. There are, though, two key problems with his argument.

First, Le Grand repeatedly interprets actual market conditions as mimicking the way that markets and firms would ideally behave. For instance, he lambastes critics like Pollock (2004) for obsessing about big, bad multinationals when quasi-market providers could also include partnerships, workers' cooperatives, non-profit or voluntary organisations and publicly owned institutions (Le Grand, 2007, p 41). Since the 'private economy' is hardly brimming with examples of such actors (see Fitzpatrick, 1999, pp 137-47), this hardly bodes well for public sector markets either. The extent to which market monopolies provide only a simulation of choice also goes unaddressed. Furthermore, since incentives arguments are central to his case, and since profits are not of primary importance to the above actors, presumably they would not thrive in the market-driven world of the consumer queen. Nor does he fully address the possibility that incentive-driven improvements would be artificial (an improvement only in public image/brand), dishonest (a manipulation of statistics) or counterproductive (giving consumers what they want might encourage a dumbing down). Ultimately, Le Grand slips from the language of 'choice' to that of competition and 'market choice' all too eagerly.

Second, Le Grand underestimates the significance of voice (which he equates to complaining and voting). When it comes to voice, sharp, middle-class elbows are assumed to be a factor jostling the poorest to the back of the queue, but in market contexts purchasing power is assumed to be equally distributed (Le Grand, 2007, pp 33-4, 44, 60, 68, 98). (This is perhaps why he assumes exiting a market to be largely a costless process (Le Grand, 2007, pp 77-9, 83, 113).)[17] Nevertheless, Le Grand does (eventually) admit that markets might disadvantage the vulnerable and so recommends a layer of 'choice advisers' and 'care advisers' to assist the poorest to become welfare queens (Le Grand,

2007, pp 118-20). But either such advisers are *no more* knight-like than existing public sector professionals (do we need advisers to direct people to the best advisers?) or they are *as* knight-like, in which case it is unclear why GPs, nurses, teachers and so on should be treated as flawed, self-interested (though well-intentioned) producers needing the carrots and sticks of market incentives. This is not to argue against a system for referring people to independent advisers, but to do so in defence of markets only underscores the extent to which market choice and micromanagement go together. Indeed, he proposes that in a 'patient budget' system most patients would not need to be told they controlled a budget (Le Grand, 2007, pp 137-9, 145-6). What kind of empowerment is that? Le Grand interprets 'choice and competition' and 'command and control' as modular, when they are in fact entwined within the model, outlined earlier, of market re-regulation, situational engineering and social remoralisation.

Conclusion

What seems desirable is a schools' admission system that conceptualises choice in terms of equity, and balances personal preferences with social needs and efficiency with fairness. Although not perfect, the UK's pre-1988 education system resembled this equilibrium more closely than the fragmented, marketised system that has prevailed since and introduced de facto selection into public education. Recreating its best features would mean returning to a 'layered' approach of decentralised planning at local authority level where allocation is based on regional profiling, public negotiation and the mature realisation by parents that they will not always get their first choice (Tough and Brooks, 2007; cf. Brighouse, 2000, Ch 9). Elements of allocation by proximity, banding and lottery are likely to be needed, even though none provides a magic wand in itself.

New Labour was correct in its stated aim of extending choice to all. However, it was often blind to the fact that choices (like the socioeconomic interests that shape them) often conflict. Further, New Labour was content to inherit the association of choice (and more recent buzzwords like 'personalised services' and 'localism') with 'market choice' from its neoliberal predecessors. Public–private partnerships have meant the introduction of private sector methods and cultures into the public sector, rather than the other way around. Choice is deservedly popular but, as argued above, the principle of autonomy only becomes meaningful as social conditions become fairer to all; thus, even before we arrive at questions of self-harm and harm to others, we are called on to equalise social conditions in ways that often restrict the purview of 'market choice'.

The same lesson might then be applied across welfare services, with choice valued yet always subject to an equity test. Therefore, when it comes to health, social housing and care services, as well as education, the priority should first be on raising service quality and provision (in order to reduce the scarcity factor) and then on facilitating public sector relationships that do not confuse choice with competition, consumerism or commodification. If all exits from public services are blocked, quality and popular support are likely to decline, but if the emphasis is on the freedom to exit, the system either risks collapsing (as some public providers are forced to close) or reproducing socioeconomic inequalities. Choice in the public sector might therefore imply input, dialogue, better information, ease, accessibility and responsiveness, negotiation, mutual participation, co-design and user influence on service provision (Clarke et al, 2007). It should imply 'voice' long before it implies exit and withdrawal (Hirschmann, 1970).[18]

This means being less paternalistic than the statism of old and more (environmentally) paternalistic than a system of market choice; this is justified not because nanny knows which is the best school but because only by equalising the conditions of choice can everyone possess full opportunities to choose without the consequences of their decisions undermining the principle of distributive justice. We should be free to choose between a menu of alternatives and able to negotiate with the chef about how the meal is cooked, but only if everyone gets to do the same, including those whose budgets are smaller. It is not the job of welfare services to compete with market vendors for speed of access and delivery, but to embody social values that competition, profit motives and price mechanisms can replicate only imperfectly.

We will obviously not correct the economic and cultural fragmentations sketched out here and at the end of Chapter Six simply by altering admissions policies, nor even by reversing the recent marketisations of welfare systems, but we can at least begin to demonstrate that alternative models of the good society exist. There are always alternatives to the prevailing orthodoxy.

Notes

[1] Is 'paternalism' the best term to use here? Why not 'justice' or 'resources', say? Such terms are relevant, as this section spells out, but as this and the last chapter establish, we have to be concerned, too, with bad habits and the protection of interests. My position implies equipping people with the social resources that are needed for autonomy to be

exercised responsibly and diversely, rather than the finger-wagging Puritanism that seeks to restrict autonomy in the name of what the Puritan has decided responsible behaviour to be.

[2] This is a possible example of what Kamm (2007, pp 118–22) calls a 'doctrine of the triple effect', in which a non-intended good side-effect outweighs a non-intended bad side-effect.

[3] However, the period of time over which those who have been made redundant become better off presumably matters.

[4] We might decide than that those made unemployed are no longer entitled to unemployment benefit, but whether this comes from taxation or compulsion to buy private insurance market interference is being justified at some level even here.

[5] This point is made because there is a danger of fetishising capabilities and imagining that resource distribution does not matter. Take the clichéd adage that teaching someone to fish is better than simply giving him a fish. Yet there is no point in teaching people to fish if you then force them to remain at a part of the river where there are few fish to catch (see Fitzpatrick, 2008).

[6] These arguments are that: (1) government possesses a 'degree of cultivation above the average of the community'; (2) labourers do not or cannot make room for education out of their wages; and (3) the quality of voluntary schools is insufficient.

[7] This includes the autonomy of the affluent if we accept the argument that social injustice leads to externalities that affect everyone adversely (if to differing degrees).

[8] This is not to be confused with public choice theory, which is more ideologically loaded. Note, too, that envy is here deployed not as a negative emotion to be ashamed of but as a test of fairness in distribution.

[9] It is possible to imagine an egalitarian society characterised by lots of envy because agents have been given no choice in the actual allocation of goods.

[10] An example is the system introduced in the UK by Brighton and Hove Council from September 2008.

[11] If this sounds strange, consider how massive strides in communication technology risk leaving the poorest at the margins of the information society unless some kind of intervention is performed.

[12] To repeat: the problem diminishes where there is excess capacity. But whereas surplus televisions will eventually 'clear' the market, scarcity in essential goods can only be overcome if we either swallow the expense of maintaining that capacity, or allow them to clear through some kind of queuing or bidding mechanism. The first option is financially and therefore politically difficult, meaning that policy makers have to ensure that there are enough essential goods to go around but not enough to generate unused waste. The queuing option can be fair but is also politically difficult if the queues are too long, and the bidding mechanism reintroduces prices into the allocation that reproduces market unfairness within sectors that are trying to correct for such unfairness in the first place.

[13] This is not to claim, by the way, that agency only means the freedom to choose; the association is made purely for the purposes of this chapter.

[14] Alternatively, we may allow the best schools/hospitals to expand; however, this is often not realistic, desirable or efficacious.

[15] The managerialist solution is to incorporate such care into performance targets, through customer evaluation, for instance. However, this means continually trying to quantify that which is unquantifiable except by being simulated and faked.

[16] Or we might only provide vouchers to those below a certain income, as in Milwaukee.

[17] He first assumes that failure is due to lack of consumer demand, but then introduces financial mismanagement into the picture (Le Grand, 2007, p 114). But if the latter can be a cause of failure, presumably market exit *will* hurt many of the most vulnerable, in addition to having other deleterious social effects.

[18] While it is not possible to offer a critique here, aspects of this approach have appeared in social reforms in recent years. I hope to offer one in the near future.

EIGHT

Relating

This chapter carries forward the general themes already discussed into debates about family and familial responsibilities. If 'environmental paternalism' captures the idea that autonomy and paternalism are most reasonably aligned when we concentrate on creating fair social conditions, what does this imply for such debates? I have so far referred to individuals as the pertinent agents. But what of families? Does the principle of autonomy become less relevant because it seems somehow facile to portray family members as autonomous towards one another? Do paternalistic arguments strengthen or weaken when we consider interventions for, and into, families? What should we even mean by 'the family'?

This chapter examines two questions to help us gain a foothold on such matters. The second is concerned with filial obligations and the distribution of responsibilities for the health and care needs of older people; but first we address a larger, background question over which kinds of families and households government should support. While Chapters Six and Seven took Mill's utilitarian liberalism as their starting point, we draw here on literatures that relate more to virtue ethics.

Family and state

Should the state actively promote marriage?

Are some family types better than others? Should government encourage the formation of such families while discouraging and excluding others? How can we decide what 'better' means?

Two key arguments are associated with, though not exclusive to, conservatism (for example, R O'Neill, 2003). The first is that the desire for kinship and intimacy is a biological imperative, with the majority of people wishing to perpetuate their bloodline by raising children. The second is that families form the basis of social stability and wellbeing, providing the moral and emotional orientation towards tradition and authority without which children would have no self-discipline or respect for others. The best families are therefore those that raise children within norms and parameters stressing honesty, fidelity, responsibility and diligence. A married partnership offers the most appropriate environment because it communicates to children a sense of continuity, security, commitment and faithfulness. This, further, implies *heterosexual* marriage, given the family's biological, reproductive function. Commentators differ over the extent to which other household types (single parents, gay/lesbian partnerships, heterosexual cohabitees) should be permitted, but even those who accept some diversity would nevertheless make policies concerning taxation, adoption, fostering, inheritance and welfare entitlements most favourable to the married, heterosexual couple (Rauch, 2003; cf. Knight, 2003; Levin, 2005).

Ranged against this are pluralists for whom the family is a social construct whose meaning, symbols and practices shift across time and space. Most people demonstrate a desire for kinship and intimacy, but the relational forms through which those desires are fulfilled vary considerably. Families are not only about children. If a heterosexual couple decided not to have kids, this would hardly make them abnormal. People seek relationships for other purposes: companionship, mutuality and security. If people take their responsibilities to others seriously, they will do so outside the institution of traditional marriage; if they do not, there is no guarantee that marriage and children will provide the necessary glue. Better, therefore, for government to work with the grain of what people desire, which means enshrining a legal and cultural recognition of family *diversity*. Certainly, some families will do the job of raising children and offering environments conducive to social stability better than others, *but this is not because they belong to a particular category*. Previous shifts towards diversity, for example, marrying outside your class or religion, have not heralded the social collapse once predicted by traditionalists. The job of government should be to encourage the best possible families *across all categories* (Lewis, 2003; Law, 2006).

Which should we favour, tradition or diversity? The above camps inevitably overlap to some extent – some traditions are more hierarchical than others and diversity need not entail a non-judgemental relativism – but by and large, there is a threshold of belief here that requires us to make a decision. So what precisely is at stake? There are any number of relevant issues that could be explored, not least the roles played by sex and sexuality. Instead we will to look at questions concerning children. Having made much of the harm principle, if it can be demonstrated that some family types are likely to harm children, governments should presumably frame their family policies and moral cultures accordingly.

There is a body of opinion that suggests that children are disadvantaged and perhaps even damaged when raised outside the traditional, heterosexual family. Sommers (2005) blames 'radical feminism' for, first, treating gender as an inherently conflictual social relation and, second, for recommending a genderless society. As the sexes 'androgynise', our social identities become confused and malleable, she proposes. Is it therefore any wonder that children grow up equally confused and unable to form stable relationships? Without strong families, children lack an understanding of what it is to hold special duties towards others, duties that remain even when (*especially when*) we feel unhappy or frustrated with relatives. What we owe our children is of a different order to what we owe our neighbours. This is not, for Sommers, a left versus right issue. Previous generations of liberals, she declares, were also resistant to the recent ideal of family as just another social association.

Sommers gives very little evidence for any of this, however, offering mainly crude characterisations of her opponents. For example, her target shifts frequently from radical feminism to 'feminism' per se, allowing her to paint the latter with the simplistic set of goals she identifies (unfairly) with the former. And her appeals to political non-partisanship are naïve at best. Many liberals and social democrats of previous generations were hostile to gender equality and so do not offer an obvious blueprint for modern norms (Somerville, 2000), and incidentally such equality is only confusable with 'androgyny' if, like Sommers, you categorise gender roles as rigid and inflexible. As such, the family is going not through a *crisis* but a series of *adjustments* to the welcome empowerment of women and the disentangling of restrictive traditions (Friedman, 2005, p 326).

Another conservative, Almond (2003), maintains that family breakdown is largely the effect of governments being too liberal and ineffective. The state wastes money and energy by first corroding the foundations of family life (through support services for single parents, no-fault divorces and so forth) and then in dealing unsuccessfully with the resulting community erosion (increases in crime, drug use, unemployment, poverty, civic disruption) as young people internalise the values of the alienated, selfish, destructive and transitory world around them. Social order, she maintains, requires permanency in those institutions through which children gain their understanding of how to behave. Disruptions to familial solidarity – through adultery, for example – are bad enough without government creating financial incentives that emphasise state dependency while helping to remove the moral and cultural deterrents that previously held people together. Biological attachment is the essence of the family, underpinning all cultural diversity, but something that requires the correct social parameters if destructive biological urges are to be avoided (Almond, 2006, pp 9–10). It is true that 18th- and 19th-century mores often disadvantaged women, but this is a reason to improve the traditional family, not to abandon it. That some non-traditional families are successful does not expunge the fact that children from such relationships will do worse on average when it comes to education and employment. Households are *not* equal in terms of equipping children with the socio-moral bearings they need. Cohabitation, for instance, sends a message to children that belonging and care are ephemeral, dispensable bonds.

Is there any convincing evidence to back this position? Three questions appear to be important here:

(1) Is family breakdown occurring?
(2) Are children from non-traditional homes exhibiting symptoms of such breakdown?
(3) Is an overly liberal state to blame?

With regard to the first of these, the traditional division of labour has certainly changed as women have entered the labour market, according to *Social Trends* (2007, Ch 2). The proportion of couples with dependent children where only the man is working decreased in Britain from 43% in 1979 to 24% by 2006. This has accompanied a polarisation between two-earner and no-earner households (in 2006 15% of children were living in working-age households with no employment). In 2006, 24% of children in Britain were living in single-parent families, three times higher than the figure in 1972. In 2005, 24% of non-married people aged under 60 were cohabiting, twice the proportion of 1986. The number of divorces remains fairly constant, at approximately 155,000–170,000 per year, with 10% of children now living in stepfamilies; and two fifths of all marriages are remarriages (40% of divorces end in marriage). In 2005, 43% of all births were outside marriage, normally to cohabiting couples who usually go on to marry, although cohabitees with children are twice as likely to split than married partners with children. There were just over 100,000 conceptions to girls aged under 20 in 2004, 8% of whom were younger than 16, another figure that has remained fairly constant over the past quarter century.

Is there evidence here of a crisis in the family? These may be important social transformations to which some kind of governmental response is required, but do they add up to family *breakdown*? If you imagine that the divorce rate should be next to nothing, it probably does; it all depends on what you mean by 'crisis' and 'breakdown'. If such standards are unrealistic – most divorces are initiated by women, partly as a consequence of increased independence and rising expectations – and such concepts inherently panic-inducing, at what point should alarm bells start ringing? Should they start ringing at all? There is simply no conclusive answer to this and our views are inevitably contested and political.

Let us take cohabitation, for instance. For many couples, it is obviously a stage *towards* marriage instead of a *substitute*. Conservatives observe, though, that cohabitation is less stable than marriage and so arguably less conducive to the welfare of children (Jensen and Clausen, 2003); after all, if people are genuinely committed to each other, shouldn't they be discouraged from diluted alternatives? What would be the solution? We might improve the financial inducement to marry (and to stay married) through the tax and benefit systems (Morgan, 2007), but there is also research suggesting that people are not simply economic actors, reacting predictably and causally to cash incentives (Duncan and Strell, 2004). People wed, and remain so, for reasons that go far beyond the monetary. We might nevertheless introduce disincentives *against* cohabitation, for instance, cracking down on benefit claimants who cohabit. This, however, could risk undermining the independence, security, self-respect and mutuality that can make cohabitation a process whose endpoint *is* marriage. If cohabitation is indeed a cause for concern, that might equally be a reason to improve public recognition of its potential value, for example, by introducing civil partnerships, clearing a positive space within which the benefits of a further stage – marriage – could be stressed.

In short, there is no obvious sign that 'the family' is fragmenting, unless you insist on reading such an ideologically loaded term into social developments, or that the response to change should be one of moral panic and atavism. Much depends, however, on the impact of these changes on children.

To address the second question, some research suggests that children of divorced parents experience heightened anxiety and depression, declining performance in school (and later in employment) and are more susceptible to addiction and relationship breakdown (for example, Wallerstein et al, 2000; Spruijt and Duindam 2005; Storksen et al, 2005; Marquardt, 2006). Set against this is work that says the traumatic effects are not as high as the above researchers imagine (Amato, 2003; Walker, 2003). For example, Amato (2000, pp 1277-82) reports that the effects are quite variable, while Hetherington and Kelly (2002) found that about 75-80% of children from divorced homes cope reasonably well.

Negative effects are influenced not only by divorce per se but also the degree of parental conflict involved; much therefore depends on the efficacy of child-focused courts and mediation services, it being possible that divorce can *improve* children's wellbeing by reducing the stress previously experienced within hostile parental environments (McIntosh, 2003).

What about cohabitation? According to Parke (2003), 69% of US children of never-married mothers are poor, compared with 45% of children brought up by divorced single mothers. Never-married mothers are significantly younger, have lower incomes, fewer years of education, and are twice as likely to be unemployed as divorced mothers. The differences cannot be entirely attributed to family structure (contra conservatives) but neither can they be entirely attributed to low income either (contra liberal pluralists), although she adds that 'most children not living with married, biological parents grow up without serious problems' (Parke, 2003, p 8). Income can be a misleading variable, however, unless properly contextualised. For what matters is not only present-day income but also long-term, relative positions with socioeconomic distributions. Rowlingson and McKay (2005) find that marital status is fundamentally a proxy for social class, with those from poorer socioeconomic backgrounds being more likely to become lone mothers and to stay as such. Additionally, Manning and Brown (2006) conclude that children born into a first marriage enjoy much higher chances of a stable childhood, but also that much depends on the networks and resources to which children of cohabiting parents have access. Placing a simplistic emphasis on marriage per se may therefore be counterproductive, especially as we currently lack large-scale, long-term research (Bumpass and Lu, 2000, p 39).

So while divorce and cohabitation are potentially risky for the wellbeing of children, there is no consensus over what those effects are, why they occur and what the policy response should be. Conservatives can insist that there is no need for a consensus. No-one argues that parental separation is *harm-free*, implying that it ought indeed to be minimised. The problem with this stance is that if, as noted above, parental conflict within partnerships matters, in addition to conflict during and after separation, there is no easy formula for safeguarding children's wellbeing. Mennemeyer and Sen (2006, p 459) observe that making divorce more difficult would probably increase the number of unhappy marriages. The disparities reported above – whereby children whose parents have separated demonstrate higher levels of undesirable behaviour than those whose parents remain together – would probably diminish, therefore, and the conservative case would be undermined.

But what if we set even this point aside? Chapter Six discussed when and why committing harm against others might be permissible. In the case of children, some harm is inevitably part of growing up. Children need to experience a modicum of harm if they are to cope with the realities of loss, risk and disappointment, *without* those harms being so damaging that they hamper the child's development. Obviously, married and cohabiting parents experiencing difficulties need to place the child's interests first, but 'harm-freeness' per se is an unrealistic ideal.

Therefore, if the above arguments stand, accusations thrown at the state's excessive liberalness are misguided. Morgan (2007), for instance, argues that tax and benefits systems incentivise lone parenthood, encourage people to conceal their family status from the authorities and no longer contain rewards for two-parent families. Her solution is to reduce incentives at the former end of the scale and bolster them at the latter. However, as noted earlier, this economistic reading may overestimate the influence of financial support. Such support may be a factor in decision making but, due to a complex range of cultural, social and experiential circumstances, not an overwhelming one (Rowlingson and McKay, 2002). Morgan's response might be that even if this is the case, we are still justified in reorganising tax and benefit systems accordingly. But two considerations are crucial here. First, that if any pattern of incentives reflects and propagates the socioeconomic inequalities mentioned above, it is merely perpetuating unjust social conditions and obscuring social relations behind rhetorics of morals and family (see Chapter Four). Second, without clearer evidence that some family types are *inherently better than others*, we may be misdiagnosing social problems and misprescribing the solutions.

If the traditional approach is misleading, what ought to guide a more pluralistic alternative? How do we bring out the best in all families? How might we guide people while respecting family diversity?

Chapter Seven defended an 'environmental paternalism' – the idea that social justice and autonomy can be mutually reinforcing. Engineering justice by disrespecting autonomy (through a reactionary paternalism of prohibiting and banning) is to treat adults like children, such direct interventions being warranted only when harm to others is concerned (albeit with various qualifications) or when people risk self-harm *unreasonably*; autonomy without background conditions of justice means that some will lack the resources needed to realise their freedom fully. We also mentioned capabilities in this context, defined as 'the opportunity and ability both to make best use of existing resources and to maximise future ones'. Although it was noted earlier that raising children is only one role performed by a family, to the extent that families *are* child-centred we might characterise that role as one designed to nurture the capabilities of future adults. More direct interventions are legitimate where there is clear evidence children are being, or are likely to be, harmed; but for the most part the job of government is to shape the settings that enable families to perform this role as effectively as possible.[1] Education is one such setting. So while there is no space here to frame what environmental paternalism might imply for family policy per se, what might 'education for capability' imply (see Fitzpatrick, forthcoming; cf. Law, 2006)?

Many philosophers of education have offered suggestions. Murris (2000), Englund (2000) and de-Shalit (2004) have all suggested that Socratic, deliberative and philosophical methods are crucial to the development of children's reflexive awareness. Gutmann (1987), too, proposes a critical pluralism where education for citizenship means the development of the deliberative virtues so that evaluation can be made of different cultural contexts, informed choice made between different ways of life and people are able to enter into a public space distinct from the private worlds of self-interest. What matters is not only democratic process but also the formation of a moral character where participants are willing to acknowledge as legitimate even those outcomes of deliberation with which they have disagreed.

What seems crucial in such debates is a distinction between critical *thinking* and critical *rationality*. For Winch (2004), critical thinking implies the identification of logical plausibility and validity in arguments, while critical rationality involves contextualisation and evaluation of authoritative arguments. Winch further distinguishes between weak and strong forms of critical rationality. The weak involves choices limited to the social ends, norms, goals and opportunity sets already made available to us; the strong suggests that ends can be subject to scrutiny, negotiation and reconstitution. According to Winch, without a conception of weak rationality we risk inviting an 'anything goes' subjectivity that disembeds all forms of existing social value; but without a conception of strong rationality we undermine the very rationale of deliberative critique, which is to push forward new horizons of social life and meaning. He proposes that social welfare must imply both the preservation of society's 'moral heritage' as well as its gradual revision (Winch, 2004, pp 477-81). While the precise balance is itself open to discussion, education must aim to teach both weak and strong forms of critical rationality and therefore of autonomy.

So while the notion of 'moral character' may be important, this need not propel us towards a hierarchically conservative direction (Brighouse, 2000, Chs 4 and 5; see also the argument on pp 79-80). Certainly, we might prefer moral education to imply directives about, and inculcation into, a pre-determined set of virtues. This seems to be what MacIntyre (1981, pp 181-7) had in mind when he recommended a canonical, authority-led approach to education. But moral character can also refer to aptitudes and capacities. The directive approach closely prescribes a range of choices within a given context of authority and subordination, while the aptitude approach is more liberal and Kantian; the former is concerned with the content of decisions, the latter with the process of decision making between diverse equals. We must presumably make some reference to both. Without basic 'instruction' in some theory of the good, and in the virtues needed to realise it, we cannot properly appreciate the nature of what is being transmitted to us from previous generations; yet if we go too far in that direction we invoke a moralistic scale of values in which those with the power to proclaim themselves morally superior dictate to those 'lower' down the scale (LaFollette, 2007, Ch 10).

An egalitarian politics sensitive to differences therefore suggests more of an aptitude-based approach, albeit one ring-fenced by virtue criteria (Kupfer, 1998). What we inherit from the past is inevitably multiple, messy, varied and contestable, and education should aim to nurture citizens capable of recognising and dealing with this by improving their *discursive capacity*. For while at present the ideal is to dovetail education with the needs of a competitive economy, so the aim would be to improve the quality of democratic debate by teaching the skills of communicative inquiry and interdependency, assisting democratic interaction, such as interaction between experts and laypeople, and opening up public spaces designed to reduce the opaqueness and improve the accountability of governance. Critical rationality quickly shades into notions of intersubjective discourse, or the democratic conversation across both space and time.

For instance, Nussbaum (1998) sees critical and self-critical examination as vital, a recognition of human interdependency that implies empathy towards others. Education systems must therefore promote the examined life rather than instrumental rationality, meaning that learning about interacting with otherness (whether physically, intellectually or imaginatively) is good not only for others but for one's own culture.

So should the state actively promote marriage? No, because it is not obvious that it needs to or can do so effectively. If marriage has the multiple benefits its defenders claim for it, financial inducements to marry are excessively economistic, and penalising non-traditional families may do more harm than good. Divorce and cohabitation may be evidence of people not treating relationships seriously, but they may also be evidence of people taking responsibilities to themselves and their children *more* seriously by refusing either to jump into, or remain indefinitely within, relationships inimical to wellbeing. The task instead should be to bring out the best in all family categories. This means shaping social environments and systems accordingly. Because it is not the intention here to offer a full theory of distributive justice, social resources with regard to the family have not been discussed, nor a comprehensive account of family policy presented, but this chapter proposes that the principle of capability is vital to that of education, and that this supports a liberal, aptitude-based approach rather than one that aims to instil given virtues within uncritically receptive minds. This sketches the basis of what a pluralistic approach to the family should resemble.

Parents and children

We have reviewed two theories of the family, one that constructs a hierarchy of family types stressing biological ties and another that attempts to work with the grain of pluralism but where the capabilities and wellbeing of children are significant values. These alternatives will reappear, slightly modified, below as we now explore a key issue for future welfare reforms.

> *Who should fund the care needs of older people?*

This question is inspired by various social developments: the implications of ageing populations for the expenditure and organisation of health and care services (Comas-Herrera et al, 2006) and the changing nature of family relationships and obligations due to divorces and remarriages (Coleman et al, 2005). Additionally, as more of us spend a greater proportion of our lives in the 'third age', what would be an appropriate distribution of responsibilities, one that does not compromise the goal of gender equality? Our discussion will not address these weighty and multifaceted issues directly, but will, instead, explore a principal philosophical foundation that would assist such debates (see Collingridge and Miller, 1997), the relevant question within applied ethics being, what do adult children owe their parents?

Two models

The 'indebtedness' model says that since you owe your life and identity to your parents, and since parents have observed their obligations to you throughout your childhood, as an adult you owe a reciprocal series of obligations to them. There are two dimensions to this model.

The first (sometimes treated as a separate 'repayment' or 'gratitude' model) involves treating reciprocity in terms of proportionality where what you owe mirrors what you derived. As your parents become your dependants, you should repay the debt you incurred when you were theirs. If yours were terrible parents, this allows for you having few if any obligations to repay. A second dimension is supported by those who view family duties as enduring, emotional bonds through which people are obliged to occupy and observe appropriate social roles, and not as a 'loan' to be repaid out of gratefulness. There are, though, two additional sub-sets within this second dimension.

Conservatives are attracted to what in the Confucian tradition is called 'filial piety' (Ivanhoe, 2006), where the performance of family duties constitutes the basis of a virtuous social order. Your obligations to your parents are inalienable regardless of how good or bad they were to you (Scruton, 2001, pp 32-3). Liberals favour a looser form of indebtedness that harks back to notions of gratitude. For instance, while arguing that parental sacrifices generate filial obligations, Wicclair (1990) proposes that because those duties are indeterminate neither heavy burdens nor specific reciprocities can be loaded on to the adult child. Finch and Mason's (1990) interviewees viewed filial obligations as resources to inspire rather than rules demanding conformism.

Before examining the indebtedness model, it would be useful to appreciate an alternative 'friendship model', one adopted by English (2005) when pondering what adult children owe their parents. Nothing, she concludes.

Her position is simple. Relationships between parents and grown children can involve positive emotions (love, forgiveness, generosity, trust) and negative ones (possessiveness, resentment, guilt, insecurity), but whether positive or negative these are highly personalised, subjective characteristics that cannot be easily or accurately exposed to moral evaluation. We can identify signs of affection and cruelty as virtuous and wicked, respectively, and we can argue about the grey areas in between, but for the most part our ethical telescopes cannot penetrate very far into emotional relationships. The language of justice and citizenship does not apply therefore, according to English. My parent does not have a 'right' to be looked after by me if she has the 'flu, nor do I possess a formal duty to do so. True, if I am neglectful, my parents will no doubt complain, but this will be on the grounds of emotional inattentiveness and not because I have failed to perform citizenship-like responsibilities. So while she is willing to talk broadly of filial obligations, English resists notions of owing and indebtedness.

Better to conceive of adult children and parents as actual or potential friends than as debtors. It would be nice if Bob rang his parents once a month, but, if he doesn't, we cannot force him to feel something for his parents if the feeling isn't there, for any such coercion would contradict the willed, emotional belonging that sincere love inherently implies.[2] By extension, while we may encourage we should not *require* children to look after their ageing parents. Responsibilities for funding and organising your future care needs presumably falls on your shoulders, therefore, and (although this would require additional justification) on the state.

The friendship model proffered by English seems to derive from the virtuists' intuition that vast areas of human life cannot be subjected to the moral callipers wielded by Kantians and consequentialists. It suggests that we need to distinguish between two senses of obligation. There are those that imply the 'enforceable performance of activities where non-compliance can legitimately attract penalties', as when I fail to hand over £10 in exchange for the book you are selling me. But there are also many obligations we cannot legislate for ethically. Some of these are supererogatory (acts we should perform even though they exceed what is strictly speaking expected of us) and some simply derive from sensations and instincts that are immune to the obedience-invoking injunctions of 'ought' and 'ought not'. We can perhaps nurture and cultivate these sentiments (as Hume would term them), but we cannot enact them into being.

Is the friendship model convincing? Those who hold to the indebtedness model bridle at the suggestion. For a conservative like Sommers (1986, 2005), obligations cannot derive merely from voluntary acts of assent. Yes, you and I may choose to marry and have kids but these decisions create dense, durable webs of responsibilities that we cannot choose to detach ourselves from at a later date. Morally, I cannot walk away from my children as I could walk away from a friend, since there is a 'differential pull' about the former in contrast to the latter.

Kupfer (2005), too, thinks that friendship offers a misleading analogy.[3] First, the equality required for friendship cannot pertain between parents and children because the former will always possess more autonomy vis-à-vis the latter. The parent has shaped the identity of, and has an intimate knowledge of, their child. Second, parents and children can never be truly independent of one another in a way demanded by friendship. There is a primitive, subconscious link that nullifies 'otherness', the separating space across which actual friends meet by deciding to reduce that distance. Kupfer proposes that these asymmetries continue to characterise relationships between parents and their adult children, meaning they can be friendly without ever *being friends*.

So for such commentators, the friendship model does not offer an accurate account of filial obligations, since the family provides a soil from which we can never really uproot ourselves. Social policies should presumably recognise and reflect the special duties family members owe to one another and not treat care as a responsibility primarily of the state or of individuals themselves. Are these criticisms reasonable?

It has already been noted why Sommers offers too restrictive a conception of the family and there is nothing more to add here. Kupfer's ideas are less dogmatic, but vulnerable to various criticisms nonetheless. What Kupfer lacks in particular is a 'socio-chronological' dimension to his account. The asymmetries that typify parent–child relationships presumably alter in character, intensity and 'gradient' as the child ages. They change in *character* as the needs and interests of parent and child evolve, in *intensity* as the child's peer groups fluctuate, and in *gradient* as the child matures into a person with their own life to lead. (And the gradient may indeed tip over so that it is the parent's autonomy that is reduced in respect of the child.) As such, Kupfer's is too broad a generalisation (Archard, 2003, pp 100-3). Furthermore, he arguably accords too much prominence to parents, ignoring the many other influences on a child's development. The education system brings children into contact with peers who will push and pull them away from their parents while offering a site within which the child can learn to deal with those family and extra-family tensions. So although Kupfer highlights the bonds of familiarity between parent and child, he does not establish that the friendship model is essentially inaccurate.

There are others who have sought a middle way between the friendship and indebtedness models. Mills (2005) thinks that the latter is too restrictive and ignores the multiple sources of, and influences on, our roles and identities. However, she is also sceptical of conceptualising families in terms of friendship, since while I can moderate a relationship with a friend as my feelings towards her fluctuate, family relationships are more resistant to such fluctuations. I still owe my wife a lift to work, even if she has just annoyed the hell out of me. For Mills, the value of families resides in the fact that the nature of each is fundamentally unchosen, as we derive our 'greatest good' from participation in relationships that are enduring and unconditional. The worth of such relationships is intrinsic, that is, what it provides is unique to it and could not come from anywhere else. So whereas the value I derive from Mike (jokey conversation, occasional favours) are *extrinsic*, because I could also receive them from becoming friends with Pete, Mills regards *intrinsic values* as superior.

It should be noted, however, that the policy outcome that Mills (2005, p 333) supports is not dissimilar to that of English. Children, she says, should only reciprocate those goods which, being intrinsic, cannot derive from anywhere else; they owe their parents continued participation in a relationship but *not* those goods and services that parents can receive from other sources. Though I may volunteer financial assistance, I am not *obliged* to pay for my mother's healthcare – though I may, on other grounds, be obliged to pay taxes to fund health services of which my mother is one recipient.

In any event, we might defend the friendship model for two reasons. First, English was speaking not of the family per se but of relationships between parents and their adult children. This distinction becomes blurred in Mills' critique and so, like Kupfer, the chronological dimension is suppressed. What counts as a 'great good' and intrinsic value when I am 12 may no longer apply when I am 23, such that inferring one from the other is facile. Second, and as noted below, friendship is not simply about the sentiments of feeling. While you cannot switch your feelings for a sibling on or off, this may also be true of close friends – and some friends may mean more to you than some relatives. But instead of denying this, the friendship model maintains that it is precisely the deep-rooted, personalised nature of feeling that makes it immune to moral legislation. Your dad may always be your dad (to invoke a soap opera cliché), but you could always disassociate yourself from him even if he will inevitably occupy your memories and reflections from time to time. Mills' distinction between what is chosen and unchosen is too severe, in other words, and so friends and family overlap to a greater extent than she admits (Keller, 2006).

Another middle way between the two models is offered by Dixon (2005). Whereas Mills leans philosophically towards the indebtedness model, Dixon seeks a reformulation of the friendship model. That friendship has for the most part to be unforced and spontaneously affectionate does not rule out the existence of additional duties. Since I am obliged to help a friend above and beyond any responsibilities I bear towards strangers, we can presumably identify certain friend-related duties that do not spring from inclination and sentiment alone. Therefore, to associate the family form with friendship does not preclude us from identifying certain duties that relations should observe towards one another. By ignoring this point, English's model cedes too much ground to Sommers and Kupfer, who are then all too willing to view the supposed loose ties of friendship as inappropriate foundations for the family. Dixon therefore advises that we view both friendships and families as embodying 'residual duties', that is, duties owed to others even after the relationship has unravelled. I may be divorcing you because our marriage is unsustainable, but I should still conduct myself respectfully towards you. Residual duties have a degree of proportionality about them – so that they may diminish and eventually disappear if you behave appallingly towards me – but they often persist even after an estrangement. This is because friendship involves striving for moral excellence and the pursuit of such excellences should continue to be my goal.

There are two potential problems with this adaptation of the friendship model. First, Dixon is wary of codifying those residual duties. In line with virtue ethics, he refrains from associating excellence with too much rule following, perhaps because virtues ought to be regarded as dispositional habits of character. Yet does this really follow? Kant (1996, pp 426–8), for instance, defines marriage as an 'equality of mutual possession' in which each party can legitimately treat the other as both a person *and* a thing. What this generates are exclusivist, conjugal rights; monogamy, in other words, a duty of which presumably still holds even if the partners are no longer, in Dixon's terms, friends. In short, we can potentially specify a baseline of obligations without surrendering what is best about the friendship model.[4]

This could provide a solution to a second criticism, which is that the friendship model offers no sanctions against the ungrateful child. In the case of a grown child who breaks all contact with parents who are loving and attentive, then the model permits this since in the complete absence of friendship there can be no obligations, even residual ones. For conservatives, this highlights the error of relying on emotional instead of biological bonds. Dixon's (2005, p 302) response is that such difficult cases are likely to be extremely rare, since there is bound to be a link, albeit a contingent one, between parents' generosity and the resulting depth of their child's friendship. Nevertheless, conservatives are likely to insist that while the completely ungrateful child is in fact rare the friendship model, by introducing any element of contingency, is too weak an account of filial obligations; such obligations have to be constant *regardless* of the degree of parent–child friendship.[5]

The Kantian argument outlined above perhaps offers a means of doing so without having to abandon the friendship model. By specifying a stable baseline of filial obligations that apply to all families, we perhaps strengthen the notion that, above this baseline, families are social–emotional networks and not a collection of biological actors inhabiting predetermined roles. The friendship model is therefore preserved by adding a pinch of Kantianism.[6]

Financial contributions

If this follows, then do adult children have an obligation, as part of that familial baseline, to contribute to the care needs of their elderly parents and, if so, how? The above amendment to Dixon's version of the friendship model gives a prima facie reason why (1) there is perhaps a baseline obligation but also suggests that (2) we should not rely on its performance to supply those needs in full.

The obligation stems from the simple observation that attending to the late-life needs of their parents is one of the most obvious duties devolving on adult children. Even in the case of estrangement, some residual duties will often persist. However, the continued centrality of friendship means that we cannot legislate for the *quality* of those obligations. For some children, it will mean becoming full-time or part-time carers; for others, it will mean visits, cards and phone calls, dealing with doctors, bureaucrats and so on, providing monetary help or any combination of these and no doubt many other activities. Together, these things suggest that the baseline obligations partly involve compulsory financial contributions. We should not demand that adult children *care* for their parents, even assuming this was workable, but a minimum *contribution* out of which care needs can be supplied might be legitimate.

Before considering what this contribution might imply in practical terms, it is important to explain how this argument fits in with preceding ones. Previous chapters have defended the liberal principle of autonomy allied to a degree of paternalism justified by the harm principle, the egalitarian redistribution of resources and the enablement of capabilities. At no point has it been proposed that autonomy emerges de novo. Indeed, social humanism points not only to the self's deterministic backgrounds, but suggests that preserving autonomy is a deep personal and social struggle. There has been an indeterminacy in deciding precisely where, as the literature has it, the 'cut' between circumstance and autonomy arises – which is to state the matter crudely, since we cannot speak of a 'cut' but of a series of interlocking meshes. Mills (1998, 2003), for instance, triumphs the value of 'unchosen' and unconditional relationships because she believes little prominence can be given to choice. But while autonomy certainly implies a background 'givenness', it also highlights the extent to which we can work, personally and socially, to reorder those backgrounds and form our individual, inter-relational identities, however contingent, ephemeral and plural those identities may be. The family is one such 'given' in the sense that it shapes us without our having initially chosen to join it. An amended friendship model captures this duality, implying that we should attend to filial obligations and its attendant virtues, without surrendering the autonomy (defined in terms of aptitudes and capabilities) that Sommers, Mills and others would have us neglect. The family is therefore a socio-emotional network combining *both* unchosen 'meta-duties' *and* voluntariness – its relationships being an example of what I have elsewhere called 'diverse reciprocity' (see Fitzpatrick, 2005a).

So what financial contributions do adult children owe (and to whom)? Option A is to 'familialise' such contributions such that, perhaps once they reach a certain income, grown children owe a percentage of this to their parents (and perhaps once parents' income falls to a particular level). Yet even apart from the difficulties of organising such a system, it impersonalises parent–child relationships, turning them into holders of rights and duties, to an extent denied by the friendship model.[7] Option B involves simply funding generous and accessible health and care services out of general taxation. This incorporates the compulsory contributions aspect of A without its excessive intrusiveness, since adult children help to fund these services through their taxes but there is no direct, mandatory transfer to their own parents. The potential attractiveness of option B does not rule out an additional option C, whereby there could be (i) specific child-related taxes that go into a general funding pot, and (ii) policies to *encourage* direct transfers.

Inheritance tax is a potential example of (i).[8] This is normally justified as an instrument for equality of opportunity (Nissan, 2001). Without redistribution from one generation to the next, existing patterns of income and wealth are entrenched and societies move even farther away from the meritocratic mobility they pride themselves on. While this principle has worth, it is fairly abstract for most people. Objections to inheritance tax no doubt stem in part from (familial) selfishness and misunderstanding of the tax system, but the generalised altruism the principle enjoins cannot help either. But there is some evidence that hypothecating it to services for 'worthy causes', like care services for older people, increases its popularity (Paxton and White, 2006, pp 28-32).

A top-up scheme might satisy (ii). Just as the state already tops up savings accounts available for specific purposes (such as the UK's Child Trust Fund), so it might top up contributions made by children to their parents' insurance schemes. I suspect that this suggestion should be a non-runner on the grounds of equity, a middle-class subsidy when social expenditure should be directed elsewhere. However, there may be other proposals that correspond to (ii) without attracting similar objections.

The friendship model therefore seems to emphasise that our financial contributions should be compulsory so long as they are indirect, that is, paid into a general pot for the supply of care services through general taxation, social insurance and inheritance tax. The care and money that children might provide directly to their parents should not be the subject of legislation or sanction, although there may be some inducement and incentive schemes worth thinking about. The weight of responsibilities for care needs therefore falls mainly to individuals, as general taxpayers and as future recipients of our own health and care services, and to all of us, rather than to particular children of particular parents,[9] *with* the proviso that funding and entitlements are consistent with the equity principle and the state is on the front line of provision (see Chapter Seven). This could imply new schemes of long-term care insurance, such as have been introduced in Germany and Japan (Parker, 2006, p 810), incorporating a redistributive element for the low-paid and those spending time outside the labour market, such as carers.[10]

This approach is likely to annoy libertarians, given their opposition to high taxes and state provision, and those conservatives who believe that children should be the principal caregivers for their parents. Some research suggests, however, that there is no trade-off to be made between filial solidarity and state welfare services, where even countries valuing strong family bonds seem to favour more welfare state assistance (Daatland and Herlofson, 2003, pp 556-7). And as women demand more independence, there is a need for statutory services to fill the care gap, for more degendered caregiving and for the state to assist individuals with their long-term care requirements. Only the most rosy-eyed free market liberals and conservatives can imagine that, respectively, individual self-help and family support are enough.

Conclusion

This chapter began with several questions into which it was intended to gain some insight. We have sketched two broad conceptualisations of 'the family' and seen how disagreements between their proponents play out across a number of debates. The approach defended (encompassing both pluralism and an amended friendship model) suggests that autonomy remains a key point of reference and that the job of families regarding their children is to nurture the aptitudes and capabilities of the adults they are gradually becoming. We have also applied the 'environmental paternalism' of previous chapters to the family indicating that, while interventions may be justified in the case of harm to others and unreasonable self-harm, for the most part governments assist families by maintaining appropriate social environments and welfare systems.

We are now going to continue to explore two particular subjects that relate to the emotional and familial bonds pertaining at the beginnings and the ends of life. These are perhaps the most controversial subjects within applied ethics. Chapter Nine deals with abortion and Chapter Ten with euthanasia.

Notes

[1] A full theory of justice would need to establish what harm means in terms of capabilities. If a child is raised to believe that some races are inferior, to what extent should social services be allowed to intervene? By and large, rather than micro-managing family relationships, we should mould social environments and welfare systems that perform the job of compensating for any deficiency in parental education.

[2] Of course, even sincere love can involve a degree of simulation. I may care about your cat because you do and I am able to love what you love; but if I hate cats, my love for you might involve some insincere toleration of the moggy. The point is that while it may involve a degree of faking, sincere love cannot *be* faked.

[3] Note that Kupfer's (1998) general support for autonomy suggests that he is more of a liberal.

[4] Incidentally, Kant did not address the question under review here, although he did argue that we do not owe our parents repayment for costs they incurred when raising us (Kant, 1996, pp 430-2).

[5] This does, however, leave conservatives vulnerable to an 'ungrateful parent objection', where we (or more probably women) are expected to remain loyal to unloving parents just because of biological links.

[6] There is no space here to offer a comprehensive account of those baseline obligations.

[7] Israel introduced such a law in 1959 but it has rarely been invoked or enforced (Iecovich and Lankri, 2002, p 122).

[8] In case it needs stating, inheritance taxes are taxes on the recipient (the child) and not the giver. American Republicans wilfully confuse the issue by referring to them as 'death taxes'.

[9] Note that all that is intended here is an elucidation of the obligations owed by adults. If, indeed, those obligations were 'impersonalised', so that contributions flow into a general pot, additional work would be needed on the grounds by which older people might draw *from* that pot. Should we universalise the services funded by that pot, or should those who are or have been parents possess more entitlements than those who never had children (perhaps because judged to have made more of a social contribution)? The numbers of the latter group will probably never be high enough to make this a problem worth worrying about, but there is a philosophical question here about the basis for the entitlements of older people that any amended friendship model would need to address.

[10] It should be added that such insurance relates to long-term care for older people. There are other forms of long-term care, such as that for disabled people, that also need to be considered.

NINE

Becoming

We now relate the themes of previous chapters – free choice, familial attachment, personal responsibility and possible harm – to two extremely controversial debates. This chapter deals with the first of these, abortion.

Despite the controversy that surrounds abortion, the aim of the chapter is to identify what can be termed a 'pragmatic consensus', or a broad field of opinion in which most of those who think about the issue probably stand. It is this that has arguably enabled abortion to become embedded as an accepted practice in many countries and which therefore deserves consideration for that reason if no other. To this end, the first half of the chapter addresses two questions that will help us to mark out the space of that consensus: should there be abortion on demand and what should the upper time limit for abortion be? The appropriateness of these questions to the pragmatic consensus should become obvious as we proceed. The chapter also explores two further questions, but we will leave these to one side for now.

Abortion on demand

Should there be abortion on demand?

There are various reasons why many feel uncomfortable with the idea of abortion on demand (Cleary, 1983; cf. Glover, 1977, pp 144-5). Wouldn't it encourage women to seek abortion on frivolous grounds? What if some used it as a form of contraception? For many, such doubts represent an insurmountable problem. So where might an ethical justification lie? On what basis could abortion on demand be permissible?

If we decide that abortion is acceptable, why should the motivations of the pregnant women be an issue? If we believe that the foetus is organically and morally indistinguishable from the rest of her body, why insist on imposing procedural hurdles?[1] Abortion is either murder or it isn't, and we don't excuse murder based on how the killer does or does not feel. So perhaps the requirement to have abortions sanctioned by medical experts and other authorities stems from nothing more than moralistic desires. To make abortion dependent on evidence of medical harm, emotional distress or worthy intentions might encourage women either to worry themselves into the first, fake the second or simulate the third – hardly a basis for ethical decision making.

Consequentialists and Kantians, of course, both downgrade the worth of factors like emotions and motivations. Some consequentialists might propose that since personal autonomy is a good, anything that interferes with this damages both the individual and her society's claim to be free; as long as someone performs a non-harmful and/or beneficial action, their motivation is irrelevant (Singer, 1993, Ch 6). For Kantians, if abortion accords with the moral law (perhaps because the sovereign autonomy of the woman is clear, that of the foetus less so), emotional factors do not matter either (Feldman, 1998). As long as we have acted in accordance with duty, our psychological gain or distress is irrelevant. Obviously, these arguments depend on whether abortion can be justified according to consequentialist and Kantian principles in the first place – a point returned to later in the chapter – but the discounting of motives seems to suggest that *if* abortion is permissible, the burden of proof lies with those who would deny abortion on demand. Do those who defend abortion but fret about the *numbers* of abortions have any solid justification for their anxieties?

If we suspected that motivations *should* matter, perhaps we should turn to virtuism. Hursthouse (1987, pp 330-9; 2002) and Little (2005) both defend abortion, but are less concerned with the ontological status of the foetus than they are with the moral climate that surrounds it (cf. Reiman, 1999, pp 57-9). Decisions about the foetus should be characterised by respect even if we decide that abortion is legitimate, they say. This means that we should disapprove of the woman who aborts because she has a world cruise planned, although, rather than deny her rights, Little suggests that she could invoke other, more virtue-respecting reasons. If this is so, whether virtuism requires more than a superficial gloss on an abortion on demand policy is far from clear.

In addition to a moral uneasiness, there are sociopolitical reasons why calls for abortion on demand have been subdued. Many of those who feel that abortion *is* or may be the taking of life (including many Catholics) do not wish to see it criminalised. Perhaps they respect individual choice, perhaps they fear a return to backstreet practices, perhaps they acknowledge the difficulty of these issues, or perhaps they oppose the amount of state action required to abolish all abortions. Whatever the grounds, the reason why the anti-abortion movement is muted in many countries is possibly because pro-choicers have formed an informal, pragmatic consensus with this kind of opinion. The cost of breaking this consensus can be seen in the US, where moral and religious conservatives have polarised the debate. Perhaps, this is only offered as an hypothesis at present, reining in on calls for abortion on demand is a price worth paying to avoid US-style enmity. If so, do not the above arguments for an on-demand policy risk undermining that valuable consensus? We can only address this question, and that of abortion on demand, once we have explored a second question.

What should the upper time limit for abortion be?

One of the acute ethical dilemmas in this debate concerns the cut-off point. When should abortions no longer be permitted? The question is partly driven by technology. The most premature baby to date was born at 22 weeks (in February 2007), which might suggest that an upper limit of 24 weeks (in the UK) is tantamount to infanticide. Presumably, the limit needs to be dropped for this possibility to be avoided. Set against this is the fact that a fifth of babies born before the 25th week of gestation have severe mental and physical disabilities, while those born earlier than 28 weeks spend 85 times longer in hospital in the first five years of their lives than full-term babies do (*The Guardian*, 2006). Table 9.1 illustrates the point.

Table 9.1 A study of survival and disability levels for babies born very prematurely

	22 weeks	23 weeks	24 weeks	25 weeks
Number liveborn (=100%)	138	241	382	424
% survived to 6 years of age	1	10	26	43
% none or mild disability (where known)	50	36	49	60
% moderate or severe disability (where known)	50	64	51	40

Source: Marlow et al (2005)

In addition, pro-choicers are correct to make two further points. The first is that in making such calls, the anti-abortion lobby's real agenda is to whittle away at current legislation and eventually scrap abortion altogether. Second, only 137 abortions were performed after 24 weeks in the UK in 2005, usually because of extreme personal or medical circumstances, and most abortions in England and Wales

(87%) are carried out before the 13th week of pregnancy. Given what is at stake, however, neither of these replies is entirely adequate. Even if anti-abortionists are wrong to want all abortions banned, this does not necessarily make them wrong about the appropriate cut-off point. Moreover, as pointed out earlier, *if* an act constitutes murder, its infrequency is hardly relevant. Which criteria are therefore relevant to this discussion?

Does independent human life begin at conception?

Anti-abortionists contend that it is immoral to abort an *independent human life* (Griffith, 2004; Lee, 2004). While each of these three words is of significance, for our purposes the key one is that of 'independence'. We could perhaps agree (but see Tooley, 1983, pp 61-77) that the zygote, embryo and foetus[2] constitute human life at various stages of development, but when does that human life become distinct and individualised? My hand is also a form of human life, but we would not say that it has rights since it is not, and has no prospect of, functioning independently.

For anti-abortionists, the answer is clear: independence begins when human life begins, at conception.[3] A zygote may be a cluster of cells that in no way resembles a fully formed human, but what is important is that it is fertilising; it has an internal dynamic that will evolve as long as the 'external conditions' are right (Lee and George, 2005, p 14). Some have argued that what matters here is the zygote's *potential* to become recognisably human (Marquis, 2002). The average infant is less intelligent, sociable and useful than I am – although I make no claims for the above-average infant – but has the potential to acquire all of the qualities we typically use to define humanness.

Yet according to critics of this argument (for example, Boonin, 2002, pp 46-9), the problem with potentiality arguments is first, that potentiality does not necessarily denote a *moral* status – since although a pile of bricks has the potential to become a house, I violate your rights more if I steal the latter than the former – and second, that potentiality resides everywhere – for example, every cell in the human body has the potential to become a living person through cloning, including the gametes of sperm and egg.

Anti-abortionists respond that conception is *the* dividing line that matters, whether this occurs through sex or because gametes are zapped with electricity (excuse the technical jargon). Later post-conception stages are secondary to this one, so rather than an ad hoc attribution of independence to one of those stages it is better to identify, as a starting line, the point at which the relevant 'internal' properties become present. It is true that a portrait is not complete until the final brush stroke, but the first drop of paint on the canvas initiates a picture that was simply not there before *any* paint was applied. And Marquis (1989) refines the potentiality argument by observing that what matters is not the characteristics the foetus acquires later on but those he sees as already present within human life from the moment of conception. In either case, the foetus has an interest in not being terminated, even if that interest is not one it can currently articulate.

But are such counter-arguments convincing? Marquis and other proponents of these arguments denounce abortion but not contraception; preventing paint from reaching the canvas is not the same as removing it once it's there. One Catholic argument against contraception (albeit not the only one) is that it prevents a potential human being from coming into existence (Finnis, 1980). When looked at teleologically, therefore, harm is committed to the person *who would have* existed, who had an interest in life but was denied it, meaning that the distinction between preventing and removing is not so great after all. Presumably, pro-choicers are entitled to borrow some of the same logic in pointing to the import of several stages of potentiality, both before *and after conception* (Glover, 1977, p 122). Conception is obviously vital, but to load everything on it is to insist on an ontology of dichotomies: a microsecond ago soul/life/independence wasn't there, a microsecond later it is.[4] Nor does reference to God necessarily guarantee this ontology, since, without loss of any cells, a pre-implantation embryo can be split into several potential individuals and then recombined into one (Harris and Holm, 2003, p 118). Does God add or remove souls according to the decisions of the scientist? It is because of the possible absurdities of this dichotomy that some prefer an ontology of gradualness, continua and incrementalism (Little, 2005, pp 28-9).

When, according to *this* ontology, does human life become independent? A popular approach here is to focus on personhood and define independence accordingly, not simply as a biological determination (Tooley, 1983; Warren, 1997; Harris and Holm, 2003; cf. Dworkin, 1993, Chs 1 and 2).

Three conceptions of personhood

First, we might propose choice as the criterion, that is, personhood is conferred on the unborn once the mother consents to the process (Rhodes, 1998). All too often, anti-abortionists establish equivalence between the foetus and the post-birth individual by saying that the former will become the latter as long as the external conditions are right (see above). Yet the woman is not just another 'external condition' but an agent with consciousness, reason, intelligence, plans, hopes and fears (Little, 2005, p 29). If this is the case, surely the agency of the woman is hardly irrelevant to what is happening inside her body.

This is the lesson frequently drawn from Thomson's (2002) famous example. Thomson asks you to imagine waking up in a hospital bed next to an eminent violinist with failing kidneys. As someone with the right blood type, you have been kidnapped and plugged into his circulatory system so that your kidneys can extract the poisons from his blood (as well as your own). The procedure of saving the violinist will take nine months. Do you have an obligation to remain? Thomson insists not. It would be charitable if you remained, but your lack of consent means that you have no such duty. The DDE enters the picture at this point (Boonin, 2002, pp 195-9). The violinist will die if you go, but this is a *foreseen* consequence of your action; your intent is simply to free yourself from a situation you did not choose (cf. Oderberg, 2000b, pp 28-31). The violinist therefore only becomes your moral responsibility if you choose to make him so. Perhaps, then, the foetus only becomes a person with independence once you recognise it as such.

It should be noted that Thomson was not attempting to offer a defence of abortion per se but only in those cases where consent was missing (rape) or where a pregnancy seriously harms the wellbeing of the mother (although a consistent anti-abortionist will still maintain that neither scenario justifies what they see as murder.) Yet her stress on voluntariness and consent has been influential. Even if you did at first agree to the medical procedure, that agreement assumed you had control of your body, a control that presumably means you can withdraw your agreement if you later change your mind. However, the analogy breaks down here, because whereas the violinist was ill before any agreement, your sexual liaison has brought a new life into the world, perhaps establishing a moral situation where you cannot withdraw your consent as easily. Furthermore, if the violinist only requires your kidneys for an hour, even if you were kidnapped you may have an obligation to remain for that hour. Voluntariness does not trump all other principles and independence may be less a specific cut-off point and more a matter of *proximity* – the violinist might not be completely well for another hour but the proximity to full recovery, or full independence, confers an obligation on you nevertheless.

What of a second candidate for personhood? Does 'viability' mark the point at which personhood begins?

Viability is often treated in a particular way (Callahan, 1986). We find a case of premature birth where the baby survived, for example, 22 weeks, the earliest recorded case. We then debate whether this should determine the cut-off point for abortion. Some people argue that at 22 weeks this baby was no longer entirely dependent on its mother's body, apply this to all foetuses and propose that any abortion at 22 weeks or later therefore constitutes infanticide.

Critics will suggest, first, that this is to make moral questions dependent on technology, as if matters of life and death reduce to technological proficiency. Second, such viability should not determine the limit, as 99% of babies born at 22 weeks do not survive (at 23 weeks, this falls to 83%), making post-viability abortion the humane option (see Table 9.1). For similar reasons, pregnancies caused by rape or that put the mother's life in danger may also justify post-viability abortions. Such criticisms have frequently been directed at *Roe vs Wade* (which was based on the principle of viability) by its supporters (Blank, 1984), since medical technology has reduced the point of viability from what it was in 1973, leaving it vulnerable to anti-abortion attacks.

But what if we use the DDE to switch the viability debate around? Abortion implies termination and termination implies killing to some and mere *discontinuance* to others. Though some have denied it (MacKenzie, 1997), the procedure that many women seek is that of discontinuance, of freeing their bodies from an unwanted incursion rather than an extinguishing of the foetus per se. The aim, in short, is withdrawal or extraction rather than annihilation. The foetus may indeed die once deprived of the sustenance provided by the woman, but this could be a regrettable side effect of the extraction *and not its direct intention*. Can this argument be used to justify abortion?

Not quite. As we have seen, consequentialism denies the DDE. If the foetus is dead, whether you killed it directly or extracted it and left it to die is hardly significant; what matters morally is the end result. *If* abortion is more beneficial than its alternative, we should not hide behind the cover of 'humane extraction'.

Both of these arguments carry force and one possible resolution is to submit that the Kantian/virtuist defence of the DDE applies in the earlier stages of the pregnancy and the consequentialist rejection of it applies to the later stages. So when we are dealing effectively with tissue, what matters is the woman's goal of extracting it and not what happens to it subsequently, but where the life of a distinct human is at stake, the consequentialist is right to deny any distinction between extraction and killing. The relevant question, of course, is when one period gives way to the other and that is precisely what we are trying to decide.

Armed with this notion of abortion as extraction, can we propose that rather than viability marking the point at which abortion is no longer permissible it denotes the point at which *a different type* of abortion is permissible? Before 20-24 weeks, let's say, the Kantian/virtuist defence applies. After 20-24 weeks extraction *but not killing* is allowed *on the grounds that the technology now exists for the foetus to potentially survive.* Technological innovation is no longer about reducing the upper limit (something pro-choicers worry about) but of altering the form of extraction practised (Gert, 1997).[5]

Before both sides lynch me let me add that this is offered merely as a thought experiment and not a realistic proposal. Anti-abortionists will continue to point to the special responsibilities they see mothers assuming at conception; pro-choicers will point out that the required technology is never likely to be universally available. The point is that if technology is allowed into the moral debate, it *may* lead us to reduce the upper limit on abortion but it *may also* cause us to permit abortion as extraction (although not abortion as killing) after that time (cf. Boonin, 2002, pp 254-60). Viability therefore offers some grounds for determining personhood and independence, but is not entirely satisfactory in offering a cut-off point. A foetus may after a certain point become a distinct human possessing rights, yet those may imply the right not to be killed *rather than* the right to continue using the mother's body.

A third candidate for personhood and independence is that of sentience, often thought to indicate when a foetus starts possessing rights that counterbalance and, in some cases, limit the mother's (Landman, 1991; Warren, 1991, pp 308-11; 2002, pp 76-9; Singer, 1993, pp 164-5; Sumner, 1997). Sentience is the capacity to experience and have sensations (no matter how primitive); it means possessing some consciousness of yourself, awareness of your surroundings and the capacity to feel pain.

Sentience is a matter of degree in two senses. First, it corresponds to the ontology of gradualness and incrementalism defended earlier; for example, within the normal course of a day people are both highly sentient (whether as a result of caffeine, sex or cold showers) and barely sentient (during sleep, drunken stupors or university lectures). Second, humans who are either non-sentient, barely sentient or who have no possibility of regaining sentience may have a different status to the rest of us; our capacity to affect their lives is one that demands responsible action if that capacity is to be more than just one of power. The moral asymmetry resides in my possession of greater free will.

The trickiness comes in assessing such degrees and in ascribing precise moral implications to them. In terms of sentience (see also Chapter Ten), what seems to matter is the development of the brain, brainstem and central nervous system. We are not simply talking about *reactions* to external stimuli – which can begin a matter of weeks after conception – since what matters is the *conscious experience* of stimuli, which, in the womb, denotes a stage when we have not yet acquired a cognitive distance from our surroundings but neither do we remain indistinguishable from them. More technically, Boonin (2002, p 115) refers to this as 'organized cortical brain activity': 'electrical activity in the cerebral cortex of the sort that produces recognizable EEG readings', or a period beginning about 25 weeks after conception. McMahan (2002, p 268) cites the period from 20-28 weeks as significant.

Reiman (1999, pp 67-8) argues that sentience is an inadequate criterion because it does not establish the moral status of abortions per se, merely ruling out painful ones. A counter-argument to this is that although sentience is itself subject to an ontology of gradualness – making it difficult to know when consciousness fully emerges – if it constitutes a credible threshold of personhood, that surely *is* relevant to the ethics of abortion. If it is the case that before the 26th week of gestation the nervous system has not developed sufficiently to allow the foetus to experience pain (according to the Royal College of Obstetricians and Gynaecologists in 1997), this is an indication – although not the only and perhaps not the most important one – that consciousness is now present. It points to a threshold of personhood and not simply to a point at which abortions have to become painless. Sentience therefore represents a period of development that is blurred and into which a margin of error has to be built but beyond which abortions become harder (although not necessarily impossible, as demonstrated below) to rule out.

Does sentience therefore dictate the upper limit for abortion? Almost. Much depends, of course, on whether we are talking about weak or strong sentience. We have already discussed how there are problems with defining sentience too weakly (it cannot simply be about reactions to external stimuli), but there are also difficulties with defining it too strongly. Tooley (1983, p 291-4) argues that what matters is not consciousness per se but also a sense of time, of perceiving that moments succeed one another and so having an interest in future continuity. The problem with defining sentience this strongly is that since newborn babies might also lack these capacities, anti-abortionists claim that abortion is, after all, equivalent to infanticide (see also McMahan, 2002, pp 338-45). And while issues concerning infanticide cannot be entirely divorced from abortion debates (see below and Chapter Ten), we need to keep them distinct nevertheless.

Even if we prefer a middle way (perhaps the idea that sentience begins around the 24th to 26th week), there may still be circumstances that allow us to breach the upper limit on abortion, for instance, where the life of the child will be shortlived and/or intolerably painful, where the life of the mother is in danger or where the pregnancy would preserve an injustice committed against the woman. Here we are faced with the kind of dilemma that consequentialist debates regularly present: in a choice between killing either two or three people, we may be entitled to kill the two and at least save one life. There may be circumstances where we know we are killing a sentient and therefore independent human life and still do so because it is the lesser of two evils: better to save the life of the mother who we *know* to be a person rather than that of the unborn child who only *may* be.

As such, abortions performed later than the upper time limit become harder *but not necessarily impossible* to justify. An intuition to err on the safe side might then caution us to place the upper limit at 20 weeks with carefully designed exceptions, that is assuming that sentience, defined neither too weakly nor strongly, begins at around 24 weeks and building in a margin of error. So reduction in the upper time limit (in terms of current UK law) may be justifiable *if* it can be demonstrated that sentience occurs at an earlier stage than previously thought and *if* consequentialist safeguards can be built in – a recognition that morality sometimes requires the lesser of two evils (Rowan, 1999, pp 178-82) .

Abortion on demand revisited

We are ready to return to an earlier question: do arguments for abortion on demand risk undermining a consensus that preserves us from US-style polarisation? The answer is 'no'. If a reduction in the upper time limit is justifiable, making abortion easier at the earlier, pre-sentient stages of pregnancy seems reasonable too. To deny this, to reduce the limit while still imposing hurdles on women, risks permitting abortion only within too narrow a timeframe, one that may not be enough for those wrestling with the personal, social and moral implications of their choice – as well as those who may be diagnosed late or those unable or unwilling to confront their condition. It is at this point that pro-choicers' fears that reductions in the upper limit are really strategies for attacking abortion per se become warranted. As such, if we concede to those uncomfortable with abortion that developments in medical knowledge and technology justify such reductions, the sine qua non has to be an easing of restrictions at the other end of the process. In the absence of such quid pro quo, pro-choicers may be entitled to dig their heels in and refuse to countenance time-limit reductions. And, of course, an easing of restrictions not only means emphasising women's choice but also facilitating its translation into action, that is, making medical and welfare services available to ensure that all women possess the same opportunities to determine what they do with their bodies (Markowitz, 1997; Shrage, 2003). (This corresponds to the egalitarian social justice included as a principle of social humanism.)

To conclude, abortion on demand is not about breaking the pragmatic consensus but of allowing it to evolve as conceptions of abortion develop from what they were in the 1960s and '70s.

If this kind of consensus is worth preserving, the map of applied ethics in Chapter Five offers it some philosophical support. Much of the sheer intractability of the debate has been sidestepped. To acknowledge the importance of intuition and social environment, as the model does, is to admit that much of what we believe may be beyond rational discourse. Parental upbringing, religious and cultural climates and simple instinct can drive us in one direction or the other, meaning it is no surprise to find consequentialists, Kantians and virtuists who are opposed to abortion.

Consequentialists may object to the social effects of what they see as the cheapening and commercialisation of life (Feldman, 1992). If a country like the UK can perform 180,000 abortions a year, if potential human beings can be disposed of so readily, activities may spill across society, inculcating an ethic in which individuals do not act for the good of others. Hare's (1989) view was that abortion is immoral because it contradicts the gratefulness we all feel for our lives. Kantians, of course, believe that someone should never be used merely as a means to the ends of another. As such, and if human sovereignty is held to begin at conception, presumably abortion risks doing so and it would hardly be moral to extinguish life because the pregnancy was the result of recklessness (Gensler, 1986; Wilson, 1988). Some virtuists, too, believe that acting responsibly means avoiding an unwanted pregnancy in the first place, but if one occurs, the possibility (however slight) of destroying another human life means that responsible agents must bring that life to full term (Oderberg, 2000b, Ch 1). In each case (though less so with virtuists for whom the experiential bonds of the mother are as important as the foetus's ontological status), moral philosophers who see an independent human life as beginning at conception, or who at least err in that direction, will take the debate in a different direction.

In short, many consequentialists, Kantians and virtuists will support abortion and many will oppose it. This re-emphasises the point made in Chapter Five that these isms can only take us so far and explains why intuition, albeit a critical and reflective intuition, is crucial to any mapping exercise. The arguments here regarding abortion reflect the intuitions of many, but they may not reflect yours. Such factors may ultimately be irresolvable rationally. But, if so, it is important to find at least some common ground, which is why a 'pragmatic compromise' is highlighted here and why we may need to see abortion on demand and upper time limit reductions as crucial to maintaining it.

Stem cells

> *Is stem cell research permissible?*

One other area remains controversial for anti-abortionists: stem cell research. Those who object to abortion are likely to object to this as well. This explains why the following discussion is brief, since many of the key issues have already been dealt with, but there are some additional questions to consider.

First, let us be clear what we are talking about. A stem cell is a human or animal cell that can produce specialised tissues and organs as well as replicate itself. Embryonic stem cells are derived from very young embryos (blastocysts) and ultimately develop into a person or an animal. Adult stem cells are found in various tissues of the adult body, such as the bone marrow, where they effect the regeneration of old or worn tissue. Adult cells are routinely used in medicine, for instance, to fight cancer. Controversy rages over the possibility of using embryonic stem cells to treat conditions like Parkinson's, since their use requires the destruction of the blastocyst. If an independent human life is created at conception, such destruction is tantamount to murder.

If, however, we decide that abortion is permissible, isn't that the end of the matter? If the pre-sentient foetus is dependent tissue, why would performing research on it be any worse than termination? As supporters often say, this is material that would have been disposed of anyway, due to the excess numbers of embryos created through IVF treatment, so surely it is best to permit research that will almost certainly aid in the alleviation of conditions such as Alzheimer's and Parkinson's. Isn't all this analogous to the abortion-on-demand arguments?

However, if there is one reason why pro-choicers might oppose stem cell research it is because there is a practice that is widely considered to be worse than killing: killing with disrespect.[6] It is one thing to end a life; it is something else to end a life through disrespect (which is arguably what the instrumentalist destruction of the blastocyst represents). This has interesting implications for the dilemma mentioned above and refers us back to discussions in Chapters Two and Three. The consequentialist argues that it is better to sacrifice one life than five. But what if that life will end in torture, and we could otherwise kill all five painlessly? Is the pain of the one worth inflicting in order to save the life of the others? Whatever your response, is there a moral parallel in the case of stem cell research? Does it imply cruelty over and above the act of termination?

In one sense, no. If in the absence of sentience no disrespect is experienced, I am presumably no more guilty of it than if I smash a brick with a hammer. On the other hand, disrespect does not necessarily have to be *felt* in order to be *performed*. If colleagues badmouth me behind my back, according to virtuism, harm is being committed, if not necessarily to me then to the moral character of my colleagues and of the workplace. Therefore, even if stem cell research can be justified in one sense we might still fear that it devalues *all* human life.[7] Natural revulsion was felt when a Liverpool hospital harvested the body parts of children who had died there without the parents' permission. Perhaps respect is not simply a matter of experienced sentience.

It is presumably for this reason that in the UK research is only permitted on embryos up to 14 days old, since we are here dealing with a cluster of cells so far removed from what we normally understand as an 'independent human life' that any moral unease will be minimal. For strict anti-abortionists, this is hypocrisy. For if we have decided that abortion up to 20 weeks (and perhaps longer) is permissible, why not allow research on a soon-to-be-aborted foetus as well? Perhaps our queasiness at doing so is because we tend to medicalise and hide from the reality of abortion. Then again, it was proposed above that killing with disrespect is worse than killing per se. If so, experimental research and the like demands an even greater margin of error before the emergence of sentience than the latter (see note 7), which means that countries like the UK are correct to limit such research to the earliest post-conception stages.

It is this form of regulation that, in addition to the kind of debates engaged with throughout this chapter and the next, hopefully ensures that life is not devalued even when we recommend its termination. The consequentialist does not advocate sacrificing one person out of contempt *but in order to respect the lives of the other four who can be saved* – although, as Chapter Four noted, the virtuist insists on additional guarantees that this is the actual motivation. The policy implication is that issues around abortion and other such sensitive areas must not be treated lightly, *not that such practices are illegitimate*. If abortion can be justified ethically, encouraging people to take it seriously implies making improvements in sex education and welfare services rather than the war on abortion clinics and women seeking terminations that religious and moral conservatives are prone to wage.

Reproduction

If some of the above arguments offer justification for abortion on demand, there are others suggesting why such policies might be resisted. Doesn't abortion on demand allow individuals to make discriminatory and disrespectful decisions about the kind of child to which they want to give birth? Might we reject abortion on demand in order to prevent that happening? Surely we should be concerned that some will choose boys over girls and non-disabled rather than disabled children.[8] After all, the previous section of this chapter allowed for late-term abortions partly on the grounds that the foetus might not survive and it is often tempting to use the phrase whereby the future child would have a 'life not worth living'. However, there are many borderline cases where this might or might not be so and perhaps the very phrase is itself evidence of bias against disability per se. Equally, we have a responsibility to reduce incidents of harm and suffering and refusing to discuss disability in this context could be seen as cowardly. There are times when the various communities of disabled people take precedence and times when the interests of the individual take over. The difficulty is in determining what should happen with *potential* people. The final question to address is therefore as follows.

> *How can the right to choose be reconciled with the right to be chosen?*

This debate has been dealt with in previous publications (for example, Fitzpatrick, 2005a, Ch 6) so a summary of this discussion is all that is required before drawing out the ethical implications more explicitly.

Biotechnology can filter out genetic properties held to be undesirable (so avoiding medical conditions and diseases) and filter in certain properties held to be beneficial (see below). The reason why this debate is of immediate and more than academic interest is because examples of the former are feared by some in the disability movement as heralding a new form of discrimination against disabled people (for example, Rock, 1996; see also Lloyd, 2001; Sharp and Earle, 2002), while the ability to perform the latter has impelled the UK to shift its position. Let us look at each of these in turn.

If we can eliminate certain genetically determined conditions, do we not have a duty to do so? If one of the aims of social policies is to prevent or at least reduce suffering and harm, doesn't the discussion end there? The problem is that we are not simply talking about a wound that can be stitched or a pain that can be anaesthetised. The concepts of 'harm' and 'suffering' are more problematic than we commonly wish to believe, loaded with assumptions and perhaps downright bias. Given the choice, you may prefer to end your life with 12 months of tolerable pain rather than a week of pain-free existence. Harm and suffering are not always bad. How much more problematic, then, when we talk about 'quality of life' (Brock, 1993). How easy it is to assume that people with, say, Down's Syndrome have too poor a quality of life, at least until friends and family assure us that this is not so. Nor is this the end of the argument. Family members may disagree about the appropriate course of action, as was the case with Terri Schiavo in 2005, when, after she had been in a persistent vegetative state for 12 years, her husband wanted her feeding tubes removed while her parents disagreed. Friends and families should not necessarily have the last word (see Chapter Ten).

Some like Shakespeare (1998; see also Kerr and Shakespeare, 2002) invoke the spectre of Nazism and argue that genetic interventions may have the following effects. The first of these is a decline in support for all disabled people as genetic disabilities become rarer. Second is the inference that those who are born bearing such disabilities have lives less worthwhile than the non-disabled. Third is an increase in 'wrongful life' and 'wrongful disability' suits as children sue their parents for the inheritance of conditions that could have been eliminated. Fourth is a reduction in human diversity as 'genetic correctness' becomes the norm. Fifth, and finally, is the possibility that genetic engineering may eventually lead to the elimination of 'social defects' (criminals, homosexuals and so on).[9] Therefore, biotechnology represents a quantum leap beyond existing forms of selective abortion.

However, supporters like Buchanan et al (2000; see also McMahan, 2005) raise a number of counter-arguments. First, avoidable suffering should be eliminated whenever possible – if we ban genetic engineering, should we not ban non-genetic techniques on the same grounds? Second, parents should have the right to know the genetic characteristics of their children and make appropriate decisions. Third, eliminating genetic disabilities need not lead to the devaluation of disabled people. Finally, if social justice requires the redistribution of undeserved *social advantages*, does it not also demand the elimination of undeserved *genetic disadvantages*?

We therefore have two options. One would regulate genetic interventions and suggest that the right to be chosen should heavily qualify the right to choose. The other option places the emphasis on the right to choose. What light, if any, can consequentialism, Kantianism and virtuism throw on the issue?

Consequentialists direct us to the importance of harm avoidance. But what kind of harm should be avoided – that to the individual or that to the group of which that individual is an actual or potential member? The more we stress the one, the more we risk neglecting the other. Harris (1998, Ch 10) and Glover (2001) emphasise the individual, since we can be more certain of when we are harming persons than of when we are harming social abstractions like groups and communities. Harris deems it a simple duty to eliminate suffering where we can and Purdy (1996) adds that parents with genetic disabilities have a responsibility not to reproduce. Glover leans in a similar direction. There are, he says, severe disabilities whose elimination is surely unproblematic and where the interests of the individual must be paramount; yet there are also cases of moderate disability where, perhaps in the interests of social diversity, the issue is not so clear. Given the choice between having a child with a moderate disability and one with no disability, Glover supports policies designed to effect the latter on the grounds of reducing harm. But if the choice is between moderate disability and having *no child at all*, the former seems preferable.

There is a prima facie plausibility here. As Singer (1993, pp 188-9) argues, banning thalidomide did not mean discriminating against people born without arms or legs (the effect the drug often caused); it simply meant avoiding preventable harm. If a woman delays becoming pregnant until that time when she can be sure her baby will not be disabled, is *she* guilty of discrimination? It would seem harsh to say so. These are the kinds of extreme and artificial examples we ought to be wary of, since they are hardly typical or illustrative of the issues at stake. We might counter them with alternative (and equally extreme) scenarios. In the case of a woman who terminates a foetus with one arm to give birth later to a baby with both arms, it hardly seems outlandish to question the ethical status of that decision and to accuse the woman of bias against disabled people.

Whereas most consequentialists seem to support selective abortion, Kantians are more split on the issue. What does it mean, in this context, to treat someone as an end? Are we violating the principle by imposing on our conception of a person a norm of physical and/or mental capacity of which disabled people are thought to fall short? Or do we violate it by insisting that, to protect the identities and interests of disabled people, personhood must encompass a broad spectrum of conditions, diseases and disabilities, even if this means that some will live lives of pain and suffering?

There are those who are in favour of selective abortion and cite the Rawlsian principle mentioned above: if social justice and equal opportunity require the redistribution of undeserved advantages and/or compensation for undeserved disadvantages, there are no compelling reasons to limit this to social goods rather than genetic goods (Buchanan et al, 2000, Ch 3). There are disabilities so severe that no social system could ever hope to compensate for them, in which case justice surely demands that those that have a genetic cause should, technology permitting, never be allowed to develop in the first place. Egalitarianism demands that such interventions be made available to all, but, as long as this condition is met, we might envisage health-related interventions becoming mandatory (Brown, 2001). Rhodes (1998) observes that Kantian autonomy implies the capacity not only to choose but also to act as an independent moral agent. As such, we are entitled to screen out those who will lack the requisite capacity.

However, operating with a similar set of Kantian principles, others are just as sure that such arguments are wrong. To place such a strong emphasis on those genetic determinants that either assist or hamper equality of opportunity is to apply a medical model that downplays the *social characteristics of impairment* (Vehmas, 2001, pp 478-9). Habermas (2003) discusses the issue in terms of how moral agency is shaped. Inevitably, our identities, beliefs and capacities are formed through processes that are initially out of our control, but, in a free society, individuals can theoretically take possession of their properties and potentially even reverse them. Biotechnology, however, makes essential properties of the self irreversible and therefore violates the principle of autonomy (Junker-Kenny, 2005). While directing most of his fire against genetic enhancements, Habermas (2003, pp 90-1) contends that we should also be wary of 'negative eugenics' (the elimination of severe genetic disorders) and certainly of progressing beyond it without the kind of public discussions he has previously defended under the heading of deliberative democracy.

It seems that little work has been done in this area by virtuists, but we can infer certain attitudes from what they have said about disability (for example, MacIntyre, 1999, pp 136-40). In particular, virtuists question reliance on 'independence' and its implicit fetishisation of the individual. Instead, we ought to recognise *dependency* as the natural and normal condition of being human, in which case disability signifies a different kind of dependency and not one we should subject to normative criteria that allow us to screen out those deemed too expensive or too difficult to care for. A care ethic valorises the person whose needs and interests may be different and does not ask whether he or she must first qualify for love, friendship and help. It is care that makes us members of the moral community and not membership of the latter that qualifies us for care. It is concerned with what those possessing differing physical and mental abilities contribute to our sense of what it means to be human and is not concerned with costs and burdens.

That said, it is also possible to *defend* selective abortion using virtuist principles. There is surely a risk that we become indifferent to harm and suffering on the grounds that at least they permit us to act charitably and demonstrate our virtues. Perhaps it is possible to care more for a foetus who will develop certain conditions and syndromes by not allowing the person who would experience them to ever develop. Virtuists surely need to avoid the 'Mother Teresa Problem', where suffering is justified because it enables us to share in God's grace.[10]

My own view (see Fitzpatrick, 2003, pp 165-74) is that we should err on the side of precaution and be absolutely clear that when abortions and genetic screenings are performed it is medical needs that predominate. This probably puts me closer to Shakespeare, Kerr and Habermas than any of the other authors mentioned above. There are certain conditions we should not wish on anyone but nor should we eliminate that diversity which lies within an acceptable framework of wellbeing and quality of life. McMahan (2005, p 98) is correct to observe that we should not value diversity for its own sake – for example, we should not *cause* people to be disabled in the name of increased diversity – but nor should we be so concerned to screen out impairments that we apply biotechnological fixes to what are essentially social relations.

What does this imply for the right to choose? One alternative is to reduced its scope, heavily qualifying what I said earlier about abortion on demand. This is not to propose that women with certain types of foetus should be forced to bear them, but it might be that some forms of information should not be made available. You have a right to abortion on demand but not necessarily to information that might impel discriminatory choices.

If this goes too far, if people *do* have a full right to information about their bodies, another option is to improve public awareness and counselling services, to dispel the many myths that circulate about the 'burden' of raising disabled children, while also improving the social services that are available for the assistance needed. By swinging the pendulum back to the right to choose, there remains the possibility, of course, that discrimination against disabilities will remain and a 'negative eugenics' will persist. Yet it is doubtful if anything better can be obtained by operating, however indirectly, a politics of coercion.

Do similar arguments apply when certain characteristics are screened *into* the foetus? This is the case with so called 'saviour siblings'. These would derive from embryos selected to have the same tissue type as an existing brother or sister affected with a disease, so that donations of their umbilical cord stem cells or a bone marrow transplant could be used to treat that sibling. On the one hand, this enables an already existing child to obtain treatment that ameliorates and perhaps cures the disease; on the other, the second child is arguably being created for instrumentalist reasons and, obviously, cannot consent to this use of his or her tissues. Saviour siblings were originally opposed by the UK's Human Fertilisation and Embryology Authority, unless the second child was at risk of the same condition as the first, but was subsequently endorsed by it and by the Human Genetics Commission *even where there is no risk to the second child*.

A consequentialist would probably favour this development (Sheldon and Wilkinson, 2004). The long-term effects on the children are difficult to estimate. On the one hand, perhaps the second child would be disregarded by the parents – its main work having been performed – and suffer the psychological harm of knowing it had been born as a glorified tissue donor; on the other hand, perhaps the parents would love it all the more since it would have enabled a much-loved child to live or live a healthier life. What *can* be anticipated are the shorter-term beneficial consequences for the first child and, if harm avoidance is desirable, that seems reason enough. Since people already become pregnant for any number of reasons (some of them selfish), is this reason any worse?

Nor can Kant be easily invoked to argue the contrary. If the saviour sibling were created *solely* as a means to help the first child that would violate Kant's principle of autonomy, but that principle *does* permit a degree of instrumentalism as long as the individual is *also* respected as an end. What would matter is how the second child were treated throughout the rest of its life and since that cannot be known in advance it would seem harsh to use the possibility of bad parenting to condemn the first child to ill health and perhaps death (Glannon, 2001, pp 118-20). From a virtuist stance, Scott (2006, p 169) has voiced a similar argument.

Nevertheless, the 'slippery slope' objection cannot be ignored (for example, Bowring, 2003, Ch 8); as we become acclimatised to more genetic interventions, we risk sleepwalking into a moral climate where what is, and was previously perceived as being, ethically unacceptable becomes the norm. The task here is to retain the social humanist principles of egalitarianism (in this case, an equality of wellbeing between the first and second child) and intersubjectivism (so that we do not have to fear the slope and can decide what is and is not acceptable on the basis of open, public debate – see Chapter Ten). Again, therefore, the contention here is that the right to choose is paramount and that in some instances procedures should help to determine the genetic characteristics of the embryo being chosen.

Conclusion

This chapter has explored four questions that are key to contemporary debates surrounding abortion and reproduction. The ethics of abortion has not been reviewed in full but enough has been said, with sentience as a vital determinant of personhood, to propose that abortion on demand is a means of *preserving* the 'pragmatic consensus', especially if we decide that the upper time limit should be reduced. Embryonic stem cell research is therefore justified also, although incorporating a wider margin of error beneath the period of emerging sentience seems wise. And, finally, emphasis has also been placed on the right to choose, this should be contextualised carefully and systematically by an ethic that, except in the case of extreme harm and suffering, respects the right to be chosen and values the social diversity that differential abilities bring.

Notes

[1] A critic might question this analogy by observing that we do not (generally) allow surgeons to amputate limbs just because a patient requests it. However, this is because such requests derive from an extreme psychological trauma or sexual fetish. If you equate such conditions to that of being pregnant and wanting a termination, this might say more about you than anyone else.

[2] For simplicity's sake, and unless otherwise indicated, the term 'foetus' is used to denote all pre-birth stages.

[3] There are differences between those who interpret conception and those who interpret implantation as important. However, for reasons of simplicity, we will concentrate here on the former.

[4] Theists are, of course, entitled to draw comparisons with death where there must presumably be a microsecond's difference between (earthly) life and not-life. We will return to this point in Chapter Ten.

[5] This argument was first formulated by Heather Gert, though I formulated it independently.

[6] It is assumed here that torturing someone to death is worse than killing them painlessly.

[7] This is not necessarily an argument for treating the embryo as having intrinsic value. Kamm (2007, pp 230-3) observes that a duty to perform q does not equate to the 'directed duty' to perform q for a specific entity. For instance, Kant's principle of humanity presumes against instrumentalist reasoning, which is surely easier to maintain in the case of demonstrable sentience than in the case of low/questionable sentience, followed by that of the potential to develop a capacity for sentience and finally that of no potential for sentience. In short, the younger the embryo, the more we are permitted to treat it instrumentally, which, in the case of stem cell research, implies a wider (pre-sentient) margin of error than applies with mere termination. The discussion of intrinsic value in Chapter Ten relates to the first of these.

[8] We will concern ourselves here with the latter distinction.

[9] This is not to say that that could ever be scientifically possible, but political dogmas are rarely concerned with scientific realities.

[10] At a 1994 prayer breakfast, Mother Theresa accused contraception and abortion of reducing the amount of love in the world (www. luisprada.com/Protected/mother_teresa_on_abortion.htm).

TEN

Dying

This chapter completes and complements the life-and-death debate begun in our analysis of abortion. Euthanasia has hovered on the outskirts of social policy's radar, with most governments reluctant to focus on such a controversial subject. As degenerative conditions become more prevalent and average life spans creep upwards, however, it seems likely that euthanasia will become more and more crucial to social policy debates in the 21st century.

This chapter will therefore be mainly concerned with the following question:

Is euthanasia justified and, if so, when?

First of all, what do we mean by euthanasia? The term implies deliberately assisting someone to die in order to benefit that person (Kuhse, 1993). It is usual to distinguish between its active and passive forms, although we will see shortly why that distinction is not always easy to maintain. *Active euthanasia* involves killing someone through direct actions, while *passive euthanasia* occurs when someone is allowed to die, whether through direct action (for example, by withdrawing medication) or non-intervention; active and passive euthanasia are therefore often categorised as 'killing' and 'letting die', respectively.[1] The question of whether they are continuous with one another or qualitatively distinct is crucial, as we shall see. This distinction cuts across a further one, between voluntary, non-voluntary and involuntary euthanasia. Voluntary euthanasia occurs with the fully informed request of the adult, whether this is made currently or has been made in the past. Non-voluntary euthanasia occurs *without* such consent, for example, when a coma patient is insentient, thought incapable of recovery and has left no prior instructions. Involuntary euthanasia occurs when someone's life is ended even though they are indicating (or have in the past indicated) their wish to go on living, or when they are capable of giving consent but are not asked to. These various categories are charted in Table 10.1.

As simple as this table may appear, it contains a legal and ethical minefield. Can we make pragmatic and moral distinctions between active and passive euthanasia? How do we decide whether someone is fully

Table 10.1: Euthanasia matrix

	Passive	Active
Voluntary	(1)	(2)
Non-voluntary	(3)	(4)
Involuntary	(5)	(6)

informed or competent enough to make relevant decisions? What constitutes consent, particularly when communicative powers are lacking? How far can proxies and doctors be permitted to respond to changing circumstances after the patient becomes insensible? What should happen when proxies and doctors disagree? These questions, and many others, can only be considered briefly in what follows, but we can at least develop a framework to clarify our thinking.

We begin by querying one of the distinctions just drawn. How distinct are passive and active euthanasia, and what ethical implications follow? There are basically four positions we could adopt. We could propose that there is no morally significant difference between passive and active euthanasia, which might lead us to suppose either (a) that euthanasia can be justified or (b) that it cannot. Alternatively, we might argue that there *is* an important difference between passive and active euthanasia that might be offered either (c) in support of euthanasia or (d) in opposition to it. These positions are illustrated in Table 10.2.

Passive and active euthanasia

Those who hold position (a) argue that there is no morally significant difference between passive and active euthanasia and that both types can thereby be justified (Glover, 1977, Chs 14–15; Singer, 1993, Ch 7; 2003).

Table 10.2: Euthanasia perspectives

Can euthanasia be justified?	Are passive and active euthanasia equivalent?	
	Yes	No
Yes	(a)	(c)
No	(b)	(d)

One of the most famous contributions to the debate was made by Rachels (2005). Rachels denied that killing is morally worse than letting someone die. Imagine that Smith stands to gain financially from the death of his six-year-old cousin. One night while the child is taking a bath, Smith enters the bathroom and drowns him. Jones, too, has a cousin from whose death he would benefit. He is outside the bathroom when he hears the child being accidentally knocked unconscious and slipping beneath the water. Jones could assist him but instead waits while the child drowns. Smith killed his cousin while Jones allowed his cousin to die when he could have intervened. Is there a difference? Rachels claims not, for in both cases the outcome was the same. It is true that Smith acted while Jones neglected to act, but that is irrelevant to the fate of the cousins. In short, what Rachels denies is the DDE. To a Kantian, it would be important that Smith intended the death of his cousin while Jones merely foresaw the death of his, but if what matters are the consequences of our actions *and inactions*, this is irrelevant. Killing and letting die are morally equivalent.

Rachels therefore argues that because it is widely accepted that certain forms of passive euthanasia are legitimate and because there is no ethical difference between the passive (letting die) and the active (killing), active euthanasia can be justified too. We will see in a moment that it is possible to reject the legitimacy of passive euthanasia, although increasingly fewer people do so. Doctors and nurses observing a do not resuscitate (DNR) order are practising a kind of passive euthanasia by respecting a patient's previously expressed wishes and not intervening.[2] Since there are few people who would question the validity of DNR orders, demanding that all lives be saved in all circumstances whatever the wishes of the individuals concerned, Rachel's premise seems persuasive and, if his reasoning is correct, a prima facie case for active euthanasia can be made. Indeed, he observes that because there are instances where the withdrawing of life support would induce a long and painful death, *active* euthanasia could sometimes be preferable.[3]

Does Rachels' argument hold? Nesbitt (2005) argues not, pointing out that we are more at threat from Smith-type persons than we are from Jones-type ones. Within the context of Rachels' scenario, this hardly offers much comfort to the cousins but there is a reasonable point here. Note that the equivalence between Smith and Jones lies not only in the outcomes but also in the selfish *motivations* Rachels attributes to them. What happens if we alter the vignette so that Jones is merely regrettably neglectful? We might still want to censure Jones but can hardly place him in the same dock as Smith. Does this mean we should prefer the DDE after all? Not necessarily, for reasons given below. Before we review why this is, what of position (b)?

This involves agreeing that killing and letting die *are* morally equivalent but that euthanasia is *not* thereby justified. We might, for example, interpret life as sacred, as a gift from God (Keown and Keown, 1995). This argument runs up against two problems, however.

First, perhaps God acts on the world *through* human agency, such that rather than violating God's commandments the doctors and nurses observing a DNR order are helping a soul return to its source. Second, if life should be preserved at all costs, this must be so regardless of the degree of pain and suffering involved. Better to keep someone alive in tortuous agony than to offer them release (Kuhse, 1998). This offends against a common intuition that life is not always worth preserving and that someone's best interests can be served by allowing them to die as painlessly as possible, with dignity. If it is possible to end life before God wishes it (an anti-euthanasia argument), why is it not also possible to preserve life beyond the point God wishes (a pro-euthanasia argument)?

A more secular version of the sanctity of life argument is to suppose that life has 'intrinsic value' and must always be preserved (Somerville, 2002, p 82; Kass, 1990, 2003). If someone is about to commit suicide, our first instinct is to help them live rather than leaving them to die and surely this is a sign that we recognise and respect life's intrinsic value. Or is it? Perhaps the real issue is that we do not initially know anything about the suicide's background. They may be momentarily depressed and about to commit a terrible mistake. In the absence of such knowledge, our default position should always be to talk someone down from the ledge and ask them to think again. But not all suicides are the same. If someone is mentally sound and competent, having given much thought to what they are intending to do, perhaps we respect their life more by allowing them to end it. Some will allege that the wish to die is itself evidence of mental unsoundness, but this is to deprive individuals of their capacity to weigh benefits and harms. The 'intrinsic value of life' is a meaningless phrase if it implies depriving people of those properties that are also intrinsic, for example, the power to choose and control that life (Dworkin, 1993, p 214-17).

A more persuasive defence of position (b) is the 'slippery slope' argument where euthanasia is held to induce undesirable consequences that were not originally intended (Dworkin et al, 1998, Ch 7; Wilkinson, 2005). This is a consequentialist argument that says because x will either definitely or probably lead to y, through a series of causal intermediate steps ($x1$, $x2$ and so on), the undesirability of y means that x should not be allowed even if x is generally benign.[4] For example, some fear euthanasia may cheapen life so there is no longer a presumption in favour of saving it, in which case relations of trust between doctors and patients may fade. This might further devalue those groups (frail older and disabled people especially) whom it is already too easy to view as social and economic burdens; in some cases, it may lead relatives, medical professionals or insurance companies to exert subtle pressures on them to seek euthanasia, or for the latter to assume that they are a burden and reach the same conclusion even in the absence of such pressures. It is then argued that legislative and administrative measures to avoid these possibilities will always be inadequate (Keown, 2002, pp 70–80). The slippery slope argument may concede the premise that some forms of passive euthanasia are morally legitimate but then suggests either that these should nevertheless remain illegal or that that legal permissibility be restricted to a minority of highly exceptional cases that would keep us poised at the summit of the slope rather than tumbling down it (Beauchamp, 2002).

We will return to this line of reasoning later but it is important to note immediately why we should not overreact to it (Battin, 2005, pp 25–9). First, there is no compelling evidence from those places where euthanasia or physician–assisted suicide has been legalised that unintended negative consequences begin to emerge (Marquet et al, 2003; Patel, 2004; Tooley, 2005, p 175; cf. Keown, 2002, Pt 3). According to the *European Journal of Cancer Care* (2003, p 302), the number of cases in the Netherlands where a doctor ended a patient's life without an explicit request was the same in 2001 as in 1995, suggesting that the supposed 'slope' is somewhat flat. (As we will see later, however, this is not the end of the matter.) This is confirmed by Smith (2005), who goes on to suggest that cases of non–voluntary and involuntary euthanasia *decline* when euthanasia is permitted. There are certainly worries that doctors are failing to report euthanasia (Onwuteaka-Philipsen et al, 2005) but such possibilities apply as much, and perhaps more, to those places where it is illegal yet still practised de facto.

The logical argument for slippery slope reasoning is also questionable (Lillehammer, 2002). LaFollette (2007, pp 131–9) observes that its advocates squeeze *x* and *y* together too quickly, without attending to the intermediate steps (*x1, x2* and so on) because doing so distracts from the rhetorical intent of their argument. Amarasekara and Bagaric (2004, pp 409-11; see also Neuberger, 2005, p 12), for instance, anticipate that legalising voluntary euthanasia would turn hospitals into 'killing fields', a bizarre assertion that treats euthanasia as a licence for suicide pills to be sold over the counter.

Imagine that we allow killing in the form of self-defence as long as the death of the other person was not our intention. Has this increased the amount of murders and killings in society? Note how this scenario allows those who are guilty to *claim* they were acting only in self-defence and so evade justice (and no doubt some do) but this is different from positing that self-defence *increases* violent crime by, for instance, devaluing human life. Yet it is not difficult to imagine a world where the proposed introduction of a self-defence plea is being debated and slippery slope proponents objecting to it on precisely those grounds. So if falling down the slope is not inevitable in that possible world vis-à-vis self-defence, why should it be in ours vis-à-vis euthanasia? As Dworkin

(1993, pp 197-8) puts it, the slippery slope argument focuses on the harms that *may* occur if euthanasia is legalised but is curiously silent on the harms that *do and will occur* if it is not. Its proponents tend not to recognise that slopes can slide in many directions; by downgrading compassion and autonomy in favour of 'life', Amarasekara and Bagaric (2004, pp 410-11) come awfully close to denying anyone the right to die (also Callaghan, 2005, pp 186-9).

So it is wishful thinking to believe that because the slippery slope *could* occur, it *does* occur. That said, it is also possible to believe that because it *doesn't*, it *couldn't*, but this would obviously be fallacious reasoning too and, as such, very few pro-euthanasia advocates deny the need for safeguards, a subject we return to later.

If the reasons why killing and letting die are morally similar, what are the reasons for treating them as dissimilar? We have, in fact, already covered them. Chapter Two posited the argument that sending poisoned food to a hunger-stricken country is not the same as neglecting to send any food, *even in those cases where the number of resulting deaths is the same*. My inaction may be regrettable but to claim it is equivalent to sending poisoned food would appear to justify murder in those cases where the murderer can allege that he has not killed any more people than would have died anyway. As Nesbitt proposed, my Jones-type behaviour is unfortunate but surely less so than Smith-type murders. This is the kind of argument advanced by Foot (1978, Ch 3; 2002, pp 78-86) in her defence of the DDE. As noted in Chapter Four, Foot's position is not based on the acts/omissions distinction – for example, that foreseeing the effects of omissions is of lower moral import than intentional actions (since it is possible to murder via omission) – but on a theory of causal sequences. She defends passive but not active euthanasia (even when voluntary) on the grounds that the former is a refusal to intervene in a sequence that is already progressing, whereas the latter initiates a new casual series of events and so imports a degree of agency and moral responsibility that is harder to justify.

Foot's conclusions place her midway between (c) and (d) in Table 10.2 (also Cavanaugh, 2006, pp 183-90). But Chapter Four also criticised Foot's claim by raising the possibility that it is harder than she allows for to distinguish between those acts that originate a causal sequence and those that do not (Norcross, 2005, pp 456-8). If this is the case, the distinction Foot proposes between passive and active euthanasia is harder to maintain than she imagines and trying to retain it perhaps implies that Foot would prefer you had a long and painful death by natural causes than a quick and painless one due to human agency.

While not addressing the DDE explicitly, Gunderson (2004, pp 283–5) defends position (c) from a Kantian perspective. Where someone has lost their rational agency irretrievably, euthanasia is justified both when they have left an advance directive requesting it (to ignore that directive would violate that person's dignity) and when no such directive has been left (if we have good reason to believe it is what that person would have willed). Killing, we might infer from Gunderson, does occupy a different moral dimension to letting die, but that does not means the former cannot be justified too.

A position closer to (d) is occupied by some of those committed to a care ethic (Young and Cullen, 1996, pp 134–46; Wolf, 2003) and a virtue ethic (Oderberg, 2000b, Ch 2; cf. van Zyl, 2000). This is generally to suggest that although life can become difficult, painful and sometimes intolerable, there is always value to it. Euthanasia is condemned as a capitulation to existing social attitudes and welfare systems that fail to embody the duty to, and the need for, care. Those close to the end of their lives or the limits of their tolerance should be offered alternatives other than death and the social resources required to make these realistic should be made available. The Vatican (1994, p 254) insisted that:

> The pleas of gravely ill people who sometimes ask for death are not to be understood as implying a true desire for euthanasia; in fact it is almost always a case of an anguished plea for help and love.

Such a care ethic would reject introducing a *system* of euthanasia, although it might sometimes permit humanitarian exceptions to the general rule (Somerville, 2002, p 34). The Vatican document just cited permits the suppression of pain even if this results in death as long as it was the relief of pain that was genuinely sought (the DDE, in short).

The care ethic is absolutely correct to observe that people's desire to live is influenced by their sense of hope in others and in their future. In this sense, the palliative care movement has been immensely beneficial. Yet palliative care is not always enough (Materstvedt et al, 2003), perhaps because pain cannot always be managed, or because the level of pain suppression may create a state ethically indistinguishable from death – typically called 'terminal sedation' – or because care may intrude on an individual's rights, for, in addition to a right to be cared for, *I must have a right not to be cared for if I so wish*. Even if I am not in much pain, I may desire to let go of a life that has become otherwise intolerable. To presume otherwise, as the Vatican citation suggests, is to replace my desires with those 'true desires' imposed on me by others.

Some Kantians also occupy position (d). Kant (1991, pp 85, 91–2) himself rejected suicide, first, because it would point self-interest (whose function is the furtherance of life, he says) in a contradictory direction, towards its destruction and, second, because escape from an intolerable situation involves treating oneself as a means and so denying one's status as an end. Such arguments presumably extend to euthanasia debates. Velleman (1999) argues that euthanasia is done for a conception of the good rather than for the sovereign individual who can formulate such conceptions, equivalent to succumbing to temporal imperatives and transient feelings. As such, it does not derive from the deepest moral principles of duty (although Velleman argues more against an *institutional* right to die). But is suicide a self-contradiction? It is if Kant is correct in assuming that self-interest is necessarily oriented around the continuance of life. But if the life that is to be continued is rationally and reasonably judged to be intolerable, the autonomous self should presumably seek its own end (Tooley, 2005, p 331). If I can exert my autonomy to avoid a future state where I will be alive but have lost autonomy, does this not satisfy Kantian principles?

What can we conclude from this discussion? The moral equivalence Rachels draws between Smith's action and Jones' inaction sounds persuasive, though this is partly because they have been given similar motivations. When our motivations are less malicious, we are presumably also less culpable than Jones even when our inactions have negative consequences. This suggests that Rachels' anti-DDE position fails. On the other hand, I am still not convinced that Foot's distinction between killing and letting die is persuasive, since her theory of causal sequences is too overdrawn.[5] I am therefore inclined to agree with Norcross (2005, p 452) that there are possible examples where killing and letting die *are* morally equivalent and possible examples where they *are not*. This perhaps means that we have a strong case for allowing passive euthanasia and a prima facie case for permitting active euthanasia subject to further consideration. We have not yet explored this issue in any depth, however, and to do this we need to return to Table 10.1.

Voluntary and involuntary euthanasia

Let us make sense of this table by first dealing with the least contentious cells.

Cell (1) falls into this category, since there are few who have argued against the morality of voluntary passive euthanasia (VPE). As we saw earlier in respect of 'sanctity of life' and 'intrinsic value' arguments, it is possible to construct such views but it has been suggested that they are weak. The real issue with VPE concerns the point at which it becomes permissible.

Terminal illness is an obvious condition, although even this does not settle the matter. Some might argue that the terminal illness must be combined with intolerable pain for VPE to be permissible; that is, the terminally ill should not be encouraged to terminate their lives when their death might still be years away. But who is to decide what is intolerable? Leaving the decision entirely to the patient might risk them ending their life too soon; but giving too much power to others might risk ignoring the genuine distress the patient is experiencing. Should pain even be a consideration? What if a terminally ill person is in no pain but simply finds their life to be unbearable and wishes to regain control, if only of the manner of its ending? And if we permit such arguments, why limit ourselves to terminal illness as a qualifying condition? Perhaps the prospect of living several more decades in a debilitating condition is enough to make some desire death – the fact that we salute those who do learn to cope with such conditions does not mean we should penalise those who cannot or do not want to try. To argue for VPE is to assume that if we respect people's capacity to make decisions about how they live, we should similarly respect their decisions about how they are to die. Certainly, we ought to counsel individuals on such a momentous decision but ultimately respect the individual's autonomy. Of course, autonomy need not imply an atomistic view of the individual and the social humanism defended in Chapter One incorporated an ethic of intersubjectivism and interdependency. But if autonomy can mean attending to the relational aspects of individuality, while nevertheless continuing to prioritise the latter, VPE can be justified.

Does this 'respect for autonomy' argument shed light on the other cells? What of (5) and (6)? It is common for involuntary euthanasia to be ruled out of hand. If someone indicates, or has indicated in the past, their desire to go on living, even in extremely adverse circumstances, this decision presumably demands as much respect as in the case of cell (1). But is it possible to imagine scenarios where we might violate the autonomy principle? Imagine that someone has expressed a desire to go on living in *all* future circumstances, and we are not even allowed to let them die as a side-effect of relieving extreme pain. An accident happens and to protect their brain functions medics initiate a chemically induced coma. Though barely sentient, an EEG detects that this person as experiencing an incredibly high level of pain that is likely to last the rest of their lives.[6] If we respect their original wish, we are condemning them to such pain, but if we do not, we are disrespecting their autonomy. Yet while it is true that people cannot always anticipate their own best interests in the future, the dilemma might recommend that more effective advice be given when people are making decisions about their possible futures. Ultimately, if that advice is comprehensive and the above kind of decision made nevertheless, overriding such autonomy on the grounds that 'others know best' does indeed set a dangerous precedent. As such, there appears to be nothing in the literature in defence of involuntary euthanasia.[7]

If we can therefore dispense with cells (1), (5) and (6), what of the others? If the 'respect for autonomy' argument holds, does it justify cell (2), voluntary active euthanasia (VAE)? Yes, as long as we can draw a moral parallel between passive and active euthanasia (Tooley, 2005); we also noted Rachels' observation earlier that performing active euthanasia may sometimes be *more* ethical. Worries about discrimination against older or disabled people cut both ways. Somebody who is able and willing can commit suicide and, while we may urge them to think again, we no longer make attempted suicide illegal. So why deny similar freedoms to those who are in some way incapacitated? If we allow them to refuse treatment and promise not to intervene in their deaths, should we not also intervene actively to hasten their deaths if they wish? Why should we prefer them to experience a long and possibly troubled death to a short and untroubled one?

A possible objection is that the former death will urge people to seek VAE only as a last resort, whereas making the exit door easier to walk through will only encourage more people to do so. But such 'moral hazard' could equally be used to propose that euthanasia needs appropriate regulatory and counselling systems that will draw out the decision-making stage (so that short-term impulses are insured against) but will respect people's informed choice. The same consideration applies to fears that those perceived as 'burdensome' will come to see themselves that way and so desire an early death, whether due to subtle social or family pressures. This is true of the decisions people already make about their deaths, but without having available the regulatory and counselling systems that a step towards de jure euthanasia would necessitate.

Another possible argument against VAE, where past but not current consent has been expressed, is that someone may make a living will authorising their termination but then change their mind, without being subsequently able to alter that will. Yet in the case of cells (5) and (6) we ruled out violations of autonomy where the patient's previously expressed wishes were clear. So why would we do so when someone has made a decision in favour of termination?[8] The argument that the intentional termination of life should *never* be permitted excludes the possibility that termination can sometimes be the best of two undesirable options and denies us all the freedom to make this determination for ourselves.

So while it would be facile to equate killing and letting die (contra Rachels), neither do they occupy distinct moral dimensions (contra Foot). Although we cannot automatically assume the justifiability of VAE from that of VPE, and so might make the relevant safeguards more stringent still, 'respect for autonomy' suggests that we should assist an individual to die if they are unable to act alone and if, being fully informed, they have demonstrated a rational preference for death over life as being in their best interests.

Non-voluntary euthanasia

What of cells (3) and (4)? It is over discussions of non-voluntary euthanasia that controversies really bite. This is because the individual has left no living will (or similar documentation) and it is not clear what they would have wished. There may well be cases that are, strictly speaking, non-voluntary but nevertheless fall into either the voluntary or involuntary cells. This occurs when a patient has left no formal instructions but it becomes evident from friends and family what their expressed preferences were in such matters. But what should happen when loved ones give conflicting accounts? What should happen when doctors and families differ? Should we always presume in favour of life, even if this means someone existing forever in a persistent vegetative state (PVS), for instance? Should we treat babies differently from adults? How minimal does consciousness have to be for it to be worth preserving?

A respect for autonomy argument is no longer enough, since it is unclear what the individual wished or would have wished. We have to make decisions about 'best interests' without guidance from the individual whose interests are at stake. These issues are obviously profound and few can honestly pretend that there are perfect solutions to them.

To make sense of all this, let us begin by asking a profound and startling question: when do we die? The question is relevant because if euthanasia involves 'assisting someone to die' and autonomous choice is out of the picture, the ontology of dying and death comes to the fore as a means for determining the morality of assisted dying. For example, if someone is judged to be essentially dead already but their organs are 'alive', we may not be committing euthanasia at all.

Fortunately, we already have a handle on this difficult question. In Chapter Nine, we contrasted two views of life, with some believing it begins (presumably instantaneously) at conception and others preferring an ontology of continuance where the person whose life it is only emerges incrementally (with sentience being an important component). I aligned myself with the latter position and so justified a politics of abortion. That parallel disagreements emerge in the euthanasia debate should hardly surprise. Those opposed to abortion are usually opposed to euthanasia, and vice versa, though there is any range of nuances we need not be concerned with here.[9] Questions of personhood and identity therefore reappear at the end of life.

On the face of it the advantage lies with those who favour an ontology of dichotomies. If I was not yet conceived on 1 January but was by 3 January, perhaps these 'bookends' can be gradually narrowed down to the second (or the microsecond?) when I was conceived and so came into existence. Similarly, I am alive today but (probably) won't be in a hundred years' time. Here, too, this alive–dead dichotomy could presumably be narrowed down following my death to a precise moment when I ceased to exist. This ontology presumes strongly in favour of preserving life both after its instantaneous creation and before its instantaneous demise. Certainly, we do not always prefer to preserve life – in cases of just war, self-defence or capital punishment, for example – yet as a general principle the preservation of life is a universal default position. Even many of those who waive it in the case of VPE will not be willing to do so with VAE (since killing is held to be *always* wrong). So why would we ever consider waiving it in the case of non-voluntary euthanasia?

In a milestone contribution to recent debate McMahan (2002, pp 424-40; see also Quinn, 1988, pp 926-35; cf. Hershenov, 2005) draws a distinction between our biographical and biological lives. Although we depend on our organisms for existence, we are not identical to them, he claims; it is possible for me to die biographically without having died biologically. In either a PVS or irreversible coma, I may have lost my identity, the very qualities that were me, so what is left is a hollow shell. My body remains but my consciousness *and capacity for consciousness* has gone. This distinction is crucial. When do I die biographically? Not when consciousness per se is lacking, since this may also be the case with certain forms of coma from which recovery can be confidently expected. It is when the *capacity* is lacking that I die biographically.

Those who collapse the biographical and the biological together may insist that the lower functions of the brain have to go for the brain to be considered dead, in other words, once the brain can no longer regulate temperature, breathing and so on because electrical activity has ceased. McMahan, however, agrees with those who propose that the whole brain does not have to be dead for the capacity for consciousness to be lost. Because the mind can expire when whole brain death has *not* occurred (as with PVS) and because the organism can survive whole brain death (when kept alive for organ transplantation), whole brain death is a necessary but not a sufficient condition of death per se. Biographical life, insists McMahan, is more a question of possessing functioning cerebral hemispheres; once those are destroyed, so is the person's capacity for consciousness, although not necessarily the biological life that person once 'inhabited'.[10]

Other opponents of whole brain death nevertheless reject McMahan's arguments by insisting that we remain alive prior to the demise of the circulatory, respiratory and nervous systems, even when someone's brain is entirely dead (Potts et al, 2000; Oderberg, 2000b, pp 85-93). Life is interpreted here as a 'functional whole' or an 'organic unity'. Yet what has to be missing for these holisms to collapse? Potts et al (2000, p 4) distinguish between the whole organism (each and every cell of the body) and the organism as a whole (the body's functional integration). Death per se does not equate to the elimination of the former, they argue, since this implies that I could be alive centuries from now as long as some of my cells survive till then; death therefore implies the termination of the latter. But can we really distinguish between the two so easily?

My cells contain DNA, after all, perhaps implying that if they did survive my DNA could be cloned in the future. If life resides in the body's systems rather than in my person, that clone would presumably be me since its integrative systems would be as identical as our hair and eye colour. But most of us would probably not treat the clone as a resurrection of myself, since the physical resemblance would be less important than our different biographies (personalities and memories). Equating human life with its 'meat' is either excessively materialist or a way of replacing the brain with what some assume really animates the meat, that is, a soul, a concept that possesses religious and emotional resonance for many but is without empirical foundation.

Why is McMahan's a potential argument for non-voluntary euthanasia? Objectors to the latter say that in the absence of choice we should always presume in favour of life. But if life is multidimensional and dispersed across a number of brain-dependent levels, what should we presume in favour of? If biological life is our baseline, we ought to preserve anything that falls short of whole brain death or perhaps even systems death. But if that means preserving an organism long beyond the point where personhood and identity (the capacity for consciousness and autonomy) have vanished, we may prefer something closer to McMahan's formulation and so justify euthanasia on the grounds of respect and compassion. With adults, this implies states such as deep coma and some instances of PVS (Horton, 1996); with babies, it is usually taken to mean cases of anencephaly (where there is no brain or spinal cord and the skull does not close)[11], although it might also be extended to some prematurely born babies facing severe disability.[12]

None of these conditions necessarily means overriding the decisions of relevant individuals. In 2004, Leslie Burke challenged guidelines permitting the withholding of artificial feeding and hydration for the purpose of ending his life at some point in the future. Although this was subsequently overturned by the European Court of Human Rights, it seems to me that his wishes ought to have been paramount, and although he was advised to make a living will these are not currently binding on medical decisions. In 2003-04, the parents of Charlotte Wyatt, a child experiencing multiple organ failure, opposed the wishes of their doctors who preferred not to revive her. This case is more difficult for, although the courts found for the parents, the child survived with severe disabilities. So it is not obvious that such decisions should *never* be overridden and, indeed, where family members disagree with one another and/or with doctors, someone is going to be overruled (as with Terry Schiavo in 2004-05). In short, the opinions of proxies cannot rule out the justified use of non-voluntary euthanasia in some circumstances.

We therefore have three categories relevant to non-voluntary euthanasia: x, where the circulatory, respiratory and nervous systems have terminated; y, where the whole brain is dead; and z, where the higher brain functions have irretrievably gone.

Category x treats the biological integrity of the self as crucial. Some religious commentators in particular see the self as a temporal and spatial unity of organic, metaphysical and cognitive ingredients (Jones, 2000), in contrast to the secular tendency to regard the self as dispersed and more loosely integrated (cf. Ramsay, 1997, pp 32-7). For the former, that dispersal dangerously invites the chaos they see as endemic within modern society. Chapter One defined as a principle of social humanism the compatibilist idea that while the determinisms of socio-material interactions provide the conditions of the self (its freedoms, its cultures), it cannot be entirely identified with them. In the present context, that means treating the conscious self as dependent on brain and body, as inhering within its material substratum, but without being fully condensable to them. Life can remain within brains and systems, but, without the capacity for consciousness, individuals, as persons, cannot. The presumption here is not in favour of a Cartesian dualism, but of a fluid and 'motionary' conception of personhood.

By placing an emphasis on the brain, category *y* appears to be ethically safe (as if we can leave matters to the MRI machine) but it, too, reduces human life to physical matter and so might be criticised on the same grounds as category *x*.

Category *z* therefore introduces a clearer 'quality of life' or 'best interests' argument based on the biographical self's capacity for consciousness, but does risk a moral (and legal) fuzziness that could leave too much control in the hands of family members, doctors, health managers and courts. To debate this, we must first acknowledge a fourth possible category where a terminal patient is biographically alive but in intolerable pain and unable to communicate their wishes. This returns us to the slippery slope argument.

In the Netherlands, about 0.7% of deaths occur without consent that is both current and explicit. For Bok, this is an example of how euthanasia *does* lead us down the slippery slope and so should be opposed (Dworkin et al, 1998, pp 122-4), while Battin (2005, p 51) counters that in half of those cases a desire for a death rather than unbearable suffering had been expressed previously and lives were foreshortened usually by a matter of hours or sometimes days. Resolving the dispute partly depends on knowing how often similar incidents happen in countries without euthanasia, for proponents of the latter are entitled to suggest that it codifies and reveals practices that occur widely anyway (particularly the shortening of life) and that we are more likely to tumble down the slope *without* the transparency and protections afforded by euthanasia (Magnusson, 2004; van Delden et al, 2005; cf. Seale, 2006). Even if this hypothesis fails, we are still left with many terminal patients experiencing intolerable pain and suffering and, as we saw above, Catholicism permits us to put such individuals out of their misery on DDE grounds.

Therefore, it seems that the opponents of euthanasia, too, make room for 'quality of life' and 'best interests' considerations. Amarasekara and Bagaric (2004, pp 418-19) oppose a best interests defence but they displace it on to a level they see as more fundamental than that of experiences: 'existence is a pre-condition to the enjoyment of any rights or interests'. But existence, it could be argued, is not a *sufficient condition* and surely we can only valorise 'life' by respecting the person to whom that life belongs or once belonged. So if we should respect the best interests of, say, a consciousness experiencing pain, why not also for those whose biographical identities have vanished? The response, of course, is that we are no longer talking of ending the self's pain but of ending the self; yet if we accept category z, it is no longer clear whether there is a self still present.

While there may always be moral and legal cracks into which difficult cases fall, proponents believe that euthanasia narrows and reduces these cracks, first, by making public and regulating more effectively practices that occur surreptitiously anyway (Gastmans et al, 2006) and second, by placing greater emphasis on living wills and advance directives.

Safeguards and advance directives

How can we safeguard against abuses?[13]

It has been suggested here that non-voluntary euthanasia can be justified in certain circumstances. Critics will see this as confirming the moral descent they fear happens once euthanasia is on the agenda; supporters will view it as relocating us to a new territory that may well be more ethical than the ad hoc practices currently prevailing. For the latter, this territory is marked and enabled by a set of moral and legal safeguards.

Pakes (2005a, p 82) draws attention to the cultural differences that are likely to affect regulatory practices:

> Jurisdictions looking to introduce euthanasia or physician-assisted suicide legislation might want to consider both 'archetypes of governance'. [One] is more suited to situations in which opinions are polarised and the legislation controversial: a strict and transparent framework is probably the only achievable model – if that. In societies where euthanasia and/or physician-assisted suicide are less controversial and widely regarded as a natural extension of ethical medical conduct, a flexible approach in which practice can develop over time might be more appropriate.

Despite these differing cultures and archetypes (a strict framework versus flexible development), there are several principles that have been proposed to ensure safeguards and that might underpin cross-cultural debates (Pakes, 2005b; Dahl and Levy, 2006). The following is only a brief summary.

- The consultation process should take account of what those family members being consulted about the termination of a relative's life might stand to gain financially as a result of their death.
- There should always be realistic and humane alternatives to termination (for example, pain control measures), especially where it is believed that minimal biographical life is still present, on the condition that pain levels are judged to be manageable.
- Where biographical life is absent, there must be a clear consensus among several independently appointed experts that this is so and is irreversible. The risk of misdiagnosis must be minimised. (Euthanasia opponents are fond of pointing to exceptional cases, such as people waking up from PVS, but such cases could hinder us from *ever* taking life-or-death decisions.)
- The relevant physicians and consultants should be a mix of those who know/knew the patient's general outlook on life and those who have not treated the patient previously. This is to ensure that decisions are both sensitive to the patient's wishes and taken objectively.
- A national system of counsellors overseen by a review board should be available. The latter would also advise governments and courts on various moral and legal implications of euthanasia practices and other relevant developments, for example, in medical technology.
- Recourse to the legal system should be a last resort where consensus has not been forthcoming.
- Expense (to the state, the hospital and so on) should be of no consideration. Although it is possible to imagine scenarios where every extra hour of life costs a horrendous sum, where a health system is fully funded and not dependent on individuals' personal health insurance such matters can be largely bracketed. (Obviously, the issue of cost has ramifications for medical and health care ethics reaching far beyond euthanasia debates.)
- The point is to avoid discrimination against vulnerable groups. Such discrimination may be economic and more likely to occur in healthcare systems that are effectively biased against the poor. (They may also result from disadvantaged groups being over-represented among those seeking voluntary euthanasia because they see it as an escape from unjust conditions.) Therefore, euthanasia should not be introduced in certain social contexts where basic economic and social justice is absent, determination of which obviously needs additional debate.
- There is a debate about proportionate versus disproportionate means of life preservation that is bypassed here. The former offers the patient a reasonable hope of beneficial treatment, whereas the latter does

not. It is legitimate for the latter to be withheld if patients or their proxies decide as such. However, a politics of redistributive equality demands that disproportionate means not be withheld on financial grounds.

Such principles obviously refer to decisions that have to be made at a particular point in time. To what extent can they be forestalled by greater use of living wills made at an earlier time, which may reduce incidents of non-voluntary euthanasia?

Fagerlin et al (2002) and Bok warn against placing too much faith in living wills (Dworkin et al, 1998, p 119), although they do not dismiss the possibility of improvements. It is difficult to imagine such directives anticipating each and every possible scenario and such wills would surely need to have been updated (or reconfirmed) within a recent timeframe, to avoid the possibility of them reflecting preferences about which the patient has subsequently changed their mind.

Nevertheless, as populations age, it is difficult to imagine living wills not becoming more prevalent, more binding on medical decisions and therefore a site of government action and regulation. To argue that a patient's advance directive undermines a doctor's duty to care is to elevate care for a life over care for the person whose life that is (see van Delden et al, 2005). A doctor's duty is to help the individual. In almost all cases, this will mean preserving life but, in the contexts of ageing populations, improved medical technology, improved access to information and increasing democratisation and individualism, doctor–patient relations of trust and negotiation become more deliberative and less paternalistic. Battin (2005, pp 39-41) estimates that directives will be made at earlier stages of our lives, as the reflection of individuals' personal philosophy, instead (as is usually the case now) of being made at the onset of terminal conditions.

As such, there is an argument for making living wills compulsory. As populations age and as degenerative conditions increase in volume, perhaps completing one could become an obligation of citizenship. For just as we increasingly require people to make some financial provision for their old age, so we could require people to anticipate the moral dilemmas that the euthanasia debate throws up. Another argument for compulsion is that it would enable people to clarify where they stand on organ donation. Traditionally, most countries have operated an 'opt-in' scheme (informed consent), where those willing to donate their organs are centrally registered (and usually carry a donor card). Increasingly, many countries have introduced an 'opt-out' scheme (presumed consent), whereby every person is assumed to be willing to become a donor unless they specifically register their unwillingness (Abadie and Gay, 2006). The latter seems to address the lack of available organs and so save lives (many potential donors surely fail to offer informed consent out of inertia), though it does raise fears that in the event of technological malfunction, bureaucratic error or medical arrogance organs might be removed from those who had no wish to donate them. A system of compulsory living wills might offer a happy medium if they can also be used for people to indicate their un/willingness to donate organs and, as a more personalised document, might be less vulnerable to error than an opt-out register.

On the other hand, we are talking about such a culture shift that perhaps it cannot be forced on us in one compulsory step. While making every effort to publicise the importance of living wills, perhaps those who do not complete one would have to rely on the kind of regulatory principles suggested earlier. It is also the case that many individuals will be unable or unwilling to comply with a compulsory scheme and I doubt if the sensitive ethical reflections demanded by the euthanasia issue can sustain the heavy-handed approach that any system of compulsory compliance ultimately requires.

We might therefore prefer government to guide and encourage a culture shift where, as euthanasia debates become more central to social policy discussions, living wills are regulated (so that each conforms at least to a basic standard of information), become more enforceable and their value publicised, without us losing sight of their inherent limitations.

Conclusion

We began by reviewing the distinction between passive and active euthanasia. It was suggested that while passive and active forms could not be equated, they do not occupy radically different moral planes. This was used to propose that if voluntary euthanasia is justified, it can be permitted on active grounds as well as passive ones. The main arguments against voluntary euthanasia require us to proceed with care but do not rule out proceeding at all, in contrast to involuntary euthanasia for which there is no compelling rationale. The real difficulty lies in debating non-voluntary euthanasia where explicit consent is missing. There are, however, examples where this might be permissible, for example, where biographical life has irretrievably disappeared, in the case of intolerable pain, or where premature babies or those with severe birth defects face suffering. Drafting regulatory principles to minimise abuse is possible, although it is facile to believe that abuse and errors will never occur – as is the case whether or not we legalise euthanasia. When prolonging life means prolonging suffering too, it may sometimes be more ethical to shorten both, even if this means killing rather than simply letting die.

Notes

[1] I am agnostic as to whether physician–assisted suicide is a form of euthanasia. There is a family resemblance. Consider the following scenarios. In scenario A, a doctor prescribes lethal medicine for you; in B, the doctor prevents a nurse from injecting you with an antidote; in C, the doctor administers the lethal medicine; and in D, the doctor does none of the above. On the one hand, A (physician–assisted suicide) is more similar to B and C than to D. On the other hand, Frey argues that what matters is who acts last in the 'chain of death' (Dworkin et al, 1998, Ch 2). In scenario A, you act last whereas in C the doctor acts last, meaning there is a considerable difference between prescribing and administering. Then again, scenario B (analogous to passive euthanasia) clouds the issue over who acts last; and is there a significant difference between me pushing the button on a suicide machine (A) and you doing it for me (C)? Therefore, physician–assisted suicide has one foot inside and one foot outside the euthanasia camp and the literature tends to reflect this.

[2] Many may prefer not to refer to this *as* euthanasia, if only because the word continues to make some morally uncomfortable.

[3] A claim relevant to voluntary euthanasia but less so to non–voluntary euthanasia as the case for legalising the latter is that there is no person/ self left.

[4] Of course, many, if not most, consequentialists will support position (a) on the grounds that slippery slope reasoning is often too wishful and so should not dictate policy. It is also possible for Kantianism to have its version of the slippery slope argument (Hughes, 2000).

[5] Admittedly, there is no full explanation here as to why Foot's account is superior to other recent alternatives (Quinn, 1993, pp 149-74; Kamm, 2007), as this seems too much of a detour for this book.

[6] Another example is of a devout Christian who has repeatedly stressed the desire to go on living under all circumstances. He is trapped in a burning building and I must decide whether to shoot him and

foreshorten his life by 30 seconds or respect his wishes and let him die painfully in the flames. On the one hand, shooting him would be humane, but, on the other hand, perhaps such extreme scenarios cannot be generalised to matters of policy.

[7] Some confuse involuntary euthanasia with non-voluntary euthanasia, which may be due to outdated or confused terminology, although is sometimes a wilful misuse by those whose agenda is to criticise euthanasia per se.

[8] It might be that living wills would have to have been authorised within a recent timeframe to ensure that they continue to reflect the patient's wishes.

[9] Someone might oppose abortion as the destruction of innocent life but favour certain types of euthanasia out of respect for that person's autonomy.

[10] The ontology is therefore similar to that used in Chapter Nine to defend sentience as that point where the capacity for consciousness *emerges*.

[11] Most cases of anencephaly can now be detected in early pregnancy, where the requisite services exist, of course.

[12] In 2006, a report by the Nuffield Council on Bioethics recommended that babies born at 22 weeks (where the survival rate is 1%) should not be routinely resuscitated, while at 23 weeks (survival rate of 17%) it should involve negotiation between doctors and parents. It did not support euthanasia, although it equated this with *active* euthanasia.

[13] We are still discussing non-voluntary cases here. Although many of the principles discussed in this section apply also to voluntary cases, the consent of the patient takes priority there, with the qualification that counselling must occur several times over a period of weeks to ensure that the patient is not succumbing to temporary impulses, depression or other psychiatric ailment, ignorance of alternatives and so on. This would also need to include discussion of possible new treatments within a realistic timescale for the patient. For a discussion of voluntary euthanasia regulation, see Janssen (2002).

ELEVEN

Sharing

In the last five chapters, we have explored some weighty and controversial subjects. At no point, however, have we addressed the existence of state welfare or the underlying assumptions of modern social policies. What if the affluence on which advanced welfare systems depend is in some way immoral? What if it derives from historical injustices and/or contemporary exploitation? What if the price of our affluence is a world in which malnutrition and premature death is rampant? What if we (continue to) fail to do anything about this deplorable state of affairs? And what if our lassitude is due not only to addictive consumerism, corporate domination, post-ideological politics and moral inertia, but also to an attachment to welfare services that absorb resources that could be directed elsewhere? Don't our responsibilities to address global impoverishment outweigh obligations to compatriots and neighbours, perhaps even friends and relatives? Isn't the welfare state *morally unaffordable*?

This chapter explores two issues that relate to this question of how resources should be globally redistributed. One deals with whether migration and cultural diversification require a two-tiered conception of welfare entitlements; the other deals with whether domestic social justice is compatible with global distributive justice. Given the novelty of some of these debates, we will draw on our three moral philosophies more selectively than before.

The fairness hypothesis

Should we restrict the welfare rights of recent migrants?

Should we limit the welfare entitlements of non-UK citizens residing in Britain? Why is this question even worth considering? Debates about migration somehow manage to become ever more raucous. This is partly because the left has been exercised with them. Some argue that, given their long-standing internationalism, the continued salience of national identity has rendered social democrats unable to deal properly with questions of cultural, ethnic and religious tensions (Phillips, 2006). Their scepticism has left them deaf to people's genuine anxieties about sociocultural change and so impotent to suggest forward strategies. They have become lost in politics of identity, recognition and difference to such an extent that principles of universalism, solidarity, trust and redistribution have been undermined (Rorty, 1998; Barry, 2001). The former have led to a multiculturalism that erodes the basis of the welfare services and mutualist institutions that depend on the latter. Only by stressing a renewed sense of common identity and national citizenship can social democrats wrestle the debate away from conservatives, ultra-nationalists and racists.

Are these allegations reasonable? Are recognition and redistribution basically zero-sum? Can we only defend comprehensive state welfare by retreating from liberal policies on migration and multiculturalism?[1] We will assume that there is a challenge here that ought to be examined, one traditionally associated with the right but some elements of which have leaked into the left. This takes the form of a 'fairness hypothesis'.[2]

People will only support the welfare state politically and financially if they see it as being fair. Fairness is undermined if from day one of their arrival in Britain non-British residents possess the same set of entitlements as British citizens. This is because citizenship has to be earned through a demonstrated commitment to the nation (work contributions, length of residence, willingness to learn the national language and customs and so on). Therefore, without stronger and visible conditions on access to welfare services, the post-war settlement will finally unravel and social solidarities will break down. Tightening the criteria on entitlement is one such condition. This could mean (as now) granting entry only to those with sufficient personal funds; it could also imply a probationary period of limited entitlement so that British citizens can be reassured that non-British residents who are or may be intending to remain in the long term really want to participate in national life and are not here for a free ride. The main points of the fairness hypothesis therefore are:

1. the welfare state depends on a sense of fairness, implying mutuality and reciprocity;
2. this sense is undermined if entitlements are granted fully and automatically to all;
3. people feel it is unfair if non-British residents have such entitlements immediately;
4. any such entitlements should be restricted;
5. this could imply a probationary period during which access to welfare services is only minimal, for example, limited to emergency care.

These points can be reformulated as the following questions:

- Are the premises of the fairness hypothesis reasonable (points 1 and 2)?
- If so, do they extend to issues of inward migration and any subsequent cultural diversification within Britain (point 3)?
- If so, should we restrict entitlement, possibly through a probationary period (points 4 and 5)?

The fairness hypothesis as stated above could be accepted (in full or in part), rejected or revised depending on our answers to these questions.

Migration

Let us start with asking whether the fairness hypothesis carries any empirical or theoretical substance in terms of migration policy. According to Banting et al (2006, pp 79-80), what matters is not so much the size of the migrant population but its rate of growth: the higher the rate, the more downward pressure there is on social expenditure.[3] *Why* this is is not clear, but it may be that rapidly increasing diversity erodes trust and thereby support for welfare spending, given the extent to which people tie rights to desert and associate migrants with a lack of deservingness (van Oorschot, 2006).[4] Miller (1995, pp 128–9) proposes that high rates of immigration leave insufficient time for a process of mutual adjustment to occur, leading to a backlash within the receiving community. In California, such a backlash led to Proposition 187, designed to deny illegal immigrants access to various welfare services (it was later struck down in 1999).[5] While disagreeing with Miller on many other subjects, Kymlicka (2006, pp 61, 136-9) includes a probationary period in a possible multicultural conception of liberal nationhood.

Set against this it is not difficult to find evidence that migration has economic benefits (TUC, 2004; Ernst and Young, 2006). By adding to consumer demand, migrants may expand markets and create growth and jobs. Therefore, it has sometimes been argued that countries like Britain with ageing populations need an influx of younger workers from elsewhere in order to fund the bills for health, social care and pensions that they cannot supply for themselves (Farrant and Sriskandarajah, 2006). (It should be noted, however, that if a substantial proportion of that influx settles, any economic benefits will deplete as those workers grow older.) As such, by increasing national affluence, migrants expand the pot of money from which services can be funded. Many governments have certainly sold the benefits of migration this way, though not without running into the objection that it is not only gross domestic product (GDP) that matters. For instance, the fairness hypothesis may hold if people still feel that the benefits of added growth are going not to themselves but to those migrants who have not done enough to earn them.

What about more theoretical arguments (see Blake, 2005; Seglow, 2005)? Let's start by reviewing the main reasons why some favour relatively open migration (ROM) (Carens, 2003; Kukathas, 2003, 2005; Benhabib, 2004; Hayter, 2004). The first (a sort of Kantian cosmopolitanism) states that freedom implies freedom of movement such that restricting people geographically is as unwarranted a restraint as preventing them from moving jobs. There is no significant distinction between moving from Paris to Marseille, and moving from Paris to London. Migration has characterised historical development and only our fairly recent obsession with national boundaries precludes us from seeing this.

Second, there are (virtuist) humanitarian reasons in two senses. Migrants typically want to make a better life for themselves and we owe them this opportunity as fellow humans, a category that trumps local and contingent ones of nationality. Also, we ought to welcome those fleeing adverse circumstances as a reflection and nurturing of our compassion and care towards others.

Finally, ROM is a matter of justice. Due to their historical dominance, western countries have not only grabbed the lion's share of the world's resources but have also exported the resulting negativities (poverty and pollution) to those we continue to exploit. Since there are limits to the effectiveness of foreign aid, we should acknowledge open migration as a form of global redistribution. Migrants from poor countries often send a slice of their new earnings back to relatives. If our socioeconomic position is fundamentally a matter of luck (see Chapter One), you do not deserve your nationality any more than you deserve your class. We should treat national borders as contingent and assess migration according to its consequences for developing nations.

What would the implications of ROM be for welfare rights? Some believe that it would have to be accompanied by two-tiered citizenship, as now, such that migrants would not qualify for full welfare entitlements all at once (Legrain, 2006, pp 150–5). Kukathas (2005, p 219) goes further, observing:

> One of the reasons why open immigration is not possible
> is that it is not compatible with the modern welfare state.

While one obvious response to this is to say, 'so much the worse for open immigration,' it is not less possible to ask whether the welfare state is what needs rethinking.

This is because humanitarianism should take precedence over local institutions of social justice. Either we allow ROM or we redistribute resources globally to such an extent that state welfare can no longer be funded to its current levels. This inverts the terms of our debate. It is not that we ought to limit welfare rights to recent migrants but that we should radically redefine welfare rights for *everyone* in developed countries. Therefore, the fairness hypothesis is confirmed (migration and state welfare *do* conflict); but instead of worrying about the erosion of support for state welfare, we should welcome it as an opportunity to rethink redistributive priorities.

Is this true? Can the welfare state only be defended in the context of global injustice? We will leave these questions hanging until later. For now, we review the arguments of those who favour relatively closed migration (RCM) (Walzer, 1983, pp 38–51; 2003; Miller, 2005).[6]

Freedom, they declare, can never be treated as an absolute (you have no right to cry 'fire!' in a theatre). So why should freedom of movement be different? Your freedom to walk the streets does not give you the right to enter my home just because you want to. Private space matters and, in global terms, this translates into national space. You may have a right to move but that only becomes a specific entitlement to live in Zoob if the people already inhabiting Zoob wish to admit you. This means that humanitarianism is not necessarily best served by throwing open the doors. Migrants who make it to another country are typically the wealthiest, most resourceful or perhaps just the luckiest members of all those who would move if they could. Why reward these characteristics when we would do better to direct resources towards the most disadvantaged on universalistic and objectivist grounds? Therefore, justice demands systematic and comprehensive forms of global distribution rather than the limited, arbitrary redistribution that open migration can deliver.

Those advocating RCM have several additional arguments that relate to the fairness hypothesis. In particular, they point to the potentially disruptive effects of migrating *cultures*. For when individuals move, it is not only their bodies that travel, but also their way of life. People cannot easily leave their habits, symbols, languages, affiliations, customs and loyalties behind. As a consequence, the receiving community may feel alarmed at the influx of foreign cultures. If this is added to feelings of unfair resource allocation, the solidarities, mutualities and familiarities on which social, civic and political stability depends may become fragmented. Therefore, a probationary period during which welfare rights are restricted could be justified as a means of stressing to potential migrants the level of commitment they need to demonstrate if they choose to come.[7] This is primarily about national cultures, not racial ones; it should apply as much to Brits emigrating to the Costa del Sol.

There are two counter-arguments to RCM we need to mention. If culture is important, the above distinction between nation and race is fragile. With ethnicity being a crucial component of human identity, to suggest that indigenous national cultures have a de facto veto on migration policy is to risk collapsing the categories of 'nation', 'race' and 'culture' into one another. Proponents of RCM are aware of this, but it is not clear whether they have done enough to exclude such illegitimacy from their model. For example, Miller (2005, p 204) proposes that precedence should be given to those 'whose cultural values are closer to those of the existing population', but that race and sex *do not* count as relevant criteria. Yet it is just not obvious that this emphasis on national cultural values will always hold the line Miller wants it to hold if the character of the 'existing population' is the relevant arbiter.

RCM also risks treating cultures as delicate entities liable to shatter without strong protection. National identity in most countries like Britain is historically dynamic, pluralistic and indeed *dependent* on the new energies, perspectives and cultures of those who come to settle from elsewhere (Davies, 1999, pp 870-1; Parekh, 2000, pp 230-6). Chapters Six to Eight defended a paternalism that seeks to enable rather than prohibit and perhaps migration policy requires a similar principle, where people are given the resources to manage changes in social identities rather than being encouraged to fear the otherness that cultures must embrace if they are not to desiccate and shrivel. This means ensuring that resources are sufficient to go round. We should not obsess about cultural tensions when the real problem is the scarcity of the resources around which those tensions become manifest. (We return to this later.)

Where does this leave us? A far as points 1 to 3 of the fairness hypothesis are concerned, the empirical evidence is perhaps inconclusive. It is true that the depressive effects of cultural diversification on welfare spending are noted by some, but this may be because the former's economic and non-economic benefits have not yet worked their way through the culture (Putnam, 2007, pp 159-65). Something interesting happens at the social theoretical level, however. Points 1 to 3 are supported by advocates of RCM so, if we agree with them, we have a prima facie reason to debate the merits of points 4 and 5. Furthermore, when proponents of ROM like Legrain and Kukathas suggest that state welfare needs a radical rethink, we may indeed conclude that welfare rights cannot continue in their current form. Legrain advocates the restriction of welfare entitlements as a practical necessity, while Kukathas retains the basics of the fairness hypothesis (points 1 and 2) but seeks to invert its implications (challenging point 3).

Does this mean that points 1 and 2 should be accepted and, if we judge Kukathas to be taking too radical a step, point 3 as well? Not quite. By building on counter-arguments introduced earlier, this chapter will argue that we should not be diverted by migration issues to the extent that Miller and colleagues have allowed themselves to become. It will then propose that arguments for two-tiered entitlement are dependent on certain social preconditions being in place if they are to possess any cogency whatsoever. Finally, it will suggest that the trade-off proposed by Kukathas ('rethink welfare instead of migration') is not as severe as he imagines. To see why, we first need to explore the fairness hypothesis as it relates more directly to matters of citizenship and cultural integration.

Citizenship and culture

As well as pertaining to migration policy (who qualifies for entry into a country and why), the fairness hypothesis relates to issues of citizenship and cultural integration (what are the rights and responsibilities of diverse communities within national borders?). Social policies typically attempt to effect what might be called 'universalism plus'. Universalism of provision and access is thought to be necessary for reasons of equality and solidarity, though a totally blind universalism may be socially *exclusive* (Williams, 1989). Within a universalist framework, sensitisations to particular contexts and interests have been implemented. This can imply tests of needs, income, work and so on and the provision of additional resources to certain groups and categories. For advocates of the fairness hypothesis, a citizenship test is a legitimate addition (points 3 to 5). For some on the right, this is justified if a clear sense of national identity and belonging is to be preserved. Others on the left meanwhile may feel it necessary in order to *defend* communal diversity.

There are two recent contributions to this debate that need to be examined so that we can properly appreciate what is at stake here. Both raise concerns about the erosive implications of communal and cultural diversity, maintaining that unless we are careful a laissez-faire attitude to social integration will finish the job, started by the free market right, of discrediting the social democratic welfare state.

Welfare on the defensive

Dench et al (2006) are among those who point an accusing finger at state welfare. In the immediate post-war years, they observe, the welfare state was based on principles of solidarity, desert and family unity, which promised a New Jerusalem occupied by those who had visibly earned its benefits. Sometime in the late 1960s, however, this began to change. Solidarity was replaced with a catch-all universalism, desert was displaced by 'need' and family gave way to a centrally and bureaucratically managed individualism. In the context of migration and ethnicity, this has fuelled racial tension, distrust and urban deprivation. But the blame for this lies not with the white working class or ethnic minorities but with a something-for-nothing culture of individual entitlement that ignores values of community, family and participative citizenship.

This has been a high profile piece of research that draws attention to debilitating sea changes in post-war reform (particularly the decline of social insurance, the rise of means testing and the demise of class politics) and to possible deficiencies in the management of welfare services. However, Dench and colleagues follow those such as Halsey et al (2000) and Field (2003) in drawing heavily on a communitarian, underclass discourse about which we should be wary. Three principal criticisms can be made (cf. Bourne, 2006).

First, their account of these changes is highly assumptive and impressionistic, lacking much by way of depth, counter-argument or data triangulation. For instance, although they take themselves to be swimming against the orthodoxy, their diagnosis and prescriptions (revive communal values and make welfare more conditional) have dominated government thinking since at least 1979. Their unwillingness to analyse what might be wrong with this social philosophy – one they seem to regard as having been miraculously dispelled by the 'new political elite' (Dench et al, 2006, p 218) (liberal lefties and welfare bureaucrats, apparently) – contributes to the lack of argumentative balance. Theirs is a concern with 'the moral economy'; the neoliberal economy barely registers. So although they acknowledge the role played by scarcities in welfare provision, this is rarely allowed to qualify their hostility towards the principle of need. And while social insurance schemes have eroded, to attribute this to the 'triumph' of left libertarianism, hostile to the entire notion of reciprocal contributions, is bizarre (Dench et al, 2006, pp 106, 207).

Second, their reliance on something resembling rational actor theory lends their analysis a curious 'a-cultural' flavour. They need this framework to attribute responsibility for failures of integration to welfare systems and not to individuals or group solidarities. Bangladeshis, they claim, are rightly dismissive of 'state charity' but behave perfectly rationally in taking advantage of it and so cannot be blamed for the dependency thereby created. But this rationalistic analysis allows them to avoid any sociocultural critique. Liberals, they declare (without any supporting evidence), are quick to accuse working-class people of racism to justify failed policies; but in this rush to wipe racism from the picture, Dench and colleagues' analysis lacks precision and consistency. For instance, in the course of four pages they swing from maintaining that racial hostility '*does not require* a psychological interpretation' to saying that it is about '*more than* personal pathologies' (Dench et al, 2006, pp 183-7; italics added). They are willing to attribute white resentment towards Bangladeshis to misperception, myth and rumour, but similar antagonism towards state welfare is given a nodding affirmation. Policy makers and practitioners are, by contrast, offered no voice at all.

Finally, family and community are presented both as deep sources of identity *and* as fragile entities that services free at the point of use have managed to destabilise. Like cultural conservatives, Dench et al (2006, pp 97, 106-7, 118-9) leap from observing that the state offers *alternatives* to family/community support, to asserting that the state thereby *undermines* family and community, hence their presumption that state welfare leads to family breakdown, rather than enabling family diversification (see Chapter Eight). To what extent should we make kinship and community affiliation the bedrock of society if it is really true that entitlements to impoverished housing and means-tested benefits can so easily undermine such bonds? Is the solution to weaken those entitlements further? Do the loving arms of relatives and neighbours really only open when there is an anti-welfare state? Or is this assumed line of causation running from state welfare to family/community too simplistic?

Another, not dissimilar, critique comes from Goodhart (2006, p 16; cf. Pathak, 2007) whose thesis can be stated briefly:

> ... the more different we become from one another – the more diverse our ways of life and our religious and ethnic backgrounds – and the less we share a moral consensus or

> a sense of fellow feeling, the less happy we will be in the
> long run to support a generous welfare state.

Among his policy solutions, Goodhart recommends a more overt
contract with migrants in the form of welfare conditionality, a revival of
insurance contributions and giving greater visibility to the probationary
period during which new arrivals do not qualify for full political and
welfare rights. Goodhart regards solidarity and diversity as a zero-sum
game and argues that we must rein back on the latter in order that the
former can revive from the weakened state he considers it to be in.
Progressive integration and nationalism are needed to preserve state
welfare while warding off the threat of the far right.

Goodhart, though, provides little support for this zero-sum reading.
Other than relying on Dench and colleagues, several polls and focus
groups that do not seem to have queried popular myths or media
panics, and research that applies to the USA at best (see Taylor-Gooby,
2005), there is remarkably little evidence to justify the strenuousness
or urgency of Goodhart's thesis. Ultimately, the 'solidarity or diversity'
trade-off is a simplistic depiction of a complex picture. Solidarity is just
one of the many values that state welfare is meant to embody (others
including justice, security and economic growth) and is generated by
a wider series of attachments than just national ones. The welfare state
has historically *utilised diversity*, in order to reconstruct and revitalise
social, civic and moral solidarities, rather than suppressing it (Sassen,
1999, Chs 5-6). Solidarity is crucial and diversity has to reconfigure
rather than dissolve social bonds, but Goodhart's dichotomised analysis
obscures more than it illuminates.

Dench et al and Goodhart make some interesting points (one of
which we return to below), but as a generalised condemnation of
approaches to citizenship and social integration the charge does not
stick. Should we therefore reject points 3 to 5 or are there more
cogent accounts to be found? Although it is possible to envisage other
targets, much of the sound and fury accompanying these debates
has zeroed in on multiculturalism. The objection is that that both in
principle and practice multiculturalism has failed to deliver the level
of integration into, and identification with, a national community
that is required for social cohesion. Having explored multiculturalism
elsewhere (for example, Fitzpatrick, 2005a, pp 192-8), only a summary
of that discussion is offered here in order to concentrate on its specific
relationship to state welfare. But let's first be clear what we are talking
about.

Multiculturalism does not equate to cultural separatism and relativism. Can it categorically be asserted that no advocates of the former have defended the latter? No. But to characterise anything in the terms laid down by some of its loopier defenders is hardly reasonable. What gets criticised (and less frequently defended) as multiculturalism is often a caricature. Sen (2006, pp 156-60; cf. Giddens, 2007, pp 153-7) terms this caricature 'plural monoculturalism', implying not the creative interaction of cultures but a federation of separate, homogeneous traditions, each defined in terms of singular identities. Britain contains both successful and ineffective examples of multiculturalism, but to treat the concept as equivalent to separatism and relativism may be a way of applauding the 'national monoculturalism' of the French, civic republican model without having to examine *its* deficiencies in any depth. Instead, multiculturalism should be thought of as the fact of cultural diversity, both within and between communities, which is treated as making or potentially making a positive contribution to the societies within which it is found, and which may therefore require policies of special recognition and support for various groupings.

There are many possible versions of multiculturalism depending on how these elements are balanced and interpreted (Kelly, 2002). Equally, there are many ways of criticising multiculturalism that accept large swathes of all them. Critics like Okin (1999), Barry (2001) and Miller (1999, pp 261-4), for instance, accept the fact of diversity and no doubt believe in its potential for positive contributions. What they doubt is whether liberalism requires much more than equal treatment and fair procedures for all – although Okin and Miller (2000, pp 53-61; 2002) advocate feminist and republican perspectives, respectively. To define our identities as predominantly cultural leads us down a blind alley, they say, both because 'culture' is a notoriously slippery term and because attempts to pin it down invariably lead to a homogenisation of culture and of identity. Cultural identity risks leaving individuals in group-specific silos and so, ironically, makes it harder to envisage cultural interaction. A common but also pluralised conception of citizenship is already offered by liberalism, which therefore does not need multiculturalism. Multiculturalism may not be *equivalent* to separatism, but the former certainly contains embryos of the latter.

Have we therefore now received the generalised critique that Dench and colleagues and Goodhart could not supply? Not all of multiculturalism's critics would support points 3 to 5 (although some would); they might indeed contend that by reifying group identity it is multiculturalism itself that invites such a divisive backlash. That said, Miller (2006, p 332) cites research where 58% of respondents support providing welfare to migrants only if they 'demonstrate commitment to the country'. Miller uses such evidence not to reject multiculturalism per se but only those radical versions of it that separate diversity from integration. A 'moderate multiculturalism' would provide special treatment to cultural groups only when it demonstrably assists integration into the 'wider community'.

This returns us to the 'precedence problem' noted above where, in respect of migration, Miller believes that precedence should be given to those whose cultural values are closer to those of the existing population. This is risky proposition, for if by cultural values we mean values expressed by an indigenous population, we risk pandering to some unsavoury attitudes. If, however, we mean values to which we aspire, and sometimes manage to demonstrate, we are left with a degree of contestability that the notion of *precedence* cannot capture. Should we exclude non-Christians because most of the country (even atheists) shares Christian values; or should precedence refer to the religious *pluralism* that enabled Britain to emerge relatively unscathed from the religious wars of the 16th and 17th centuries? What is this 'wider community', exactly? Miller (2006, pp 334-5) cites negative perceptions of cultural diversity in arguing for a moderate multiculturalism. While we must take account of such negativity, however, there is a difference between fighting against such perceptions and pandering to them.

So while the cultural identity objection is certainly worth attending to, it all depends on how 'thick' or 'thin' we interpret the cultural waters in which we swim. Earlier work (Fitzpatrick, 2005a, pp 192-8) has critiqued those communitarians and postmodernists who regard the cultural environment as quite dense, opaque and viscous, some of whom go on to support multiculturalism (Parekh, 2000) and some of whom do not (Rorty, 1998). But whatever the direction taken, such 'thick' interpretations risk the homogenisation noted above. But rather than either reject or dilute multiculturalism as, respectively, Barry and Miller advocate, Phillips (2007) has shown that it can be based on thin conceptions of culture. This means abandoning cultural determinism and viewing people everywhere as shaped by cultures that are themselves the product of individual agency and so rife with complexity, tension and pluralism. Phillips has not provided the last word in this thick/thin debate, a distinction that may never be subject to final calibration, but she does establish that it is possible to defend a politics of recognition and special support to an extent that multiculturalism's critics are not willing to countenance.

Trade-offs, politics and insurance

We have therefore explored a series of critiques about citizenship, social integration and cultural diversity, designed to support a strong emphasis on national identity and belonging, and found none of them especially convincing. But even if we do prefer multiculturalism, does this necessarily rule out points 3 to 5 of the fairness hypothesis? Perhaps a probationary period of partial entitlement for recent arrivals is necessary if people are to eventually accept and value the national, religious and ethnic diversities that those arrivals add to British life. (This is not necessarily about restricting immigration, since some advocates of ROM, like Legrain, support partial entitlement.) Is there any evidence for making this case?

To date, the most extensive discussion of state welfare in relation to multiculturalism has been provided by Banting and Kymlicka (2006). They outline two trade-offs. The 'heterogeneity/redistribution trade-off' maintains that ethnic diversity undermines redistributive policies. If people do not feel connected to one another, the reasoning goes, they will be reluctant to fund services for each another. The 'recognition/redistribution trade-off' states that a concern with the politics of recognition and difference drains attention and energy away from a politics of redistribution (Fraser and Honneth, 2003). If these trade-offs are real, perhaps support for redistribution requires that people visibly qualify for membership of the polity and that might necessitate either a probationary period or some equivalent alternative.

But the contributors to Banting and Kymlicka (2006) propose not so much that those trade-offs have no purchase, more that they are over-generalised. Redistribution *can* be undermined by diversity and a politics of recognition but more importantly *there is no inherent logic at work*. Multiculturalism may threaten trust and solidarity, but it may equally support them. There are too many factors to justify simplistic generalisations, much depending on how multiculturalism is made to work (Schierup et al, 2006, p 252). (It is an anti-multiculturalist polemic that could make it harder to preserve social trust and solidarity.) If those trade-offs capture much of what is at stake in the fairness hypothesis do we now have reason to reject the hypothesis in its entirety?

The answer is, not really. Banting and Kymlicka might be wary of attributing an inherent logic to multiculturalism, but they leave open the possibility that, whether for reasons of poor management, communication, scarce resources or a combination of these and other local factors, multicultural practices may sometimes malfunction. So while we should not raise the fairness hypothesis to the status of a commandment, neither should we entirely reject it.

This is all very well, but does it mean that we at least have reason to reject points 4 and 5? As noted earlier, Banting et al (2006, pp 79-81) report that rapid immigration exerts downward pressure on social spending. However, they and Crepaz (2006, p 113) find that this is then counteracted by an *upward pressure in those countries operating strong multicultural policies* – in other words, the latter maintain and indeed strengthen relations of trust and solidarity. There are two ways of interpreting this with regard to points 4 and 5. One is to observe with Legrain (2006, p 254-7) that if multiculturalism is successful in this respect, it is because even countries operating strong multicultural policies retain restrictions on welfare entitlements for new arrivals (Sigg et al, 2002, p 212; see also Sainsbury, 2006). In short, partial entitlements *are* necessary if multiculturalism is to be pro-redistributive.

There is another interpretation, which is to observe that such partiality makes social integration harder by marking some out as second-class citizens. Access to welfare services is required in order for everyone to perform the tasks of social participation that we demand from one another. Without sufficient public goods and social resources, individuals are hamstrung and unable to participate fully in national life. Without benefit entitlements, for instance, many migrants will be less able to survive and negotiate the hazards of low-wage labour markets and so more likely to remain at the margins of the economy. The fairness hypothesis has therefore got things the wrong way round. We cannot delay the provision of full welfare rights until we are satisfied that immigrants have passed certain tests *because inclusive participation will not occur without access to the very rights which are integral to national life.*

On the one hand, partial entitlements might therefore assist multiculturalism to maintain upward pressure on social spending and support for redistribution. On the other hand, they might feed hostility towards second-class 'others' and so hamper social participation and cultural interaction. Is there any way of resolving this impasse?

As noted earlier, Dench and colleagues and Goodhart both lamented the decline (in Britain) of social insurance, the principle that common risks should be commonly pooled and that an upper tranche of welfare entitlements have to be earned by paying contributions into that pool. Why this principle declined in Britain is a story for another time but it has undoubtedly weakened the inclusivity of state welfare. We have expanded selectivist and punitive measures without the ladder-climbing, solidarity-inducing incentives that social insurance schemes can provide at their best. True, much depends on their design (Kreiger,

2003). Social insurance can entrench socioeconomic inequalities and needs to factor in participative activities (especially caring) that go beyond paid work; it has also been argued elsewhere that minimum welfare entitlements still need to be fairly generous (Fitzpatrick, 1999, 2005a; see also Bay and Pedersen, 2006). In short, and as noted earlier, we should not apply culturalist analyses to social conflicts when much of the blame lies with a scarcity of economic resources and political empowerment. That said, properly designed social insurance could stress what anti-multiculturalists want to be stressed (solidarities through civic participation and interaction) without marking out either minority communities or recent arrivals as 'problem populations'.[8]

So should we restrict the welfare rights of recent migrants? No. But by instituting upward steps of contributory insurance (keeping in mind the qualifications just made), perhaps we can bolster support for redistributive solidarity, inspiring new synergies between diversity and trust, recognition and redistribution and even class and ethnicity (Carens, 2000, p 14; 2005), without the exclusionary and discriminatory obsessions, directed towards ethnocultural others, that have poisoned the atmosphere of recent public debates (Rex, 2004).

In short, any potential clash over cultural diversity should be contextualised by just distributions of socioeconomic resources and primary goods. Much of the recent sound and fury accompanying debates about migration and inclusive (multicultural) citizenship occurs within a neoliberal context of social inequality and public scarcity. Get rid of the context and the tone of those debates can change. This is not to claim that cultural and ethnic tensions are dissolved by social equality – given the recent experiences of countries like the Netherlands (Nannestad, 2004) – but it is to claim that we should not be mesmerised by the former either.

The fairness hypothesis therefore has its basis in what people do and should expect of one another as inhabitants of the same social space. Points 1 and 2 capture widespread intuitions about the reasonableness of what White (2003) calls 'the civic minimum'. But, points 3 to 5 take us into dangerous territory where a distinction between British and non-British is ossified. We may indeed feel it necessary to have upward steps of welfare entitlements through contributory insurance. These could address some of the fears many people have about rapid social change without either pandering to them or using them as justifications for new forms of exclusion in a mobile, globalising environment.

Global justice

One question has been left hanging in the air. How open or closed should migration policies actually be? As we saw above, one argument for ROM is that it is an effective means of redistributing from affluent to developing countries. But the following discussion concentrates on a more fundamental issue, as it seems that we need some idea of *how much* redistribution to effect before we can properly decide on the means of doing so. It will be assumed that we *should* be redistributing resources globally without analysing this assumption (see Nussbaum, 2006, pp 264-70).[9]

Instead, we will concern ourselves with two questions:

- Does global redistribution require a principle of symmetry?
- How demanding is global redistribution?

These questions are designed to shed light on the final ethical question of this book.

> **To what extent is global justice in tension with (domestic) welfare states?**

First, we need to consider what the 'principle of symmetry' is. Robert Goodin (2002a, p 565) offers a blunt definition:

> If the rich countries do not want to let foreigners in, then the very least they must do is send much more money to compensate them for their being kept out.

Let's assume that x is the sum of y and z. The principle of symmetry is neutral between the respective values of y and z, merely insisting that they should always yield x. You are allowed to have more y and less z, or vice versa, so long as x is always the result. If x stands for given amount of resources to be redistributed globally, y stands for migration from developing to affluent countries and z stands for (let's say) foreign aid from affluent to developing countries, the principle pictures inward migration and foreign aid as counterbalances on scales designed to redistribute resources. As long as x is yielded, it doesn't matter whether you have massive aid and modest migration, or massive migration and modest aid, or any number of middle-way alternatives. Of course, if migration and aid are both unpopular with western electorates, we might decide to reduce the value of x to make them more palatable;

however, doing so may violate the normative obligations to be debated shortly.

So does global redistribution require a principle of symmetry? If mass immigration is unpopular, should we raise foreign aid to compensate?[10] If so, by how much? If aid is unpopular, are we obligated to open our borders more? To address these questions, we need to envisage the reasons why we might wish to violate the principle.

Figure 11.1: The principles of symmetry and asymmetry

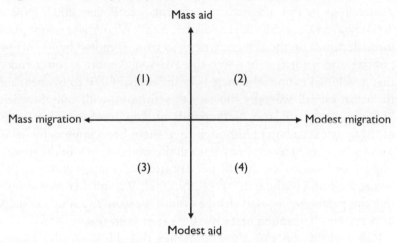

Take Figure 11.1. For obvious reasons the principle of symmetry applies to quadrants (2) and (3). There are in addition two zones of 'asymmetry'.

In quadrant (1), we would favour massive migration *and* aid. Why? Perhaps because the value of x should be so high that it cannot be satisfied by a y/z counterbalance. Imagine that we had completely open borders so that potentially tens of millions of people a year were migrating to the west. This might still not solve global poverty (for instance, some developing countries might collapse due to a massive brain drain) such that rather than reduce foreign aid, as the principle of symmetry suggests, *we ought to raise it further.*

In quadrant (4), we favour modest migration and aid, perhaps because we determine the value of x to be actually quite low. Maybe we are not to blame for conditions in developing countries or maybe we can discharge our compensatory obligations at a fairly low level. We don't need to counterbalance y and z because we can yield x easily enough without having to devise trade-offs between them.

The principle of symmetry therefore seems appropriate for scenarios where our obligations are high but not so high that they are potentially unrealistic (quadrant (1)) and where we have to be sensitive to the needs and interests of affluent populations though not to the extent that the bar is set so low we imagine we have relatively little to do (quadrant (4)). It all seems to hinge on how high or low x should be.

This brings us to our second question: how demanding is global redistribution? Let us consider three options to help tackle this issue: minimum demandingness, medium demandingness and maximum demandingness (for alternative treatments, see Pogge, 2002; Dower, 2003; Satz, 2003, pp 629-37; LaFollette, 2005). All of these might place more demands on the affluent west than those imposed by its current policies and priorities. In 1969, the Pearson Report recommended that developed countries donate 0.7% of annual GDP to overseas aid. In fact, most fall woefully short of this amount, with only Sweden, Norway, Denmark, the Netherlands and Luxembourg currently meeting or exceeding it. Although there have been improvements in some indicators in recent years, it is still the case that 19% of the world's population exist on less than $1 per day and 10.5 million children died before their fifth birthday in 2004 (UN, 2007). We will therefore assume that this paradigm needs to change even if we were to adopt a strategy of minimum demandingness only. Let's start with that.

Rawls (1999, pp 113-20) exemplifies this thinking (also Miller, 2000, pp 172-9; Arthur, 2005). This is surely something of a surprise. Presumably the Rawlsian difference principle applies to the global context as well? If we make decisions about principles of justice behind a veil of ignorance, shouldn't this also exclude knowledge of our nationality? And wouldn't we then define the 'least well-off' in global and not just domestic terms such that we have an obligation to effect some degree of global equality (Beitz, 2000; Buchanan, 2000)? Yet Rawls does not go down this road.

First, he is basically a prioritarian (Fitzpatrick, 2005a, pp 33-8) in that once the least advantaged are able to live worthwhile lives, the remaining gap between rich and poor matters less. In terms of global justice, once people have a 'working liberal or decent government', no further redistribution is warranted. Second, for Rawls, justice implies fairness and fairness implies a large degree of independence and self-determination. To impose strong egalitarian requirements on countries risks undermining that independence. The need for harmony amid global diversity demands that we recognise the many different ways in which people can choose to live together. Of course, this will often imply liberal constitutions and democratic polities but it is also possible to imagine people content to live in benign hierarchical nations (highly religious ones, perhaps) and we need to make room for that possibility. Strong, global egalitarianism risks destabilising that divergent harmony.

Is this convincing? Rawls notes that a global redistributive egalitarianism can only be cogent if there is a cut-off point. To advocate endless redistribution is tantamount to proposing that egalitarianism ultimately demands an absolute global equality of outcomes, which hardly seems reasonable. This is a persuasive observation, since, after all, egalitarians wrestle with the question of whether and when illegitimate inequalities (requiring intervention) give way to legitimate inequalities (where no intervention seems justified). But can Rawls' goal (the 'political autonomy of free and equal liberal or decent peoples') provide that cut-off point?[11]

How many countries achieve this liberal or decent standard? We might propose that few do, as only a few countries have come close to eliminating poverty and we might claim that this is a condition of being 'liberal or decent'. Applying this criterion to global relations might then make it harder to achieve the divergent harmony that Rawls regards as vital. So perhaps we ought to allow that 'liberal or decent' standards are consistent with relatively high levels of poverty in a country like the UK where over 20% of children are poor on widely accepted measures. But if this is the case, the difference principle really does cease to matter and the attractiveness, and indeed the distinctiveness, of Rawlsian liberalism is undermined. Rawls' philosophy of minimum demandingness therefore appears too undemanding.

And what of maximum demandingness? Unger (1996) and Singer (1993, Ch 8; 2002b) have offered a compelling defence. We already know what this is. Both are consequentialists who believe there is no fundamental difference between killing and letting die. Unger (2006, pp 24–36) puts it in the following way. The owner of a vintage sedan is out driving and comes across an injured man who needs hospitalisation. However, he is bleeding so profusely that the sedan's upholstery will be damaged and need replacing at a cost of $5,000. The driver drives on. The man is picked up later and loses a leg that might otherwise have been saved. Was the driver's behaviour reprehensible? Certainly. Now imagine that a charity asks you to donate $100 in order to save the lives of 30 children. You do not do so. Was your refusal reprehensible? Some of us would say no, some yes, but even most of the latter might hesitate to treat your behaviour as equivalent to that of the driver. Yet your failure involved far less money and far more injury than the driver's.

In other words, according to Unger/Singer, our moral intuitions are far more self-serving than we like to believe. There are surely many reasons we give to distinguish between the above scenarios – the driver's obligation seems more visible and direct, and you do not *intend* the deaths of 30 children (though you foresaw that they might die) – but strict consequentialists insist that we must attend to the effects of our actions *and non-actions*. Therefore, your behaviour is actually *more* reprehensible than the driver's.

We will not dwell on this kind of argument, since we have covered the DDE enough in previous chapters (Dower, 2003, pp 646-9). For instance, if consequences are important, we might invoke those that follow from the above argument. If I have an obligation to help those who need help, there is apparently no end to this. What if the first request for $100 is followed by another? And then another and another? Presumably if lives can be saved, obligations on receiving the *n*th request for a donation remain as strong as they were at the first one. Indeed, I might only be able to legitimately refuse to hand over $100 when it is my last remaining money and any donation will lead to *my* death – so leaving me unable to help others in the future. Perhaps instead of this iterative approach, we need an aggregative one, a point beyond which I can legitimately refuse to help, even if further requests arrive and even if I could still help, since I will already have done my bit.

Such is the proposal of Cullity (2004) (see also Scanlon, 1998, pp 224-5; Hooker, 1999, pp 179-81), whose contribution to the debate might be described as one of *medium* demandingness (Wellman, 2005). If those like Unger and Singer believe we have an obligation to be more altruistic, this can only be up to the point where we assist others to be altruistic too, Cullity insists. If it is wrong to lead a non-altruistically focused life, I have no obligation to assist others to lead that kind of life (Cullity, 2004, Ch 8). I have an obligation to provide those in developing nations with the conditions necessary for leading an altruistically focused life, but no more. To put it crudely, I owe you the basics of a reasonable life, but not those resources you will use to buy non-essential commodities. This obligation is higher than that proposed by Rawls (by looking beyond national boundaries to cosmopolitan, cross-border needs and decencies), but lower than that proposed by Unger/Singer.

In truth, Cullity (2004, pp 174-86) is not much help when it comes to translating this philosophical obligation into practical specifics[12] – and anyway his analysis is pitched at the level of personal rather than collective obligation. For some assistance we can in fact turn back to Singer. Singer is receptive to the idea that we have to adapt ourselves to humanity's moral 'imperfectability' in that we will probably never achieve what the ideal of maximum demandingness lays down. So whereas in 1972 he was talking about considerable (though unspecified) amounts of redistribution (2002c, p 578), by the early 1990s this had reduced to a more manageable recommendation that 10% of income in the affluent world should go to assisting the globally impoverished (1993, pp 245 6). By the early 21st century, he mentions 1% as necessary to eliminate global poverty (2002a, pp 191-5; Pogge, 2002, pp 609-11, also 2008, p 306, n 333).

Singer's is a pragmatic stance: there is no point in asking so much of people that few donate and so we end up receiving less than if our demands were more modest. That said, the 1% figure is based on a UN definition of poverty that is quite minimalist; according to White (2001, p 346), 'Taking just 1% from rich countries ... reduces the number of poor from 1.3 billion to 1.1 billion'. A more generous conception of poverty would require more global redistribution and so higher percentages of income donated.

We might, for instance, prefer a capabilities approach, which, borrowing more from virtuism than it does from either contractualism or consequentialism, begins with the dignity of every human being.[13] Wellbeing implies a diverse array of capabilities by which resources may be converted into a functioning and flourishing life (Nussbaum and Sen, 1993; Nussbaum, 2006). These 'capabilities' are intended to be universal descriptors that nevertheless permit cross-cultural variations. Among them are being able to live a life of normal length; possess bodily health and integrity; cultivate and express imagination and thought; form emotional attachments; form and pursue a conception of the good; interact and be respected by others; relate to the natural environment; play and enjoy; and have some control over one's political and material circumstances. In short, the capabilities approach is more ambitious that the minimalist definition of poverty Singer derives from the UN, but could hopefully be operationalised in such a way that we are not committed to an open-ended series of redistributive donations. In other words, it potentially provides a Rawlsian cut-off point (Crocker, 2002).

So, here we have the intriguing possibility of a medium demandingness drawing on Singer's pragmatic consequentialism and a virtuist capabilities approach to supply a Rawls-inspired cut-off point for global egalitarian redistribution. It implies redistribution of more than 1% of affluent countries annual income but probably no more than 10%, on Singer's estimate, and possibly much less (depending on the level of commitment 'capabilities' translate into).

Two implications follow from this. First, we have no compelling reasons to abandon the principle of symmetry in the direction of either quadrants (1) or (4) – although in the light of the previous discussion, we might see the principle as swinging closer to (4) than to (1). This does not mean we should adhere rigidly to the principle   Goodin (2002a, p 569) notes that 'differential treatment' can be justified because there may be times when it is prudent to restrict migration without increasing aid to compensate – but that it is needed as a regulative ideal. The principle suggests that the question 'how much migration?' occurs at a secondary stage, dependent on a prior question about the extent of our globally redistributive obligations. Arguing for less migration does not get you off the moral hook, although the above discussion also suggests that our obligations are considerable without being bankrupting.

Second, to what extent is global justice in tension with (domestic) welfare states? ('Domestic' is bracketed here to distinguish this issue from those who call for a global welfare state (Townsend, 2002).) Any answer to this is inevitably political and contested. The UK in 2006 had a gross national income (GNI) of about £1,300 billion and was spending £5 billion on development assistance (excluding debt relief), or 0.38% of GNI. The key question for the future is 'how high should assistance go and how fast?', for which we might postulate three options:[14]

1. We can aim high but go slowly in order to minimise disruption to existing spending commitments.
2. We can aim lower but go quickly in order to reach the cut-off point relatively soon.
3. We can effect some compromise between 1 and 2.

This contrasts with maximum demandingness – 'aim high, go quickly' – or minimum demandingness – 'aim low, go slowly'.

The virtue of option 1 is that is more likely to carry popular support but may cost lives that would otherwise have been saved with a faster rate of assistance growth. The virtue of option 2 is that it addresses global deprivation more rapidly but, by exceeding GNI growth, either eats into other forms of expenditure or requires potentially unpopular tax rises, or both. Imagine we prefer option 3 and that this implies aid of, say, 3%. At current rates of assistance growth, the UK would reach this level around 2051. If we doubled the rate, we could reach this about 2030. This would require an annual increase of £2 billion a year (in 2006 figures) and seems manageable in terms of existing national income and expenditure. So whereas in 2006, 3% of GNI, representing £39 billion (or 6.6% of public expenditure), would present considerable problems in how to find the resources, ascending to that threshold over two or three decades seems more realistic, allowing time for adjustments to spending commitments to be anticipated and implemented.

This is not to deny there are substantial hurdles to overcome. Dedicating 6% or more of public expenditure to overseas aid means that something has to give somewhere, even with a lead-in time of more than two decades. Do we redirect social expenditure, private consumption or some mix of the two? Global justice cannot be pain-free or free of political considerations.

Conclusion

In any event, and on the above assumptions, *there is no inherent tension between welfare states and making large strides towards global justice*. Political conflict, difficult decisions and managerial challenges there may be, but there is nothing to suggest that we have to substantially rethink existing institutions and objectives, still less dismantle them. As with the earlier discussion about migration, we have obligations to the wider world, but not ones that need cause us to panic. We need a fairer and more equal distribution of global resources, but this process has to be managed if we are to be both ambitious and effective. It would be easy to demand an overnight redistribution of affluence and comforting to lambaste the selfish west for every day it fails to do so. Yet at its best state welfare has proven itself in the past to be a reasonably effective vehicle for social progress. If we are to promote the cause of global justice, we are better off investigating where the compatibilities and consistencies lie than indulging in anti-state welfare rhetoric.

We already know where the latter takes us, don't we? And you don't think it's towards greater distributive equality, do you?

Notes

[1] Some may worry that to state things in these terms is dangerous, in that it risks implying that migrants are a 'problem to be solved' (for example, Sales, 2007, p 157). There are obvious hazards to be avoided here. However, such commentators themselves make connections between migration and 'citizenship issues' where multiculturalism plays a large role (Sales, 2007, pp 106-15, 176-80; see also Entzinger, 2006).

[2] There are several caveats here. First, we are not dealing with those making temporary visits or with the descendants of migrants. Nor are we concerned with asylum seeking, as this deserves a related but much lengthier discussion. This chapter deals with the sharing of global resources and is not meant to be a comprehensive discussion of migration and so forth. Second, and similarly, it is not the intention to provide a critique of existing policies, such as the existing 'public funds' rule governing entry into Britain. It also needs to be noted that very few migrants receive benefits. Third, in an atmosphere where 'culture' is often a proxy for 'race', we need to ensure that our analysis does not breathe the same air. This means acknowledging the fact of ethnic tension without treating 'ethnicity' as synonymous with 'immigration'. We will therefore assume that all British nationals have the same entitlements, whatever their ethnicity or origin of birth, while exploring whether all recent non-national migrants should have limited entitlements – again, whatever their ethnicity or origin of birth. By 'recent migrants' is therefore meant all non-nationals who reside in Britain regardless of their eligibility for British nationality. Finally, we will not explore how any probationary period would work, that is, how people would qualify for full welfare rights.

[3] For a conservative analysis, see Coleman and Rowthorn (2004).

[4] The logic here is that if people have chosen to come here, why do they deserve additional assistance? Note that Banting and colleagues add an important qualification mentioned later.

[5] We ought to be careful here, of course. A probationary, transitional period of qualification needs to be considered on its own merits and not because of frustration with those who have either illegally entered the country or illegally remained.

[6] There are two qualifications to this. First, these commentators are generous in their attitude towards asylum seekers and would not wish to limit their numbers. Second, while proposing that national borders be 'relatively' closed, what this implies in practice can vary from commentator to commentator and may even translate into *more* migration than currently prevails. In short, it would be mistaken to depict the following arguments as akin to ultra-nationalism (but for a harder-edged position, see Browne (2002)).

[7] Note that most migrants are ignorant of the welfare rights of the country they are travelling to and there is little evidence of welfare migration/tourism (Ennew, 2006).

[8] This adds another strand to the research agenda: to what extent does the principle of social insurance either assist or impede the high levels of social trust that are associated with successful multiculturalism?

[9] Is this about correcting past injustices? Addressing needs? Some other alternative? See Satz (2003) and LaFollette (2003). For a view that we have no obligations additional to domestic ones, see Kekes (2002).

[10] Foreign aid is used as an example of z merely for illustrative purposes.

[11] This is a slight misquote, since Rawls (1999, p 118) suddenly speaks of 'liberal *and* decent' (my italics) — a typographical error, perhaps?

[12] Nor does Cullity discuss this logic when applied to domestic social justice goals.

[13] For other virtuist analyses, see Slote (2005) and, for a more conservative take, Cohen (2005), whose position is one of minimum demandingness.

[14] For an interesting overview of possible alternatives, see Glaser (2006). What follows is merely meant to be indicative. Note that 3% represents an aid budget designed to help humans per se. The question of what we need to do additionally to preserve the environment is not one that is considered here, but presumably bears implications for domestic welfare states (Fitzpatrick and Cahill, 2002).

Epilogue

This book essentially turns on three basic claims.

The first is that while attention to the foundations of moral deliberation, insight and analysis is important, we do not yet possess a firm, comprehensive theory. The belief that God is the foundation of morality is only satisfying if you leave various awkward questions to one side; and although it seems that a naturalistic approach is the way to go, such naturalism is only credible if it takes proper account of humanity's socialised being and does not merely reduce the sociocultural to the natural. So although the book's aim is not to propose a full theory of social humanism, it has highlighted three principles that are surely crucial to it and to which we have returned selectively throughout: compatibilism (Chapters One, Three, Five and Ten), intersubjectivism (Chapters One, Three, Four, Five, Eight, Nine and Ten) and egalitarianism (Chapters Four, Five, Seven, Eight, Nine and Eleven).

Suspecting that a pluralistic, multi-perspective strategy is appropriate, the book spent some time outlining three of the most prominent normative philosophies of ethics. These are summarised in Chapter Five and there is nothing more to add here. Chapter Five also defended an eclectic, pragmatic but nevertheless rigorous conjunction of consequentialism, Kantianism/contractualism and virtuism, arguing that they can all combine the abstract and the commonsensical in critically reflective methods of analysis, and that they all touch base with social humanism in one respect or another. Figure 5.1 captures the second of this book's central claims.

The third is defended mainly in Chapters Six and Seven. Having established the relevance of those philosophies to applied ethics, we saw how various concepts, frameworks and premises have played out by investigating a series of specific questions that emerge at the place where applied ethics and social policy debates intersect. Of particular importance are the meaning, scope and implications of harm, the possible ways in which interactions between autonomy and paternalism can be interpreted, and the doctrine of double effect. The 'social context' outlined in Chapters Six and Seven was not intended to be thorough because the purpose was to recommend an 'environmental paternalism', that is, a paternalism more concerned with the justice of social conditions (what Rawls called society's basic structure) and with the *enabling* of individual agency and responsibility, rather than a heavy-handed management of personal attitudes, habits and behaviour.

As such, Chapter Six issues a cautionary warning about over-medicalising debates about 'bad habits'. Health and expenditure considerations should not be ignored, especially where harm to others is involved, but there is more to life than its prolongation. Chapter Seven argues that choice does not necessarily translate into 'market choice'; that it can imply forms of negotiation and information dissemination that avoids the corroding producer–consumer dichotomies of recent public sector reforms. Chapter Eight maintains that principles of autonomy and social justice apply to the family also, that a pluralistic approach to family policies is appropriate, one incorporating a 'critical autonomy', and that familial obligations do not start or end with the family itself. Chapters Nine and Ten then twin two debates about the beginnings and endings of life. In both cases, it is suggested that self-determination should be paramount as long as an actually-existing, independent human life is not harmed and as long as various safeguards are built into euthanasia policies. Finally, Chapter Eleven is something of an outlier but it seems important to ponder whether and to what extent the terms of policy debates are changing from the domestic to the global. It finds that worries about migration, cultural diversification and global injustice do not warrant an entirely new agenda for social policy, though much work remains to be done here, obviously.

This autonomy-respecting, environmental paternalism is consistent with a social, or perhaps an egalitarian, liberalism that has fallen out of favour over the past few decades. The mainstream right and left, in many countries though certainly not all, are content to regulate and perpetually monitor the experiential and the private. 'Liberty' is becoming less of an automatic reflex and more of an outdated reference point that we are surrendering up both for the sake of consumerist convenience and because fears emerging from, and constructed around, crime and terrorism compel us to hand intimate details of the self over to governmental and quasi-governmental agencies. The same political elites who insist that it is no longer possible to manage economies sometimes seem intent on managing the other 90% of human activity instead.

Perhaps the two years spent writing this book has been a waste. Perhaps we really are in a post-liberal, post-egalitarian era. Perhaps readers 20 years from now will see it as a passé, anachronistic joke. But if so, I am happy to go down with the ship. Indeed, in this scenario we will all be sinking, although not all of us will realise that we are drowning. With what must be deliberate understatement, Glover (1999, p 3) ridiculed late 19th-century complacency when he observed that 'much of twentieth century history has been a very unpleasant surprise'. We have no excuse for any similar lack of foresight today. The contempt we sometimes direct towards the fin de siècle may be nothing compared with the contempt directed at us a century from now if we mess things up again. Applied ethics directs our attention to many of the challenges we face and social policy has a crucial role to play in helping us to face them.

When asked as a boy to select a puppy from a litter, I chose the one that sloped up to me the last, that was laconic and languid and thought it was *my* job to impress *him*. That's why I named him 'Snoopy'. It was years later before I made an obvious association with another childhood hero, one who surpassed even Einstein. Charlie Brown is forever being invited by Lucy to kick a ball that she, very graciously, offers to hold in place for him. Charlie eventually overcomes his suspicions and memories of previous broken promises. He runs, he kicks, and because Lucy has swiped the ball away from him at the last moment he swings into the air and falls on his arse. As he looks up at the sky, Charlie vows never to be fooled again. *He vows this every time!* Is it that Charlie can't learn from experience? Or is it that the exhilaration of the run, the thrill of the risk, is worth the eventual pain and humiliation? If you think the former, if you think success only comes when the ball arcs away into the distance, you don't know at whom Charlie's exasperated sigh, 'Oh, good grief!', is actually being aimed.

References

Abadie, A. and Gay, S. (2006) 'The impact of presumed consent legislation on cadaveric organ donation', *Journal of Health Economics*, vol 25, no 4, pp 599-620.

Adnett, N. and Davies, P. (2003) 'Schooling reforms in England', *Journal of Education Policy*, vol 18, issue 4, pp 393-406.

Adonis, A. and Pollard, S. (1998) *A Class Apart*, Middlesex: Penguin.

Allison, H. (1990) *Kant's Theory of Freedom*, Cambridge: Cambridge University Press.

Almond, B. (2003) 'Family', in H. LaFollette (ed) *The Oxford Handbook of Practical Ethics*, Oxford: Oxford University Press.

Almond, B. (2006) *The Fragmenting Family*, Oxford: Oxford University Press.

Amarasekara, K. and Bagaric, M. (2004) 'Moving from voluntary euthanasia to non-voluntary euthanasia', *Ratio Juris*, vol 17, no 3, pp 398-423.

Amato, P. (2003) 'Reconciling divergent perspectives: Judith Wallerstein, quantitative family research, and children of divorce', *Family Relations*, vol 52, no 4, pp 332-9.

Amato, P.R. (2000) 'The consequences of divorce for adults and children', *Journal of Marriage and the Family*, vol 62, issue 4, pp 1269-87.

Apple, M.W. (2001) 'Comparing neo-liberal projects and inequality in education', *Comparative Education*, vol 37, no 4), pp 409-24.

Aquinas, T. (1993) *Selected Philosophical Writings*, Oxford: Oxford Paperbacks.

Archard, D. (2003) 'Children', in H. LaFollette (ed) *The Oxford Handbook of Practical Ethics*, Oxford: Oxford University Press.

Aristotle (1955) *Nichomachean Ethics*, Middlesex: Penguin.

Arneson, R. (1989) 'Paternalism, utility and fairness', *Revue Internationale de Philosophie*, 43, pp 409-37.

Arneson, R. (2003) 'Equality, coercion, culture and social norms', *Politics, Philosophy and Economics*, vol 2, no 2, pp 139-63.

Arthur, J. (2005) 'World hunger and moral obligation', in D. Boonin and G. Oddie (eds) *What's Wrong?*, Oxford: Oxford University Press.

Bailey, J. (1997) *Utilitarianism, Institutions and Justice*, Oxford: Oxford University Press.

Balaguer, M. (2004) 'A coherent, naturalistic, and plausible formulation of libertarian free will', *Noûs*, vol 38, no 3, pp 379-406.

Ballet, J. and Jolivet, P. (2003) 'About the Kantian economy', *Social Science Information*, vol 42, no 2, pp 185–208.

Bane, M.J. and Mead, L. (2003) *Lifting up the Poor*, Washington, DC: Brookings.

Banting, K. and Kymlicka, W. (eds) (2006) *Multiculturalism and the Welfare State*, Oxford: Oxford University Press.

Banting, K., Johnston, R., Kymlicka, W. and Soroka, S. (2006) 'Do multiculturalism policies erode the welfare state? An empirical analysis', in K. Banting and W. Kymlicka (eds) *Multiculturalism and the Welfare State*, Oxford: Oxford University Press.

Barber, B. (2007) *Consumed*, New York, NY: W. W. Norton and Co.

Baron, M. (1995) *Kantian Ethics Almost Without Apology*, London: Cornell University Press.

Baron, M. (1997) 'Kantian ethics', in M. Baron, P. Pettit and M. Slote (eds) *Three Methods of Ethics*, Oxford: Blackwell.

Barry, B. (1995) *Justice as Impartiality*, Oxford: Oxford University Press.

Barry, B. (2001) *Culture and Equality*, Cambridge: Polity.

Barry, B. (2005) *Why Social Justice Matters*, Cambridge: Polity.

Bartlett, W., Roberts, J.A. and Le Grand, J. (eds) (1998) *A Revolution in Social Policy*, Bristol: The Policy Press.

Battin, M. (2005) *Ending Life*, Oxford: Oxford University Press.

Baum, B. (2003) 'Millian radical democracy', *Political Studies*, vol 51, no 2, pp 404–28.

Bauman, Z. (2001) *Community*, Cambridge: Polity.

Bauman, Z. (2005) *Work, Consumerism and the New Poor* (2nd edn), Buckingham: Open University Press.

Bay, A.-H. and Pedersen, A. (2006) 'The limits of social solidarity', *Acta Sociologica*, vol 49, no 4, pp 419–36.

Beauchamp, T. (2002) 'Justifying physician assisted deaths', in H. LaFollette (ed) *Ethics in Practice* (2nd edn), Oxford: Blackwell.

Beckman, L. (2001) *The Liberal State and the Politics of Virtue*, Edison, NJ: Transaction Publishers.

Beitz, C. (2000) 'Rawls's law of peoples', *Ethics*, 110, pp 669–96.

Benhabib, S. (1992) *Situating the Self*, Cambridge: Polity.

Benhabib, S. (2004) *The Rights of Others*, Cambridge: Cambridge University Press.

Benn, P. (1998) *Ethics*, London: Routledge.

Bentham, J. (1962) *The Complete Works* (vol 2), edited by John Bowring, New York, NY: Russell and Russell.

Bentham, J. (2000) *Introduction to the Principles of Morals and Legislation*, Ontario: Batoche Books.

Berkowitz, P. (1999) *Virtue and the Making of Modern Liberalism*, Ewing Princeton, NJ: Princeton University Press.

Berlin, I. (1991) 'John Stuart Mill and the ends of life', in J. Gray and G. Smith, (eds) *J. S. Mill – On Liberty*, London: Routledge.

Blackburn, S. (2001) *Being Good*, Oxford: Oxford University Press.

Blake, M. (2005) 'Immigration', in R. Frey and C. Wellman (eds) *A Companion to Applied Ethics*, Oxford: Blackwell.

Blank, R. (1984) 'Judicial decision making and biological fact', *The Western Political Quarterly*, vol 37, no 4, pp 584-602.

Blom, B. (2001) 'The personal social services in a Swedish quasi-market context', *Policy & Politics*, vol 29, no 1, pp 29-42.

Bloom, A. (1988) *The Closing of the American Mind*, New York: Simon & Schuster.

Bookchin, M. (1997) *The Murray Bookchin Reader*, edited by Janet Biehl, London: Cassell.

Boonin, D. (2002) *A Defence of Abortion*, Cambridge: Cambridge University Press.

Bourne, J. (2006) 'Labour's love lost?', *Race and Class*, vol 48, no 1, pp 93-9.

Bowles, H. and Gintis, S. (1998) *Recasting Egalitarianism*, London: Verso.

Bowring, F. (2003) *Science, Seeds and Cyborgs*, London: Verso.

Bracci, S. (2002) 'Seyla Benhabib's interactive universalism', *Qualitative Inquiry*, vol 8, no 4, pp 463-88.

Brady, M. (2004) 'Against agent-based virtue ethics', *Philosophical Papers*, vol 33, no 1, pp 1-10.

Brandom, R. (ed) (2000) *Rorty and His Critics*, Oxford: Blackwell.

Brighouse, H. (2000) *School Choice and Social Justice*, Oxford: Oxford University Press.

Broadie, S. (1991) *Ethics with Aristotle*, Oxford: Oxford University Press.

Brock, D. (1993) 'Quality of life measures in health care and medical ethics', in M. Nussbaum and A. Sen (eds) *The Quality of Life*, Oxford: Clarendon Press.

Brown, J. (2001) 'Genetic manipulation in humans as a matter of Rawlsian justice', *Social Theory and Practice*, vol 27, no 1, pp 83-110.

Browne, A. (2002) *Do We Need Mass Immigration?*, London: Civitas.

Buchanan, A. (2000) 'Rawls's law of peoples', *Ethics*, 110, pp 697-721.

Buchanan, A., Brock, D., Daniels, N. and Wikler, D. (2000) *From Chance to Choice*, Cambridge, Cambridge University Press.

Buckley, W. (2002) 'The war on drugs is lost', in H. LaFollette (ed) *Ethics in Practice*, Oxford: Blackwell.

Bumpass, L. and Lu, H.-H. (2000) 'Trends in cohabitation and implications for *children*'s family contexts in the United States', *Population Studies*, vol 54, issue 1, pp 29–41

Burgess, S., Propper, C. and Wilson, D. (2005) *Choice: Will More Choice Improve Outcomes in Education and Health Care?*, University of Bristol: Centre For Market And Public Organisation.

Butler, J., Laclau, E. and Zizek, S. (2000) *Contingency Hegemony Universality*, London: Verso.

Cain, J. (2004) 'Free will and the problem of evil', *Religious Studies*, vol 40, issue 4, pp 437–56.

Callaghan, D. (2005) 'A case against euthanasia', in A. Cohen and C. Wellman (eds) *Contemporary Debates in Applied Ethics*, Oxford: Blackwell.

Callahan, D. (1986) 'How technology is reframing the abortion debate', *Hastings Center Report*, 16, pp 33–42.

Card, R. (2004) 'Consequentialist teleology and the valuation of states of affairs', *Ethical Theory and Moral Practice*, vol 7, no 3, pp 253–65.

Carens, J. (2000) *Culture, Citizenship and Community*, Oxford: Oxford University Press.

Carens, J. (2003) 'Who should get in? The ethics of immigration admissions', *Ethics and International Affairs*, vol 17, no 1, pp 95–110.

Carens, J. (2005) 'The integration of immigrants', *Journal of Moral Philosophy*, vol 2, no 1, pp 29–46.

Carr, D. (2003) 'Character and moral choice in the cultivation of virtue', *Philosophy*, 78, pp 219–232.

Cavanaugh, T. (2006) *Double Effect Reasoning*, Oxford: Clarendon Press.

Chan, D. (2000) 'Intention and responsibility in double effect cases', *Ethical Theory and Moral Practice*, vol 3, no 4, pp 405–34.

Clarke, J., Newman, J., Smith, N., Vidler, E. and Westermarland, L. (2007) *Creating Citizen-Consumers*, London: Sage Publications.

Cleary, R. (1983) 'Some thoughts on the ethics of abortion on demand', *Dialogue*, 25, pp 60–8.

Cohen, A. (2000) 'Does communitarianism require individual independence?', *Journal of Ethics*, vol 4, no 3, pp 283–305.

Cohen, A. (2005) 'Famine relief and human virtue', in A. Cohen and C. Wellman (eds) *Contemporary Debates in Applied Ethics*, Oxford: Blackwell.

Cohen, G.A. (1995) *Self-Ownership, Freedom and Equality*, Cambridge: Cambridge University Press.

Coleman, D. and Rowthorn, R. (2004) 'The economic effects of immigration into the United Kingdom', *Population and Development Review*, vol 30, no 4, pp 579-624.

Coleman, M., Ganong, L., Hans, J., Rothrauff, T. and Sharp, E. (2005) 'Filial obligations in post-divorce stepfamilies', *Journal of Divorce and Remarriage*, vol 43, nos 3-4, pp 1-27.

Collingridge, M. and Miller, S. (1997) 'Filial responsibility and the care of the aged', *Journal of Applied Philosophy*, vol 14, no 2, pp 119-28.

Comas-Herrera, A., Wittenberg, R., Costa-Font, J., Gori, C., Di Maio, A., Paxtot, C., Pickard, L., Pozzi, A. and Rothgang, H. (2006) 'Future long-term care expenditure in Germany, Spain, Italy and the United Kingdom', *Ageing and Society*, vol 26, no 2, pp 285 302.

Considine, M. (2003) 'Governance and competition', *Australian Journal of Political Science*, vol 38, no 1, pp 63-77.

Copleston, F. (1985) *A History of Philosophy* (vol 2), New York, NY: Image-Doubleday.

Copp, D. (1992) 'The right to an adequate standard of living', *Social Philosophy and Policy*, vol 9, no 1, pp 231-261.

Copp, D. and Sobel, D. (2004) 'Morality and virtue', *Ethics*, vol 114, no 3, pp 514-54.

Corson, D. (2002) 'Teaching and learning for market-place utility', *International Journal of Leadership in Education*, vol 5, issue 1, pp 1-13.

Craig, D. (2006) *Plundering the Public Sector*, London: Constable.

Crepaz, M. (2006) '"If you are my brother I may give you a dime!" Public opinion on multiculturalism, trust and the welfare state', in K. Banting and W. Kymlicka (eds) *Multiculturalism and the Welfare State*, Oxford: Oxford University Press.

Crisp, R. and Slote, M. (eds) (1997) *Virtue Ethics*, Oxford: Oxford University Press.

Crocker, D. (2002) 'Hunger, capacity and development', in H. LaFollette (ed) *Ethics in Practice*, Oxford: Blackwell.

Cullity, G. (2004) *The Moral Demands of Affluence*, Oxford: Oxford University Press.

Cummiskey, D. (1996) *Kantian Consequentialism*, Oxford: Oxford University Press.

Daatland, S. and Herlofson, K. (2003) '"Lost solidarity" or "changed solidarity": a comparative European view of normative family solidarity', *Ageing and Society*, vol 23, issue 5, pp 536-60.

Dagger, R. (2006) 'Neo-Republicanism and the civic economy', *Politics, Philosophy and Economics*, vol 5, no 2, pp 151-73.

Dahl, E. and Levy, N. (2006) 'The case for physician assisted suicide', *Journal of Medical Ethics*, vol 32, no 6, pp 335-8.

Danley, J. (1979) 'Robert Nozick and the libertarian paradox.', *Mind*, vol 88, no 1, pp 419-23.

Darwall, S. (2002) *Welfare and Rational Care*, Princeton, NJ: Princeton University Press.

Darwall, S. (ed) (2003a) *Consequentialism*, London: Routledge.

Darwall, S. (ed) (2003b) *Contractarianism/Contractualism*, Oxford: Blackwell.

Darwall, S. (2006) *The Second-Person Standpoint*, Cambridge, MA: Harvard University Press.

Darwin, C. (2004) *The Descent of Man*, Middlesex: Penguin.

Davey Smith, G., Dorling, D. and Shaw, M. (2005) 'Health inequalities and New Labour', *British Medical Journal*, vol 330, April 23, pp 1016-21.

Davis, M. (2001) *Late Victorian Holocausts*, London: Verso.

Davies, N. (1999) *The Isles*, London: Papermac.

Davies, N. (2000) *The School Report*, London: Vintage Books.

Davies, T. (1997) *Humanism*, London: Routledge.

Dawkins, R. (2006) *The God Delusion*, London: Bantam.

Deacon, A. (2002) *Perspectives on Welfare*, Milton Keynes: Open University Press.

Dean, H. (2006) *Social Policy*, Cambridge: Polity.

Dean, M. (2007) *Governing Societies*, Buckingham: Open University Press.

Dench, G., Gavron, K. and Young, M. (2006) *The New East End*, London: Profile Books.

Dennett, D. (2003) *Freedom Evolves*, London: Allen Lane.

Dennett, D. (2006) *Breaking the Spell*, London: Allen Lane.

de-Shalit, A. (2004) 'Political philosophy and empowering citizens', *Political Studies*, vol 52, issue 4, pp 802-18.

de Waal, F. (2006) *Primates and Philosophers*, Princeton, NJ: Princeton University Press.

Dixon, N. (2005) 'The friendship model of filial obligations', in D. Boonin and G. Oddie (eds) *What's Wrong?*, Oxford: Oxford University Press.

Dodson, K. (2003) 'Kant's socialism: a philosophical reconstruction', *Social Theory and Practice*, vol 29, no 4, pp 525-38.

Dowding, K. and John, P. (forthcoming) 'The value of choice in public policy', *Public Administration*.

Dower, N. (2003) 'World hunger', in H. LaFollette (ed) *The Oxford Handbook of Practical Ethics*, Oxford: Oxford University Press.

Doyal, L. and Gough, I. (1991) *A Theory of Human Needs*, London: Macmillan.

Driver, J. (2001) *Uneasy Virtue*, Cambridge: Cambridge University Press.

Dubos, R. (1998) *So Human an Animal*, Edison, NJ: Transaction Publishers.

Duncan, S. and Strell, M. (2004) 'Combining lone motherhood and paid work: the rationality mistake and Norwegian social policy', *Journal of European Social Policy*, vol 14, no 1, pp 41-54.

Dworkin, G., Frey, R. and Bok, S. (1998) *Euthanasia and Physician-Assisted Suicide*, Cambridge: Cambridge University Press.

Dworkin, R. (1993) *Life's Dominion*, London: HarperCollins.

Dworkin, R. (2000) *Sovereign Virtue*, Cambridge, MA: Harvard University Press.

Eckersley, R. (1992) *Environmentalism and Political Theory*, New York, NY: Suny Press.

Economics and Philosophy (2001) *Symposium on Amartya Sen's Philosophy* vol 17, no 1, pp 1-88.

Egan, B. (2001) *The Widow's Might*, London: Social Market Foundation.

Eisner, M. (2006) 'Banning smoking in public places', *Journal of the American Medical Association*, vol 296, no 14, pp 1778-9.

Elster, J. (1982) 'Sour grapes – utilitarianism and the genesis of wants', in A. Sen and R. Williams (eds) *Utilitarianism and Beyond*, Cambridge: Cambridge University Press.

Elster, J. (1985) *Sour Grapes*, Cambridge: Cambridge University Press.

English, J. (2005) 'What do grown children owe their parents?', in D. Boonin and G. Oddie (eds) *What's Wrong?*, Oxford: Oxford University Press.

Englund, T. (2000) 'Rethinking democracy and education: towards an education of deliberative citizens', *Journal of Curriculum Studies*, vol 32, no 2, pp 305-13.

Ennew, C. (2006) 'Welfare tourism', in T. Fitzpatrick, H.-J. Kwon, N. Manning, J. Midgely and J. Pascall (eds) *The International Encyclopaedia of Social Policy*, London: Routledge.

Entzinger, H. (2006) 'Changing the rules while the game is on', in Y.M. Bodemann and G. Yurdukal (eds) *Migration, Citizenship, Ethnos*, Basingstoke: Palgrave Macmillan.

Ernst and Young (2006) *Item Club Special Report*, December.

Etzioni, A, (1992) 'On the place of virtues in a pluralistic democracy', *American Behavioral Scientist*, vol 35, nos 4-5, pp 530-40.

European Journal of Cancer Care (2003) 'News', *European Journal of Cancer Care*, vol 12, issue 4, pp 302-7.

Fagerlin, A., Ditto, P., Hawkins, N., Schneider, C. and Smucker, D. (2002) 'The use of advance directives in end–of-life decision making', *American Behavioural Scientist*, vol 46, no 2, pp 268-83.

Farrant, M. and Sriskandarajah, D. (2006) 'Migration, moving beyond numbers', in M. Dixon and J. Margo (eds) *Population Politics*, London: Institute for Public Policy Research.

Feinberg, J. (1986) *Harm to Self*, Oxford: Oxford University Press.

Feldman, F. (1992) *Confrontations with the Reaper*, Oxford University Press.

Feldman, F. (1997) *Utilitarianism, Hedonism, and Desert*, New York, NY: Cambridge University Press.

Feldman, S. (1998) 'From occupied bodies to pregnant persons', in J. Kneller (ed) *Autonomy And Community*, New York, NY: Suny Press.

Field, F. (2003) *Neighbours from Hell*, London: Politico's.

Finch, J. and Mason, J. (1990) 'Filial obligations and kin support for elderly people', *Ageing and Society*, 10, pp 151-75.

Finnis, J. (1980) *Natural Law and Natural Rights*, Oxford: Clarendon Press.

Fitzpatrick, T. (1999) *Freedom and Security*, Basingstoke: Macmillan.

Fitzpatrick, T. (2001) *Welfare Theory*, Basingstoke: Palgrave.

Fitzpatrick, T. (2002a) 'The two paradoxes of welfare democracy', *International Journal of Social Welfare*, vol 11, no 2, pp 159-69.

Fitzpatrick, T. (2002b) 'Critical theory, information society and surveillance technologies', *Information, Communication and Society*, vol 5, no 3, pp 357-78.

Fitzpatrick, T. (2003) *After the New Social Democracy*, Manchester: Manchester University Press.

Fitzpatrick, T. (2005a) *New Theories of Welfare*, Basingstoke: Palgrave.

Fitzpatrick, T. (2005b) 'The fourth attempt to construct a politics of welfare obligations', *Policy & Politics*, vol 33, no 1, pp 3-21.

Fitzpatrick, T. (2008) 'From contracts to capabilities and back again', *Res Publica*, vol 14, no 2.

Fitzpatrick, T. (forthcoming) 'Exploring the links between deliberative democracy, critical rationality and social memory', draft paper available from the author.

Fitzpatrick, T. and Cahill, M. (eds) (2002) *Environment and Welfare*, Basingstoke: Palgrave.

Foot, P. (1978) *Virtues and Vices*, Oxford: Blackwell.

Foot, P. (2001) *Natural Goodness*, Oxford: Clarendon Press.

Foot, P. (2002) *Moral Dilemmas*, Oxford: Clarendon Press.

Foster, P., Gomm, R. and Hammersley, M. (1996) *Constructing Education Inequality*, Brighton: Falmer Press.

Foucault, M. (1989) *The Order of Things*, London: Routledge.

Fraser, N. (2001) 'Recognition without ethics?', *Theory, Culture and Society*, vol 18, nos 2-3, pp 21-42.

Fraser, N. and Honneth, A. (2003) *Redistribution or Recognition?*, London: Verso.

Frey, R. (ed) (1984) *Utility and Rights*, Oxford: Blackwell.

Friedman, M. (1962) *Capitalism and Freedom*, Chicago, IL: Chicago University Press.

Friedman, M. (2005) '"They lived happily ever after": Sommers on women and marriage', in D. Boonin, and G. Oddie (eds) *What's Wrong?*, Oxford: Oxford University Press.

Furedi, F. (2001) *Paranoid Parenting*, London: Allen Lane.

Galston, W. (2003) 'After socialism', in E.F Paul, F. Miller and J. Paul (eds) *After Socialism*, Cambridge: Cambridge University Press.

Gastmans, C., Lemiengre, J., van der Wal, G., Schotsmans, P. and De de Casterle, B. (2006) 'Prevalence and content of written ethics policies on euthanasia in Catholic healthcare institutions in Belgium (Flanders)', *Health Policy*, vol 76, no 2, pp 169-78.

Gaynor, M. (2006) *What Do We Know About Competition and Quality in Health Care Markets?*, University of Bristol: Centre for Market and Public Organisation.

Gelfand, S. (2004) 'The ethics of care and (capital?) punishment', *Law and Philosophy*, vol 23, no 6, pp 593-614.

Gensler, H. (1986) 'A Kantian argument against abortion', *Philosophical Studies*, vol 49, no 1, pp 83-98.

George, A. (2004) 'Is "property" necessary?', *Res Publica*, vol 10, no 1, pp 15-42.

Gert, H. (1997) 'Viability', in S. Dwyer and J. Feinberg (eds) *The Problem of Abortion* (3rd edn), Belmont, CA: Wadsworth.

Gibbons, S., Machin, S. and Silva, O. (2006) *Choice, Competition and Pupil Achievement*, IZA Discussion Paper, no. 2214, Forschungsinstitut zur Zukunft der Arbeit: Bonn.

Giddens, T. (2007) *Over to You, Mr Brown*, Cambridge: Polity.

Gillett G. (1999) 'Dennett, Foucault, and the selection of memes', *Inquiry*, vol 42, no 1, pp 3-23.

Glannon, W. (2001) *Genes and Future People*, Oxford: Westview Press.

Glaser, D. (2006) 'The limits to global redistribution', *Global Society*, vol 20, no 2, pp 137-54.

Glauser, R. (2003) 'Le problème du mal dans la philosophie analytique de la religion', *Revue Internationale de Philosophie*, 57, pp 285-311.

Glover, J. (1977) *Causing Deaths and Saving Lives*, Middlesex: Penguin.

Glover, J. (1999) *Humanity*, London: Jonathan Cape.

Glover, J. (2001) 'Future people, disability, and screening', in J. Harris (ed) *Bioethics*, Oxford: Oxford University Press.

Goodhart, D. (2006) *Progressive Nationalism*, London: Demos.

Goodin, R. (1986) *Protecting the Vulnerable*, Chicago, IL: University of Chicago Press.

Goodin, R. (1989) *No Smoking*, Chicago, IL: University of Chicago Press.

Goodin, R. (1995) *Utilitarianism as a Public Philosophy*, Cambridge: Cambridge University Press.

Goodin, R. (2002a) 'Free movement: if people were money', in H. LaFollette (ed) *Ethics in Practice*, Oxford: Blackwell.

Goodin, R. (2002b) 'Permissible paternalism: saving smokers from themselves', in H. LaFollette (ed) *Ethics in Practice*, Oxford: Blackwell.

Gould, J. (2002) 'Better hearts: teaching applied virtue ethics', *Teaching Philosophy*, vol 25, no 1, pp 1-26.

Gould, S. (2002) *Rocks of Ages*, London: Vintage Books.

Gray, J. (1983) *Mill on Liberty*, London: Routledge and Kegan Paul.

Gray, J. (2000) *Two Faces of Liberalism*, Cambridge: Polity.

Gray, J. (2002) *Straw Dogs*, London: Granta.

Griffin, J. (1986) *Well-Being*, Oxford: Clarendon Press.

Griffith, S. (2004) 'The moral status of a human fetus', *Christian Bioethics*, vol 10, no 1, pp 55-61.

Grotius, H. (2005) *Rights of War and Peace* (vol 1), Indianapolis, IN: Liberty Fund.

Gunderson, M. (2004) 'A Kantian view of suicide and end-of-life treatment', *Journal of Social Philosophy*, vol 35, no 2, pp 277-87.

Gutmann, A. (1987) *Democratic Education*, Princeton, NJ: Princeton University Press.

Gutmann, A. (1989) 'Undemocratic Education', in N. Rosenblum (ed) *Liberalism and the Moral Life*, Cambridge, MA: Harvard University Press.

Gutmann, A. (2000) 'What does "school choice" mean?', *Dissent*, Summer, pp 19-24.

Guyer, P. (2005) *Kant's System of Nature and Freedom*, Oxford: Clarendon Press

Habermas, J. (1977) 'A review of Gadamer's truth and method', in F. Dallmayr and T. McCarthy (eds) *Understanding and Social Inquiry*, Notre Dame, IN: Notre Dame University Press.

Habermas, J. (1990) *Moral Consciousness and Communicative Action*, Cambridge, MA: MIT Press.

Habermas, J. (2003) *The Future of Human Nature*, Cambridge: Polity.

Halsey, A.H., Dennis, N. and Erdos, G. (2000) *Families Without Fatherhood*, London: Civitas.

Halwani, R. (2003) 'Care ethics and virtue ethics', *Hypatia*, vol 18, no 3, pp 160-92.

Hardwick, C. and Crosby, D. (eds) (1997) *Pragmatics, Neo-pragmatism, and Religion*, New York, NY: Peter Lang.

Hare, R.M. (1981) *Moral Thinking*, Oxford: Clarendon Press.

Hare, R.M. (1989) 'Abortion: reply to Brandt', *Social Theory And Practice*, 15, pp 25-32.

Harris, J. (1998) *Clones, Genes and Immortality*, Oxford: Oxford University Press.

Harris, J. and Holm, S. (2003) 'Abortion', in H. LaFollette (ed) *The Oxford Handbook of Practical Ethics*, Oxford: Oxford University Press.

Häyry, M. (1994) *Liberal Utilitarianism and Applied Ethics*, London: Routledge.

Hayter, T. (2004) *Open Borders*, London: Pluto.

Heath, J. (2004) 'Dworkin's auction', *Politics, Philosophy and Economics*, vol 3, no 3, pp 313-35.

Held, V. (2002) 'Care and the extension of markets', *Hypatia*, vol 17, no 2, pp 19-33.

Herbert, D. (2004) 'Segregation and school attainment', *Dela*, 21 pp 393-403.

Herdt, J. (1998) 'Alasdair MacIntyre's "rationality of traditions" and tradition-transcendental standards of justification', *Journal of Religion*, vol 78, no 4, pp 524-46.

Herman, B. (1993) *The Practice of Moral Judgment*, London: Harvard University Press.

Hershenov, D. (2005) 'Persons as proper parts of organisms', *Theoria*, vol 71, no 1, pp 29-37.

Hetherington, E.M. and Kelly, J. (2002) *For Better or for Worse*, New York, NY: W.W. Norton and Co.

Hier, S. (2003) 'Risk and panic in late modernity', *British Journal of Sociology*, vol 54, no 1, pp 3-20.

Hill, T.E. (1992) *Dignity and Practical Reason in Kant's Moral Theory*, Ithaca, NY: Cornell University Press.

Hill, T.E. (2002) *Human Welfare and Moral Worth*, Oxford: Clarendon Press.

Himmelfarb, G. (1995) *The Demoralisation of Society*, New York, NY: Alfred A. Knopf.

Hirschmann, A. (1970) *Exit, Voice and Loyalty*, Cambridge, MA: Harvard University Press.

Holmes, S. (1997) *Passions and Constraint*, Chicago, IL: University of Chicago Press.

Holtug, N. (2002) 'The harm principle', *Ethical Theory and Moral Practice*, vol 5, no 4, pp 357–89.

Honderich, T. (2002) *How Free Are You?* (2nd edn), Oxford: Oxford University Press.

Hooker, B. (1999) 'Sacrificing for the good of strangers – repeatedly', *Philosophy and Phenomenological Research*, vol 59, no 1, pp 177–81.

Hooker, B. (2002) *Ideal Code, Real World*, Oxford: Oxford University Press.

Horton, J. and Mendus, S. (eds) (1994) *After MacIntyre*, Cambridge: Polity.

Horton, S. (1996) 'Persistent vegetative state: what decides the cut-off point?', *Intensive and Critical Care Nursing*, 12, pp 40–4.

Hudson, W. (1983) *Modern Moral Philosophy*, Basingstoke: Macmillan.

Hughes, J. (2000) 'Consequentialism and the slippery slope', *Journal of Applied Philosophy*, vol 17, no 2, pp 213–9.

Hume, D. (1969) *A Treatise on Human Nature*, Middlesex: Penguin.

Hume, D. (1998) *An Enquiry Concerning the Principles of Morals*, Oxford: Oxford University Press.

Hursthouse, R. (1987) *Beginning Lives*, Oxford: Blackwell.

Hursthouse, R. (2001) *On Virtue Ethics*, Oxford: Oxford University Press.

Hursthouse, R. (2002) 'Virtue theory and abortion', in H. LaFollette (ed) *Ethics in Practice*, Oxford: Blackwell.

Hursthouse, R. (2003) 'Normative virtue ethics', in S. Darwall (ed) *Virtue Ethics*, Oxford: Blackwell.

Hutton, W. (2003) 'New term, same classes', *The Observer*, 14 September.

Huxley, A. (1936) *Eyeless in Gaza*, London: Chatto and Windus.

Iecovich, E. and Lankri, M. (2002) 'Attitudes of elderly persons towards receiving financial support from adult children', *Journal of Aging Studies*, vol 16, no 2, pp 121–33.

Ivanhoe, P. (2006) 'Filial piety as a virtue', in R. Walker and P. Ivanhoe (eds) *Working Virtue*, Oxford: Oxford University Press.

Jackson, B. (2004) 'The uses of utilitarianism: social justice, welfare economics and British socialism, 1931–48', *History of Political Thought*, vol 25, no 3, pp 508–35.

Jacobson, D. (2000) 'Mill on liberty, speech, and the free society', *Philosophy and Public Affairs*, vol 29, no 3, pp 276–309.

Janssen, A. (2002) 'The new regulation of voluntary euthanasia and medically assisted suicide in the Netherlands', *International Journal of Law, Policy and the Family*, vol 16, no 2, pp 260-9.

Jensen, A.-M. and Clausen, S.-E. (2003) 'Children and family dissolution in Norway: the impact of consensual unions', *Childhood*, vol 10, no 1, pp 65-81.

Jones, D. (2000) 'Metaphysical misgivings about "brain death"', in M. Potts, P. Byrne and R. Nilges (eds) *Beyond Brain Death*, Hingham, MA: Kluwer Academic Publishers.

Jordan, J. (2004) 'Divine love and human suffering', *International Journal for Philosophy of Religion*, vol 56, nos 2-3, pp 169-78.

Junker-Kenny, M. (2005) 'Genetic enhancement as care or as domination?', *Journal of the Philosophy of Education*, vol 39, no 1, pp 1-17.

Kahkonen, L. (2005) 'Costs and efficiency of quasi-markets in practice', *Local Government Studies*, vol 31, no 1, pp 85-97.

Kamm, F.M. (2007) *Intricate Ethics*, Oxford: Oxford University Press.

Kane, R. (ed) (2002) *Oxford Handbook of Free Will*, Oxford: Oxford University Press.

Kant, I. (1934) *Critique of Pure Reason*, London: Dent.

Kant, I. (1991) *Groundwork of the Metaphysics of Morals*, London: Routledge.

Kant, I. (1996) *Practical Philosophy*, Cambridge: Cambridge University Press.

Kant, I. (2001) *Basic Writings of Kant*, New York, NY: The Modern Library.

Kass, L. (1990) 'Death with dignity and the sanctity of life', *Commentary*, vol 89, no 3, pp 33-43.

Kass, L. (2003) *Life, Liberty and the Defense of Dignity*, New York: Encounter Books.

Kateb, G. (1989) 'Democratic individuality and the meaning of rights', in N. Rosenblum (ed) *Liberalism and the Moral Life*, Cambridge, MA: Harvard University Press.

Katz, M. (2002) *The Price of Citizenship*, New York, NY: Owl Books.

Kekes, J. (2002) 'On the supposed obligation to relieve famine', *Philosophy*, 77, pp 503-17.

Keller, S. (2006) 'Four theories of filial duty', *Philosophical Quarterly*, vol 56, issue 223, pp 254-74.

Kelly, P. (ed) (2002) *Multiculturalism Reconsidered*, Cambridge: Polity.

Kenny, A. (1995) 'Philippa Foot on double effect', in R. Hursthouse, G. Lawrence and W. Quinn (eds) *Virtues and Reasons*, Oxford: Clarendon Press.

Kenny, S. (2005) 'Terrify and control: the politics of risk society', *Social Alternatives*, vol 24, no 3, pp 50-4.

Keown, D. and Keown, J. (1995) 'Killing, karma and caring: euthanasia in Buddhism and Christianity', *Journal of Medical Ethics*, vol 21, no 5, pp 265-9.

Keown, J. (2002) *Euthanasia, Ethics and Public Policy*, Cambridge: Cambridge University Press.

Kerr, A. and Shakespeare, T. (2002) *Genetic Politics*, Cheltenham: New Clarion Press.

Keynes, J.M. (1964) *The General Theory of Employment, Interest and Money*, New York, NY: Harcourt Brace.

Kierkegaard, S. (1985) *Fear and Trembling*, Middlesex: Penguin.

Knight, R. (2003) 'How domestic partnerships and "gay marriage" threaten the family', in J. White (ed) *Contemporary Moral Problems* (7th edn), Belmont, CA: Wadsworth.

Korsgaard, C. (1996) *Creating the Kingdom of Ends*, Cambridge: Cambridge University Press.

Kraut, R. (ed) (2006) *The Blackwell Guide to Aristotle's Nichomachean Ethics*, Oxford: Blackwell.

Krieger, T. (2003) 'Voting on low-skill immigration under different pension regimes', *Public Choice*, 117, pp 51-78.

Kuchler, F., Tegene, A. and Harris, M. (2005) 'Taxing snack foods', *Review of Agricultural Economics*, vol 27, no 1, pp 4-20.

Kuhse, H. (1993) 'Euthanasia', in P. Singer (ed) *A Companion to Ethics*, Oxford: Blackwell.

Kuhse, H. (1998) 'Critical notice: why killing is not always worse – and is sometimes better – than letting die', *Cambridge Quarterly of Healthcare Ethics*, vol 7, no 4, pp 371-4.

Kukathas, C. (2003) 'Immigration', in H. LaFollette (ed) *The Oxford Handbook of Practical Ethics*, Oxford: Oxford University Press.

Kukathas, C. (2005) 'The case for open immigration', in C. Wellman and A. Cohen (eds) *Contemporary Debates in Applied Ethics*, Oxford: Blackwell.

Kultgen, J. (1997) 'Slote's free-standing virtue ethics and its props', *Southwest Philosophy Review*, vol 14, no 1, pp 103-10.

Kupfer, J. (1998) 'Education, indoctrination and moral character', in T. Magnell (ed) *Values and Education*, Amersterdam: Rodopi.

Kupfer, J. (2005) 'Can parents and children be friends?', in D. Boonin, and G. Oddie (eds) *What's Wrong?*, Oxford: Oxford University Press.

Kymlicka, W. (2002) *Contemporary Political Philosophy* (2nd edn), Oxford: Oxford University Press.

Kymlicka, W. (2006) 'Liberal nationalism and cosmopolitan justice', in S. Benhabib *Another Cosmopolitanism*, edited by Robert Frost, Oxford: Oxford University Press.

Lacan, J. (1989) *Écrits*, London: Routledge.

LaFollette, H. (ed) (2003) *The Oxford Handbook of Practical Ethics*, Oxford: Oxford University Press.

LaFollette, H. (2005) 'World hunger', in R. Frey and C. Wellman (eds) *A Companion to Applied Ethics*, Oxford: Blackwell.

LaFollette, H. (2007) *The Practice of Ethics*, Oxford: Blackwell.

Landman, W. (1991) 'On excluding something from our gathering', *South African Journal Of Philosophy*, February, pp 7-19.

Lansley, S. (2006) *Rich Britain*, London: Politico's.

Law, S. (2006) *The War for Children's Minds*, London: Routledge.

Lawrence, G. (2006) 'Human good and human function', in R. Kraut (ed) *The Blackwell Guide to Aristotle's Nichomachean Ethics*, Oxford: Blackwell.

Layard, R. (2005) *Happiness*, London: Allen Lane.

Le Dœuff, M. (1991) *Hipparchia's Choice*, Oxford: Blackwell.

Le Grand, J. (2003) *From Knight to Knave and From Pawn to Queen*, Oxford: Oxford University Press.

Le Grand, J. (2007) *The Other Invisible Hand*, Princeton, NJ: Princeton University Press.

Le Grand, J. and Bartlett, W. (eds) (1993) *Quasi-Markets and Social Policy*, Bristol: The Policy Press.

Lee, P. (2004) 'The pro-life argument from substantial identity', *Bioethics*, vol 18, no 3, pp 249-63.

Lee, P. and George, R. (2005) 'The wrong of abortion', in A. Cohen and C. Wellman (eds) *Contemporary Debates in Applied Ethics*, Oxford: Blackwell.

Leech, D. and Campos, E. (2003) 'Is comprehensive education really free?', *Journal of the Royal Statistical Society: Series A*, vol 166, no 1, pp 135-54.

Legrain, P. (2006) *Immigrants*, London: Little, Brown.

Levin. M. (2005) 'Why homosexuality is abnormal', in D. Boonin and G. Oddie (eds) *What's Wrong?*, Oxford: Oxford University Press.

Levy, N. (1999) 'Stepping into the present: MacIntyre's modernity', *Social Theory and Practice*, vol 25, no 3, pp 471-90.

Lewis, J. (2003) *Should We Worry about Family Change?*, Toronto: University of Toronto Press.

Lillehammer, H. (2002) 'Voluntary euthanasia and the logical slippery slope argument', *Cambridge Law Journal*, vol 61, no 3, pp 545-50.

Lister, R. (2004) *Poverty*, Cambridge: Polity.

Little, M. (2005) 'The moral permissibility of abortion', in A. Cohen and C. Wellman (eds) *Contemporary Debates in Applied Ethics*, Oxford: Blackwell.

Lloyd, M. (2001) 'The politics of disability and feminism: discord or synthesis?', *Sociology*, vol 35, no 3, pp 715-28.

Louden, R. (1997) 'On some vices of virtue ethics', in R. Crisp and M. Slote (eds) *Virtue Ethics*, Oxford: Oxford University Press.

Louden, R. (2000) *Kant's Impure Ethics*, New York, NY: Oxford University Press.

Lundahl, L. (2002) 'Sweden: decentralization, deregulation, quasi-markets – and then what?', *Journal of Education Policy*, 17, pp 687-97.

Lupton, D. and Tulloch, J. (2002) 'Life would be pretty dull without risk', *Health, Risk and Society*, vol 4, no 2, pp 113-24.

Macdonald, C. and Merrill, D. (2002) 'It shouldn't have to be a trade', *Hypatia*, vol 17, no 2, pp 67-83.

MacIntyre, A. (1967) *A Short History of Ethics*, London: Routledge.

MacIntyre, A. (1971) *Against the Self Images of the Age*, London: Duckworth.

MacIntyre, A. (1981) *After Virtue*, London: Duckworth.

MacIntyre, A. (1987) *Whose Justice? Which Rationality?*, London: Duckworth.

MacIntyre, A. (1990) *Three Rival Versions of Moral Inquiry*, London: Duckworth.

MacIntyre, A. (1999) *Dependent Rational Animals*, London: Duckworth.

Mack, M. (1961) *Jeremy Bentham: An Odyssey of Ideas, 1748-92*, London: Heinemann.

MacKenzie, C. (1997) 'Abortion and embodiment', in S. Dwyer and J. Feinberg (eds) *The Problem of Abortion* (3rd edn), Belmont, CA: Wadsworth.

Mackie, J.L. (1971) 'Evil and omnipotence', in B. Mitchell (ed) *The Philosophy of Religion*, Oxford: Oxford University Press.

Macleod, A. (2003) 'Freedom and the role of the state', *Social Philosophy Today*, 18, pp 139-50.

Magnusson, R.S. (2004) 'Euthanasia: above ground, below ground', *Journal of Medical Ethics*, vol 30, no 5, pp 441-6.

Mann, W. (1998) 'Piety: lending a hand to euthyphro', *Philosophy and Phenomonological Research*, vol 58, no 1, pp 123-42.

Manning, W. and Brown, S. (2006) 'Children's economic well-being in married and cohabiting parent families', *Journal of Marriage and Family*, vol 68, issue 2, pp 345-62.

Markowitz, S. (1997) 'Abortion and feminism', in S. Dwyer and J. Feinberg (eds) *The Problem of Abortion* (3rd edn), Belmont, CA: Wadsworth.

Marlow, N., Wolke, D., Bracewell, M. and Samara, M. (2005) 'Neurological and developmental disability at six years of age after extremely premature birth', *New England Journal of Medicine*, vol 352, no 1, p 9-19.

Marquardt, E. (2006) *Between Two Worlds: The Inner Lives of Children of Divorce*, New York, NY: Three Rivers Press.

Marquet, R.L., Bartelds, A., Peters, L., Spreeuwenberg, P. and Visser, G.J. (2003) 'Twenty five years of requests for euthanasia and physician assisted suicide in Dutch general practice', *British Medical Journal*, vol 327, no 7408, 26 July, pp 201-2.

Marquis, D. (1989) 'Why abortion is immoral', *Journal of Philosophy*, 86, pp 183-202.

Marquis, D. (2002) 'An argument that abortion is wrong', in H. LaFollette (ed) *Ethics in Practice*, Oxford: Blackwell.

Materstvedt, L.J., Clark, D., Ellershaw, J., Førde, R., Boeck Gravgaard, A.-M., Mueller-Busch, H.C., Porta i Sales, J. and Rapin, C.-H. (2003) 'Euthanasia and physician–assisted suicide', *Palliative Medicine*, vol 17, no 2, pp 97-101.

Matravers, M. (2003) 'Responsibility and choice', in M. Matravers (ed) *Scanlon and Contractualism*, London: Frank Cass.

Mawson, T. (2004) 'The possibility of a free will defence for the problem of natural evil', *Religious Studies*, vol 40, issue 1, pp 23-42.

McDowell, J. (1997) 'Virtue and reason', in R. Crisp and M. Slote (eds) *Virtue Ethics*, Oxford: Oxford University Press.

McIntosh, J. (2003) 'Enduring conflict in parental separation: pathways of impact on child development', *Journal of Family Studies*, vol 9, no 1, pp 63-80.

McLellan, D. (1989) *Simone Weil*, Basingstoke: Macmillan.

McMahan, J. (2002) *The Ethics of Killing*, Oxford: Oxford University Press.

McMahan, J. (2005) 'Causing disabled people to exist and causing people to be disabled', *Ethics*, 116, pp 77-99.

McMaster, R. (2002) 'The analysis of welfare state reform', *Journal of Economic Issues*, vol 36, no 3, pp 769-94.

Mead, L. (2005a) *Government Matters*, Princeton, NJ: Princeton University Press.

Mead, L. (2005b) 'Welfare reform and citizenship', in L. Mead and C. Beem (eds) *Welfare Reform and Political Theory*, New York, NY: Russell Sage Publications.

Mennemeyer, S. and Sen, B. (2006) 'Undesirable juvenile behavior and the quality of parental relationships', *Southern Economic Journal*, vol 73, issue 2, pp 437-60.

Midgley, M. (2002) *Evolution as a Religion*, London: Routledge.

Mill, J.S. (1962) *Utilitarianism*, edited by Mary Warnock, London: Fontana.

Mill, J.S. (1985) *Principles of Political Economy*, Middlesex: Penguin.

Mill, J.S. (1989) *Autobiography*, Middlesex: Penguin.

Mill, J.S (1991) *On Liberty*, Gray, J. & Smith, G.W. (eds), London: Routledge.

Miller, D. (1995) *On Nationality*, Oxford: Clarendon Press.

Miller, D. (1999) *Principles of Social Justice*, Cambridge, MA: Harvard University Press.

Miller, D. (2000) *Citizenship and National Identity*, Cambridge: Polity.

Miller, D. (2002) 'Doctrinaire liberalism versus multicultural democracy', *Ethnicities*, vol 2, no 2, pp 261-5.

Miller, D. (2005) 'Immigration: the case for limits', in C. Wellman and A. Cohen (eds) *Contemporary Debates in Applied Ethics*, Oxford: Blackwell.

Miller, D. (2006) 'Multiculturalism and the welfare state: theoretical reflections', in K. Banting and W. Kymlicka (eds) *Multiculturalism and the Welfare State*, Oxford: Oxford University Press.

Mills, C. (1998) 'Choice and circumstance', *Ethics*, vol 109, no 1, pp 154-65.

Mills, C. (2003) 'The child's right to an open future?', *Journal of Social Philosophy*, vol 34, no 4, pp 499-509.

Mills, C. (2005) 'The ties that bind: duties to family members', in D. Boonin and G. Oddie (eds) *What's Wrong?*, Oxford: Oxford University Press.

Mills, C.W. (2000) *The Sociological Imagination*, Oxford: Oxford University Press.

Monk, R. (2001) *Bertrand Russell: 1921-70*, London: Vintage Books.

Moore, G.E. (1993) *Principia Ethica*, Cambridge: Cambridge University Press.

Morgan, P. (2007) *The War Between the State and the Family*, London: Institute of Economic Affairs.

Mulgan, T. (2001) *The Demands of Consequentialism*, Oxford: Clarendon Press.

Muller, J. (2006) 'The neglected moral benefits of the market', *Society*, vol 43, no 2, pp 12-14.

Murdoch, I. (2001) *On the Sovereignty of Good*, London: Routledge.

Murphy, M. (2003) *Alisdair MacIntyre*, Cambridge: Cambridge University Press.

Murris, K. (2000) 'Can children do philosophy?', *Journal of Philosophy of Education*, vol 34, no 2, pp 261-79.

Nagel, T. (1995) *Other Minds*, Oxford: Oxford University Press.

Nannestad, P. (2004) 'Immigration as a challenge to the Danish welfare state?', *European Journal of Political Economy*, vol 20, issue 3, pp 755-67.

Narveson, J. (1967) *Morality and Utility*, Baltimore, MD: Johns Hopkins University Press.

Narveson, J. (1984) 'Equality vs liberty', *Social Philosophy and Policy*, 2, pp 33-60.

Nesbitt, W. (2005) 'Is killing no worse than letting die?', in D. Boonin and G. Oddie (eds) *What's Wrong?*, Oxford: Oxford University Press.

Neuberger, J. (2005) *The Moral State We're In*, London: Harper Collins.

Nissan, D. (2001) 'Use inheritance tax to give a fair chance to all', *New Statesman*, 26 February.

Noddings, N. (2002) *Starting at Home*, Los Angeles and Berkeley, CA: University of California Press.

Noden, P. (2001) 'School choice and polarisation', *New Economy*, vol 8, issue 4, pp 199-202.

Norcross, A. (2005) 'Killing and letting die', in R. Frey and C. Wellman (eds) *A Companion to Applied Ethics*, Oxford: Blackwell.

Norman, R. (2004) *On Humanism*, London: Routledge.

Norton, D. (ed) (1993) *The Cambridge Companion to Hume*, Cambridge: Cambridge University Press.

Nozick, R. (1974) *Anarchy, State and Utopia*, Oxford: Blackwell.

Nussbaum, M. (1986) *The Fragility of Goodness*, Cambridge: Cambridge University Press.

Nussbaum, M. (1998) *Cultivating Humanity*, Cambridge, MA: Harvard University Press.

Nussbaum, M. (1999a) *Sex and Social Justice*, Oxford: Oxford University Press.

Nussbaum, M. (1999b) 'Virtue ethics: a misleading category?', *Journal of Ethics*, vol 3, no 3, pp 163-201.

Nussbaum, M. (2001a) 'Adaptive preferences and women's options', *Economics and Philosophy*, vol 17, no 1, pp 67-88.

Nussbaum, M. (2001b) *Upheavals of Thought*, Cambridge: Cambridge University Press.

Nussbaum, M. (2006) *Frontiers of Justice*, Cambridge, MA: Balknap Press.

Nussbaum, M. and Sen, A. (eds) (1993) *The Quality of Life*, Oxford: Clarendon Press.

Oddie, G. (2005) 'Addiction and the value of freedom', in D. Boonin and G. Oddie (eds) *What's Wrong?*, Oxford: Oxford University Press.

Oderberg, D. (2000a) *Moral Theory*, Oxford: Blackwell.

Oderberg, D. (2000b) *Applied Ethics*, Oxford: Blackwell.

Okin, S.M. (1999) *Is Multiculturalism Bad for Women?*, Princeton, NJ: Princeton University Press.

Olssen, M. and Peters, M. (2005) 'Neoliberalism, higher education and the knowledge economy', *Journal of Education Policy*, vol 20, no 3, pp 313-45.

O'Neill, J. (1998) *The Market*, London: Routledge.

O'Neill, O. (1989) *Constructions of Reason*, Cambridge: Cambridge University Press.

O'Neill, O. (1996) *Towards Justice and Virtue*, Cambridge: Cambridge University Press.

O'Neill, O. (2003) 'Constructivism vs. contractualism', *Ratio*, vol 16, issue 3, pp 319-31.

O'Neill, R. (ed) (2003) *Does Marriage Matter?*, London: Civitas.

Onwuteaka-Philipsen, B., van der Heide, A., Muller, M., Rurup, M., Rietjens, J., Georges, J.-J., Vrakking, A., Cuperus-Bosma, J., van der Wal, G. and van der Maas, P. (2005) 'Dutch experience of monitoring euthanasia', *British Medical Journal*, vol 331, no 7518, 24 September, pp 691-3.

Pakes, F. (2005a) 'The legalisation of euthanasia and assisted suicide', *International Journal of the Sociology of Law*, vol 33, no 2, pp 71-84.

Pakes, F. (2005b) 'Under seige: the global fate of euthanasia and assisted-suicide legislation', *European Journal of Crime, Criminal Law and Justice*, vol 13, no 2, pp 119-35.

Parekh, B. (2000) *Rethinking Multiculturalism*, London: Palgrave.

Parke, M. (2003) *Are Married Parents Really Better for Children? What Research Says About the Effects of Family Structure on Child Well-Being*, Washington: Centre for Law And Social Policy.

Parker, G. (2006) 'Long-term care', in T. Fitzpatrick, H.-J. Kwon, N. Manning, J. Midgely and G. Pascall (eds) *International Encyclopaedia of Social Policy*, London: Routledge.

Patel, K. (2004) 'Euthanasia and physician–assisted suicide policy in the Netherlands and Oregon: a comparative analysis', *Journal of Health and Social Policy*, vol 19, no 1, p 37.

Pathak, P. (2007) 'The trouble with David Goodhart's Britain', *Political Quarterly*, vol 78, issue 2, pp 261-71.

Paxton, W. and White, S. (eds) (2006) *The Citizen's Stake*, Bristol: The Policy Press.

Pearsall, R. (1969) *The Worm in the Bud*, London: Weidenfeld and Nicolson.

Penelhum, T. (1992) *David Hume*, Indiana: Purdue University Press.

Perri 6 (2003) 'Giving consumers of British public services more choice', *Journal of Social Policy*, vol 32, no 2, pp 239-70.

Pettit, P. (ed) (1993) *Consequentialism*, Aldershot: Dartmouth.

Pettit, P. (1997) 'The consequentialist perspective', in M. Baron, P. Pettit and M. Slote, *Three Methods of Ethics*, Oxford: Blackwell.

Pettit, P. (2000) 'A consequentialist perspective on contractualism', *Theoria*, vol 66, no 3, pp 228-36.

Pettit, P. and Brennan, G. (1993) 'Restrictive consequentialism', in P. Pettit (ed) *Consequentialism*, Aldershot: Dartmouth.

Phillips, A. (2007) *Multiculturalism without Culture*, Princeton, NJ: Princeton University Press.

Phillips, T. (2006) 'Colonisation in reverse: how globalisation is changing Britain', Hugh Gaitskell Memorial Lecture, Nottingham University, 8 February.

Pinker, S. (2002) *The Blank Slate*, Middlesex: Penguin Books.

Plantinga, A. (2000) *Warranted Christian Belief*, Oxford: Oxford University Press.

Plato (1954) *The Last Days of Socrates*, Middlesex: Penguin.

Pogge, T. (2002) 'Eradicating systematic poverty: brief for a global resources dividend', in LaFollette, H. (ed) *Ethics in Practice*, Oxford: Blackwell.

Pollock, A. (2004) *NHS Plc*, London: Verso.

Polsby, D. (1998) 'Regulation of foods and drugs and libertarian ideals', *Social Philosophy and Policy*, vol 15, no 2, pp 209-42.

Porter, J. (1993) 'Openness and constraint: moral reflection as tradition-guided inquiry in Alasdair MacIntyre's recent works', *Journal of Religion*, vol 73, no 4, pp 514-36.

Portmore, D. (2001) 'Can an act-consequentialist theory be agent-relative?', *American Philosophical Quarterly*, 38, pp 363-77.

Potts, M., Byrne, P. and Nilges, R. (eds) (2000) *Beyond Brain Death*, Hingham, MA: Kluwer Academic Publishers.

Powell, M. (2003) 'Quasi-markets in British health policy', *Social Policy and Administration*, vol 27, no 7, pp 725-41.

Prasch, R. and Sheth, F. (2000) 'What is wrong with education vouchers?', *Journal of Economic Issues*, vol 34, no 2, pp 509-15.

Purdy, L. (1996) *Reproducing Persons*, Ithaca, NY: Cornell University Press.

Putnam, R. (2007) 'E pluribus unum: diversity and community in the twenty-first century', *Scandinavian Political Studies*, vol 30, no 2, pp 137-74.

Quinn, K. (1988) 'The best interests of incompetent patients', *California Law Review*, 76, pp 897-937.

Quinn, W. (1993) *Morality and Action*, Cambridge: Cambridge University Press.

Rachels, J. (2005) 'Active and passive euthanasia', in D. Boonin and G. Oddie (eds) *What's Wrong?*, Oxford: Oxford University Press.

Ramsay, H. (1997) *Beyond Virtue*, Basingstoke: Macmillan.

Rauch, J. (2003) 'Who needs marriage?', in J. White (ed) *Contemporary Moral Problems* (7th edn), Belmont, CA: Wadsworth.

Rawls, J. (1972) *A Theory of Justice*, Oxford: Oxford University Press.

Rawls, J. (1993) *Political Liberalism*, New York, NY: Columbia University Press.

Rawls, J. (1999) *The Law of Peoples*, Cambridge, MA: Harvard University Press.

Rawls, J. (2000) *Lectures on the History of Moral Philosophy*, Cambridge, MA: Harvard University Press.

Rawls, J. (2001) *Justice as Fairness*, Cambridge, MA: Harvard University Press.

Rawls, J. (2003) 'Kantian constructivism in moral theory', in S. Darwall (ed) *Contractarianism/Contractualism*, Oxford: Blackwell.

Rees, J. (1991) 'A re-reading of Mill *On Liberty*', in J. Gray and G. Smith (eds) *J. S. Mill – On Liberty*, London: Routledge.

Reeve, A. (1990) 'Individual choice and the retreat from utilitarianism', in L. Allison (ed) *The Utilitarian Response*, London: Sage Publications.

Rehg, W. (1994) *Insight and Solidarity*, Berkeley, CA: University of California Press.

Rehg, W. (1999) 'Intractible conflicts and moral objectivity: a dialogical, problem-based approach', *Inquiry*, 42, pp 229-58.

Reiman, J. (1999) *Abortion and the Ways We Value Human Life*, Lanham, MD: Rowman & Littlefield.

Reiter, J. (1996) 'Citizens or sinners?', *Columbia Journal of Law and Social Problems*, 29, pp 443-68.

Rex, J. (2004) 'The integration of immigrant minorities, social citizenship and cultural differences', *Journal of Conflict and Violence Research*, vol 6, no 2, pp 63-84.

Rhodes, R. (1998) 'Abortion and assent', *Cambridge Quarterly of Healthcare Ethics*, 8, pp 416-27.

Ridley, M. (1996) *The Origins of Virtue*, Middlesex: Penguin.

Rock, P. (1996) 'Eugenics and euthanasia: a cause for concern for disabled people, particularly disabled women', *Disability and Society*, vol 11, no 1, pp 121-7.

Rorty, A. (ed) (1980) *Essays on Aristotle's Ethics*, Berkeley, CA: University of California Press.

Rorty, R. (1998) *Achieving Our Country*, Cambridge, MA: Harvard University Press.

Rowan, J. (1999) *Conflicts of Rights*, Boulder: Westview.

Rowlingson, K. and McKay, S. (2002) *Lone Parent Families*, Harlow: Pearson Education.

Rowlingson, K. and McKay, S. (2005) 'Lone motherhood and socio-economic disadvantage: insights from quantitative and qualitative evidence', *Sociological Review*, vol 53, issue 1, pp 30-49.

Sainsbury, D. (2006) 'Immigrants' social rights in comparative perspective: welfare regimes, forms of immigration and immigration policy regimes', *Journal of European Social Policy*, vol 16, no 3, pp 229-44.

Sales, R. (2007) *Understanding Immigration and Refugee Policy*, Bristol: The Policy Press.

Sandel, M. (1982) *Liberalism and the Limits of Justice*, Cambridge: Cambridge University Press.

Sartre, J.-P. (1948) *Existentialism and Humanism*, London: Methuen.

Sassen, S. (1999) *Guests and Aliens*, New York: New Press.

Satz, D. (2003) 'International economic justice', in H. LaFollette (ed) *The Oxford Handbook of Practical Ethics*, Oxford: Oxford University Press.

Scanlon, T. (1998) *What We Owe to Each Other*, Cambridge, MA: Harvard University Press.

Scanlon, T. (2000) 'A contractualist reply', *Theoria*, vol 66, no 3, pp 237-45.

Scanlon, T. (2003) *The Difficulty of Tolerance*, Cambridge: Cambridge University Press.

Schaler, J. (2002) 'Moral hygiene', *Society*, 39, pp 63-9.

Scheffler, S. (1994) *The Rejection of Consequentialism* (2nd edn), Oxford: Clarendon Press.

Schellenberg, J. (2004) 'The atheist's free will offence', *International Journal for Philosophy of Religion*, vol 56, no 1, pp 1-15.

Schierup, C.-U., Hansen, P. and Castles, S. (2006) *Migration, Citizenship, and the European Welfare State*, Oxford: Oxford University Press.

Schneewind, J. (1997) 'The misfortunes of virtue', in R. Crisp and M. Slote (eds) *Virtue Ethics*, Oxford: Oxford University Press.

Schwartz, B. (2004) *The Paradox of Choice*, London: HarperCollins.

Schwartz, J. (2000) *Fighting Poverty with Virtue*, Bloomington, IN: Indiana University Press.

Schwartz, J. (2005) 'PRWORA and the promotion of virtue', in L. Mead and C. Beem (eds) *Welfare Reform and Political Theory*, New York, NY: Russell Sage Publications.

Scott, R. (2006) 'Choosing between possible lives', *Oxford Journal of Legal Studies*, vol 26, no 1, pp 153-78.

Scruton, R. (2001) *The Case for Conservatism* (2nd edn), Basingstoke: Palgrave.

Seale, C. (2006) 'National survey of end-of-life decisions made by UK medical practitioners', *Palliative Medicine*, vol 20, no 1, pp 3-10.

Seglow, J. (2005) 'The ethics of immigration', *Political Studies Review*, vol 3, issue 3, pp 317-34.

Seldon, A. (2005) *The Welfare State*, edited by Colin Robinson, Indianapolis, IN: Liberty Fund.

Sen, A. (1999) *Development as Freedom*, Oxford: Oxford University Press.

Sen, A. (2003) 'Utilitarianism and welfarism', in S. Darwall (ed) *Consequentialism*, London: Routledge.

Sen, A. (2006) *Identity and Violence*, London: Allen Lane.

Sen, A. and Williams, R. (eds) (1982) *Utilitarianism and Beyond*, Cambridge: Cambridge University Press.

Sennett, R. (2003) *Respect*, London: Allen Lane.

Shakespeare, T. (1998) 'Choices and rights: eugenics, genetics and disability equality', *Disability and Society*, vol 13, no 5, pp 665-81.

Shapiro, D. (2003) 'Addiction and drug policy', in J. White (ed) *Contemporary Moral Problems*, Belmont, CA: Wadsworth.

Shapiro, D. (2005) 'Smoking tobacco: irrationality, addiction and paternalism', in D. Boonin and G. Oddie (eds) *What's Wrong?*, Oxford: Oxford University Press.

Sharp, K. and Earle, S. (2002) 'Feminism, abortion and disability', *Disability and Society*, vol 17, no 2, pp 137-45.

Sheldon, S. and Wilkinson, S. (2004) 'Should selecting saviour siblings be banned?', *Journal of Medical Ethics*, 30, pp 533-7.

Sherman, N. (1997) *Making a Necessity of Virtue*, Cambridge: Cambridge University Press.

Shklar, J. (1998) *Political Thought and Political Thinkers*, edited by S. Hoffmann, Chicago, IL: University of Chicago Press.

Shrage, L. (2003) *Abortion and Social Responsibility*, Oxford: Oxford University Press.

Sidgwick, H. (1981) *The Methods of Ethics* (7th edn), Indianapolis, IN: Hackett.

Sigg, R., Behrendt, C. and Behr, C. (2002) *Social Security in the Global Village*, Edison, NJ: Transaction Publishers.

Singer, P. (1993) *Practical Ethics* (2nd edn), Cambridge: Cambridge University Press.

Singer, P. (1999) *A Darwinian Left*, New Haven, CT: Yale University Press.

Singer, P. (2002a) *One World*, New Haven, CT and London: Yale University Press.

Singer, P. (2002b) 'Poverty, facts, and political philosophies', *Ethics and International Affairs*, vol 16, no 1, pp 121-4.

Singer, P. (2002c) 'Famine, affluence and morality', in H. LaFollette (ed) *Ethics in Practice*, Oxford: Blackwell.

Singer, P. (2003) 'Voluntary euthanasia: a utilitarian perspective', *Bioethics*, vol 17, nos 5-6, pp 526-41.

Slote, M. (1985) *Common-Sense Morality and Consequentialism*, London: Routledge.

Slote, M. (1992) *From Morality to Virtue*, Oxford: Oxford University Press.

Slote, M. (2001) *Morals from Motives*, Oxford: Oxford University Press.

Slote, M. (2005) 'Famine, affluence, and empathy', in D. Boonin and G. Oddie (eds) *What's Wrong?*, Oxford: Oxford University Press.

Smart, J.J.C. and Williams, R. (1973) *Utilitarianism: For and Against*, Cambridge: Cambridge University Press.

Smith, A. (1976) *Theory of the Moral Sentiments*, Oxford: Oxford University Press.

Smith, P. (2002) 'Drugs, morality and the law', *Journal of Applied Philosophy*, vol 19, no 3, pp 233-44.

Smith, S. (2005) 'Evidence for the practical slippery slope in the debate on physician-assisted suicide and euthanasia', *Medical Law Review*, vol 13, no 1, pp 17-44.

Smurl, J. (1980) 'Distributing the burden fairly', *Values and Ethics in Health Care*, 5, pp 97-125.

Sober, E. and Wilson, D. (1998) *Unto Others*, Cambridge, MA: Harvard University Press.

Social Philosophy and Policy (2001) *Natural Law and Modern Moral Philosophy*, special edition, vol 18, no 1, pp 1-251.

Social Trends (2007) *Social Trends 37*, Basingstoke: Palgrave Macmillan.

Somerville, J. (2000) *Feminism and the Family*, Basingstoke: Macmillan.

Somerville, M. (2002) *Death Talk*, London: McGill-Queen's University Press.

Sommers, C. (1986) 'Filial morality', *Journal of Philosophy*, 83, pp 439-456.

Sommers, C. (2005) 'Philosophers against the family', in D. Boonin and G. Oddie (eds) *What's Wrong?*, Oxford: Oxford University Press.

Soper, K. (1986) *Humanism and Anti-humanism*, London: Hutchinson.

Spruijt, E. and Duindam, V. (2005) 'Problem behavior of boys and young men after parental divorce in the Netherlands', *Journal of Divorce and Remarriage*, vol 43, nos 3-4, pp 141-55.

Storksen, I., Roysamb, E., Moum, T. and Tambs, K. (2005) 'Adolescents with a childhood experience of parental divorce', *Journal of Adolescence*, 28, pp 725-39.

Stratton-Lake, P. (2000) *Kant, Duty and Moral Worth*, London: Routledge.

Stuyven, L. and Steurs, G. (2005) 'Design and redesign of a quasi-market for the reintegration of jobseekers', *Journal of European Social Policy*, vol 15, no 3, pp 211-29.

Sumner, L. (1997) 'A third way', in S. Dwyer and J. Feinberg (eds) *The Problem of Abortion* (3rd edn), Belmont, CA: Wadsworth.

Swanton, C. (2003) *Virtue Ethics*, Oxford: Oxford University Press.

Swinburne, R. (1998) *Providence and the Problem of Evil*, Oxford: Oxford University Press.

Szasz, T. (2003) 'The ethics of addiction', in J. White (ed) *Contemporary Moral Problems*, Belmont, CA: Wadsworth.

Tännsjö, T. (1998) *Hedonistic Utilitarianism*, Edinburgh: Edinburgh University Press.

Tarrant, I. and Tarrant, J. (2004) 'Satisfied fools', *Journal of Philosophy of Education*, vol 38, issue 1, pp 107-20.

Taylor, C. (2007) *A Secular Age*, Cambridge, MA: Belknap Press.

Taylor, R. (2005) 'Self-ownership and the limits of libertarianism', *Social Theory and Practice*, vol 31, no 4, pp 465-82.

Taylor-Gooby, P. (ed) (1998) *Choice and Public Policy*, Basingstoke: Macmillan.

Taylor-Gooby, P. (2005) 'Is the future American? Can left politics preserve European welfare states from erosion through growing "racial" diversity?, *Journal of Social Policy*, vol 34, no 4, pp 661-72.

Ten, C. (1991) 'Mill's defence of liberty', in J. Gray and G. Smith (eds) *J. S. Mill – On Liberty*, London: Routledge.

Tessman, L. (2005) *Burdened Virtues*, Oxford: Oxford University Press.

The Guardian (2006) 'Early births could prompt IVF restrictions', 21 April.

Thompson, P. (1999) 'Evolutionary ethics: its origins and contemporary face', *Zygon*, vol 34, no 3, pp 473-84.

Thomson, J. (2002) 'A defence of abortion', in H. LaFollette (ed) *Ethics in Practice*, Oxford: Blackwell.

Thornton, M. (1995) 'The repeal of prohibition', in M. Tibor and D. Rasmussen (eds) *Liberty for the Twenty-First Century*, Lanham, MD: Rowman & Littlefield.

Tooley, M. (1983) *Abortion and Infanticide*, Oxford: Oxford University Press.

Tooley, M. (2005) 'In defence of voluntary active euthanasia and assisted suicide', in A. Cohen and C. Wellman (eds) *Contemporary Debates in Applied Ethics*, Oxford: Blackwell.

Tough, S. and Brooks, R. (2007) *Fair Choice, London:* Institute for Public Policy Research.

Townsend, P. (2002) 'Poverty, social exclusion and social polarisation', in P. Townsend and D. Gordon (eds) *World Poverty, Bristol:* The Policy Press.

Toynbee, P. (2003) *Hard Work*, London: Bloomsbury.

Trigg, R. (2005) *Morality Matters*, Oxford: Blackwell.

Tronto, J. (1993) *Moral Boundaries*, London and New York, NY: Routledge.

TUC (2004) *Propping up Rural and Small Town Britain*, London: TUC.

Ubel, P., Baron, J. and Asch, D. (1999) 'Social responsibility, personal responsibility, and prognosis in public judgments about transplant allocation', *Bioethics*, vol 13, no 1, pp 57-68.

Unger, P. (1996) *Living High and Letting Die*, Oxford: Oxford University Press.

United Nations (2007) *The Millennium Development Goals Report*, New York, NY: United Nations.

van Delden, J.M., Visser, J.F. and Borst-Eilers, E. (2005) 'Thirty years experience with euthanasia in the Netherlands', in T.E. Quill and M. Battin (eds) *Physician Assisted Dying*, Baltimore, MD: Johns Hopkins University Press.

van den Brink, J.C., Brandsen, T. and Putters, K. (2002) 'The smothering embrace', *Social Policy and Administration*, vol 36, no 2, pp 200-15.

van Hees (2003) 'Acting autonomously versus not acting heteronomously', *Theory and Decision*, vol 54, no 4, pp 337-55.

van Hees, M. (2004) 'Freedom of choice and diversity of options: some difficulties', *Social Choice and Welfare*, 22, pp 253-66.

van Hooft, S. (2006) *Understanding Virtue Ethics*, Chesham: Acumen.

van Oorschot, W. (2006) 'Making the difference in social Europe', *Journal of European Social Policy*, vol 16, no 1, pp 23-42.

van Zyl, L. (2000) *Death and Compassion*, Aldershot: Ashgate.

Vatican (1994) 'Declaration on euthanasia', in P. Singer (ed) *Ethics*, Oxford: Oxford University Press.

Veatch, R. (1974) 'Who should pay for smokers' medical health care? Part 1', *Hastings Center Report*, 4, pp 8-9.

Vehmas, S. (2001) 'Just ignore it? Parents and genetic information', *Theoretical Medicine*, 22, pp 473-84.

Velleman, D. (1999) 'A right of self-termination?', *Ethics*, 109, pp 606-28.

Vineis, P. et al (2005) 'Environmental tobacco smoke and risk of respiratory cancer and chronic obstructive pulmonary disease in former smokers and never smokers in the EPIC prospective study', *British Medical Journal*, vol 330, no 7486, 5 February, p 277.

Walker, J. (2003) 'Radiating messages: an international perspective', *Family Relations*, vol 52, no 4, pp 406-17.

Wallerstein, J., Lewis, J. and Blakeslee, S. (2000) *The Unexpected Legacy of Divorce: The 25 Year Landmark Study*, New York, NY: Hyperion.

Walzer, M. (1983) *Spheres of Justice*, Oxford: Blackwell.

Walzer, M. (2000) *Just and Unjust Wars* (3rd edn), New York, NY: Basic Books.

Walzer, M. (2003) 'Universalism, equality and immigration', in H. Pauer-Studer (ed) *Constructions of Practical Reason*, Stanford, CA: Stanford University Press.

Warren, M. (1991) 'Abortion', in P. Singer (ed) *A Companion to Ethics*, Oxford: Blackwell.

Warren, M. (1997) 'On the moral and legal status of abortion', in S. Dwyer and J. Feinberg (eds) *The Problem of Abortion* (3rd edn), Belmont, CA: Wadsworth.

Warren, M. (2002) 'On the moral and legal status of abortion', in H. LaFollette (ed) *Ethics in Practice*, Oxford: Blackwell.

Watson, G. (2003) 'Some considerations in favour of contractualism', in S. Darwall (ed) *Contractarianism/Contractualism*, Oxford: Blackwell.

Weil, S. (1987) *The Need for Roots*, London: Ark.

Weil, S. (2002) *Gravity and Grace*, London: Routledge.

Weithman, P. (ed) (2002) *Religion and Contemporary Liberalism*, Notre Dame, IN: University of Notre Dame Press.

Wellman, C. (2005) 'Famine relief: the duties we have to others', in A. Cohen and C. Wellman (eds) *Contemporary Debates in Applied Ethics*, Oxford: Blackwell.

West, A. and Pennell, H. (1997) 'Educational reform and school choice in England and Wales', *Education Economics*, vol 5, no 3, pp 285-305.

West, A., Hind, A. and Pennell, H. (2004) 'School admissions and "selection" in comprehensive schools', *Oxford Review of Education*, vol 30, no 3, pp 347-69.

West, E.G. (1997) 'Education vouchers in principle and practice: a survey', *World Bank Research Observer*, vol 12, no 1, pp 83-103.

White, H. (2001) 'National and international redistribution as tools for poverty reduction', *Journal of International Development*, vol 13, issue 3, pp 343-51.

White, M. (2004) 'Can homo economicus follow Kant's categorical imperative?', *Journal of Socio-Economics*, vol 33, no 1, pp 89-106.

White, S. (2003) *The Civic Minimum*, Oxford: Oxford University Press.

White, S. (2005) 'Is conditionality illiberal?', in L. Mead and C. Beem (eds) *Welfare Reform and Political Theory*, New York, NY: Russell Sage Publications.

Wicclair, M. (1990) 'Caring for frail elderly parents: past parental sacrifices and the obligations of adult children', *Social Theory and Practice*, vol 16, no 2, pp 163-89.

Wielenberg, E. (2004) 'A morally unsurpassable God must create the best', *Religious Studies*, vol 40, issue 1, pp 43-62.

Wilkinson, B. (2005) '"The right to die" by Russell Ogden: a commentary', *Canadian Public Policy*, vol 21, no 4, pp 449-55.

Williams, B. (1985) *Ethics and the Limits of Philosophy*, Cambridge, MA: Harvard University Press.

Williams, C. (ed) (2005) *Personal Virtues*, Basingstoke: Macmillan.

Williams, F. (1989) *Social Policy*, Cambridge: Cambridge University Press.

Wilson, B. (1988) 'On a Kantian argument against abortion', *Philosophical Studies*, 53, pp 119-30.

Wilson, E.O. (1998) *Consilience*, London: Abacus.

Wilson, J. (2002) 'Against the legalisation of drugs', in H. LaFollette (ed) *Ethics in Practice*, Oxford: Blackwell.

Wilson, N. and Thomson, G. (2005) 'Tobacco taxation and public health', *Social Science and Medicine*, vol 61, no 3, pp 649-59.

Winch, C. (2004) 'Developing critical rationality as a pedagogical aim', *Journal of Philosophy of Education*, vol 38, no 3, pp 467-84.

Wokler, R. (1994) 'Protecting the Enlightenment', in J. Horton and S. Mendus (eds) *After MacIntyre*, Cambridge: Polity.

Wolf, S. (2003) 'A feminist critique of physician assisted suicide', in J. White (ed) *Contemporary Moral Problems*, Belmont, CA: Wadsworth.

Wolfe, A. (2001) *Moral Freedom*, New York, NY: W.W. Norton and Co.

Wolff, J. (2002) 'Addressing disadvantage and the human good', *Journal of Applied Philosophy*, vol 19, no 3, pp 207-18.

Wood, A. (1999) *Kant's Ethical Thought*, Cambridge: Cambridge University Press.

Woodward, P.A. (ed) (2001) *The Doctrine of Double Effect*, Notre Dame, IN: University of Notre Dame Press.

Yadin, A. (2004) 'Assuming determinism, free will can only be an illusion: an argument for incompatibilism', *Iyyun*, 53, pp 275-86.

Young, M. and Cullen, L. (1996) *Good Death*, London: Routledge.

Index

Page references for notes are followed by n

Also available from The Policy Press

Policy and Politics in the Twenty-First Century series

Pensions
Michael Hill

This book provides a much-needed introductory guide to the issues surrounding pension policy, not just in the UK but worldwide, and offers a critique of some of the dominant ideas and assumptions.

PB £12.99 US$24.00 **ISBN** 978 1 86134 851 7
198 x 129mm 200 pages May 2007

The education debate
Stephen J. Ball

Stephen Ball provides a substantive account of current education policy trends and offers a way to make sense of what is happening to our experience of education, as learners, as teachers, as parents and as citizens.

PB £12.99 US$24.95 **ISBN** 978 1 86134 920 0
198 x 129mm 256 pages January 2008

The health debate
David J. Hunter

Focusing on the British NHS, this book reviews some of the key contemporary debates concerning health systems and how they have shaped the way that health care has, and is, evolving.

PB £12.99 US$24.95 **ISBN** 978 1 86134 929 3
198 x 129mm 176 pages tbc September 2008

Social justice and public policy
Seeking fairness in diverse societies
Edited by **Gary Craig, Tania Burchardt** *and* **David Gordon**

Social justice is a contested term, incorporated into the language of widely differing political positions. To date, political philosophers have made relatively few serious attempts to explain how a theory of social justice translates into public policy. This important book, drawing on international experience and a distinguished panel of political philosophers and social scientists, addresses what the meaning of social justice is, and how it translates into the everyday concerns of public and social policy, in the context of both multiculturalism and globalisation.

PB £19.99 US$36.95 **ISBN** 978 1 86134 933 0
HB £65.00 US$99.00 **ISBN** 978 1 86134 934 7
234 x 156mm 256 pages tbc June 2008

Welfare and well-being
Social value in public policy
Bill Jordan

In this original book Bill Jordan presents a new analysis of well-being in terms of its social value, and outlines ways in which this could be incorporated into public policy decisions. Using new evidence on subjective well-being from psychological research and survey data, the author argues that it is culture, rather than contract and consumption, which is the key to better quality of life and true well-being. It will be an essential text for academics and students in social theory, social welfare, public policy and governance.

PB £22.50 US$39.95 **ISBN** 978 1 84742 080 0
HB £65.00 US$110.00 **ISBN** 978 1 84742 081 7
234 x 156mm 224 pages tbc September 2008

Partnerships
Machines of possibility
Niels Åkerstrøm Andersen

Everyone is talking about partnerships:
environmental partnerships, social partnerships,
public-private partnerships, partnerships
between NGOs in Europe and the third world.
How did partnerships come to emerge almost
everywhere and at almost the same time? What
is the inner logic of partnerships? And at what point does that logic
begin to break down?

In a highly complex society, the conditions on which agreements are built
are constantly changing, demanding, first and foremost, that parties
agree to reach an agreement. Partnering is an answer to the growing
differentiation and dynamism of the societies in which we live. While
this answer holds great potential, however, it is also very fragile. It is the
aim of this book to improve our understanding of the shifting ground on
which agreements must be reached in today's hyper-complex society.

HB £65.00 US$110.00 **ISBN** 978 1 84742 026 8
234 x 156mm 176 pages January 2008

To order copies of these publications or any other Policy Press
titles please visit **www.policypress.org.uk** or contact:

In the UK and Europe:
Marston Book Services, PO Box 269,
Abingdon, Oxon, OX14 4YN, UK
Tel: +44 (0)1235 465500
Fax: +44 (0)1235 465556
Email: direct.orders@marston.co.uk

In the USA and Canada:
ISBS, 920 NE 58th Street, Suite
300, Portland, OR 97213-3786,
USA
Tel: +1 800 944 6190
(toll free)
Fax: +1 503 280 8832
Email: info@isbs.com

**In Australia and
New Zealand:**
DA Information Services,
648 Whitehorse Road Mitcham,
Victoria 3132, Australia
Tel: +61 (3) 9210 7777
Fax: +61 (3) 9210 7788
E-mail: service@dadirect.com.au